Ultimate Microsoft Cybersecurity Architect SC-100 Exam Guide

Master the SC-100 Exam with Practical Examples and Case Studies to Secure the Digital World with Microsoft Cybersecurity Expertise

Dr. K.V.N. Rajesh

www.orangeava.com

First published: May 2024

Published by: Orange Education Pvt Ltd, AVA™

Address: 9, Daryaganj, Delhi, 110002, India

275 New North Road Islington Suite 1314 London,

N1 7AA, United Kingdom

ISBN: 978-81-97223-82-2

www.orangeava.com

Dedicated To

My Beloved Mother:

Mrs. K. Subbalakhmi

My Strength and Support System

About the Author

Dr. K.V.N. Rajesh is a Microsoft Certified Trainer and serves as a Senior Subject Matter Expert at CloudThat. With an impressive background in Azure Security, Identity and Access Management, Information Protection, Microsoft 365 admin center, Defender Suite, Microsoft Cloud App Security, and various other security operations, Dr. Rajesh brings a wealth of hands-on experience to the table. With a remarkable 18 years of expertise in the realm of technical training, he is not just a seasoned professional but a passionate advocate for sharing his knowledge. Rajesh's commitment to knowledge dissemination is evident through his provision of customized training solutions, tailored to suit corporate, online, and classroom environments. His extensive proficiency extends to Microsoft 365 Security, Azure AI, and Deep Learning. Over the course of his illustrious career, he has had the privilege of training more than 10,000 enthusiastic participants, helping them acquire crucial insights into the intricacies of his subject matter.

One of his most recent and notable accomplishments is securing the top spot in the highly competitive Microsoft Azure Blogathon contest. This recognition reflects not only his expertise but also, his dedication to staying at the forefront of industry developments and sharing that knowledge with others. In essence, Dr. K.V.N. Rajesh is not just a trainer; he is a mentor, a guide, and an expert who is committed to delivering training of the highest quality. His extensive experience, coupled with his commitment to staying updated with the latest trends, makes him a valued resource for anyone seeking to master the intricacies of Azure Security, Microsoft 365, and more. His passion and knowledge are the cornerstones of his impactful training career.

About the Technical Reviewers

Oluwaseyi is an accomplished Cybersecurity Expert with over a decade of experience encompassing threat intelligence, incident response, risk management, cloud security, and policy implementation. He holds a B.Eng. in Information and Communication Engineering and an MBA, both from the University of South Wales. Oluwaseyi is certified in CISSP, CCSP, CRISC, CEH, CLPT, and other prestigious credentials, demonstrating his commitment to professional development. He actively shares cybersecurity expertise through writing and mentorship, making him a highly sought-after professional for organizations seeking to fortify their defenses.

Wojciech Ciemski, also known as Blue Team Sparan, is a valued cybersecurity expert with many years of experience in IT. As the founder of the Security Beyond Taboo® blog and vCISO and CSO, he is known for his dynamic commitment to cyber education, captivating audiences at major IT conferences. His involvement with Open Source and the Blue team underscores his commitment to advancing cybersecurity knowledge. Through his work, Wojciech embodies the spirit of innovation and community, supporting a safer digital world.

Amrit Lal is a Cybersecurity professional with over 15 years of field and domain experience in IT and Cybersecurity. He has experience in working with complex cybersecurity platforms and solutions. He has witnessed the rise of cybersecurity needs for organizations and the community. Currently, he works with organizations to build more secure cloud-based infrastructure that meets required security regulatory compliance, as per business requirements, to avoid any future security attacks.

Purav Desai has over 4 years of experience in Cyber Security, with a particular focus on Microsoft Security. He showcased his passion for technology through his PDTechHD YouTube channel in 2012. Purav has worked with Microsoft Security tooling across various industries, including Retail, Transportation, Energy, and Financial Services. Having covered a variety of Cyber domains, Purav currently works as a M365 Incident Responder in Financial Services, with a focus on Cloud Digital Forensics. His Cyber portfolio can be found at https://github.com/PuravsPoint.

Acknowledgements

The crafting of this textbook has been a collective endeavor, and I am deeply appreciative of all those who have played a part in its formation. I extend my heartfelt gratitude to my esteemed colleagues in the realm of Cybersecurity, whose wealth of knowledge and valuable perspectives have significantly enhanced the substance of this book. Special recognition is owed to the numerous participants in my training sessions, whose inquiries and feedback have been instrumental in refining the explanations and examples provided within these pages.

Furthermore, I wish to acknowledge the dedication and hard work of the editorial and production teams, whose tireless efforts have been crucial in ensuring the precision and lucidity of this textbook. Finally, I am profoundly grateful to my family for their unwavering support and encouragement throughout this endeavor.

Preface

Welcome to the world of cybersecurity architecture—a dynamic realm where technology meets strategy, and innovation intersects with vigilance. This textbook is crafted as a comprehensive guide, designed to equip both aspiring and seasoned professionals with the knowledge, tools, and frameworks necessary to navigate the complexities of cybersecurity architecture. Whether you're a student delving into the fundamentals or a practitioner seeking to deepen your expertise, this book endeavors to serve as a trusted companion on your journey.

Cybersecurity architecture transcends the mere deployment of firewalls or encryption protocols—it embodies a holistic approach to safeguarding digital assets, preserving privacy, and fortifying the integrity of systems. From conceptualizing resilient infrastructures to orchestrating robust defense mechanisms, every facet of cybersecurity architecture demands meticulous attention and strategic foresight.

Throughout these pages, we embark on an exploratory voyage through the multifaceted dimensions of cybersecurity architecture. Drawing from a rich tapestry of theoretical insights, practical case studies, and real-world examples, we aim to illuminate the intricate interplay between technological innovation, threat landscapes, and organizational imperatives.

Chapter 1. Zero Trust Frameworks and Best Practices Simplified: This chapter provides an in-depth exploration of the Zero Trust security model, offering practical insights and strategies for its effective implementation in organizational environments.

Chapter 2. Cloud Blueprint-Conforming Solutions: Readers will gain valuable insights into designing and deploying security solutions that align seamlessly with cloud architecture blueprints, ensuring enhanced protection and compliance.

Chapter 3. Microsoft Security Framework-Compliant Solutions: This chapter delves into leveraging Microsoft's security frameworks to develop tailored and compliant security solutions, addressing the unique security challenges faced by organizations.

Chapter 4. Cybersecurity Threat Resilience Design: Strategies for building resilience against cyber threats are explored in this chapter, including proactive threat detection, incident response planning, and recovery measures to mitigate potential impacts.

Chapter 5. Compliance-Driven Solution Architecture: In this chapter, readers will learn about designing security architectures that prioritize compliance with regulatory requirements and industry standards, ensuring adherence to best practices.

Chapter 6. Identity and Access Control Design: Best practices for designing and implementing robust identity and access management solutions are discussed in this chapter, offering strategies to safeguard critical resources and data.

Chapter 7. Designing Access Security for High-Privilege Users: Techniques for securing access to high-privilege accounts and resources are explored in this chapter, addressing the elevated risk associated with privileged access.

Chapter 8. Security Operations Design: Principles and methodologies for establishing efficient and effective security operations centers (SOCs) are outlined, providing insights into monitoring, detecting, and responding to security incidents.

Chapter 9. Microsoft 365 Security Design: This chapter focuses on strategies for securing Microsoft 365 environments, including email, collaboration tools, and cloud services, against evolving threats.

Chapter 10. Application Security Design: Readers will gain insights into designing and implementing secure software development practices to mitigate vulnerabilities and protect applications from exploitation.

Chapter 11. Data Protection Strategy Development: Guidance on developing comprehensive data protection strategies, including encryption, data masking, and data loss prevention measures, is provided in this chapter.

Chapter 12. Security Specifications for Cloud Services: Considerations and recommendations for defining security specifications and requirements when deploying and managing cloud services are discussed, ensuring a secure cloud environment.

Chapter 13. Hybrid and Multi-Cloud Security Framework: This chapter explores best practices for securing hybrid and multi-cloud environments, offering strategies for managing security across diverse cloud platforms.

Chapter 14. Secure Endpoint Solution Design: Strategies for designing and deploying robust endpoint security solutions to protect devices from malware, ransomware, and other cyber threats are presented in this chapter.

Chapter 15. Secure Network Design: Principles for designing secure network architectures, including segmentation, encryption, and intrusion detection/ prevention measures, are discussed to mitigate network-based attacks.

This textbook is not merely a compendium of theories and practices; it is a call to action–a rallying cry for cybersecurity architects to embrace their pivotal role as guardians of digital ecosystems. As we delve into the intricacies of risk management frameworks, threat modeling methodologies, and resilient design principles, let us remember that our mission transcends the confines of code and algorithms–it encompasses the preservation of trust, the empowerment of societies, and the advancement of human progress.

In a world where the boundaries between virtual and physical realities continue to blur, the significance of cybersecurity architecture cannot be overstated. As stewards of this discipline, let us embark on this journey with unwavering resolve, boundless curiosity, and a steadfast commitment to excellence.

Together, let us navigate the ever-shifting currents of cyberspace, forging a future where security is not merely an afterthought, but a fundamental pillar upon which the digital world thrives.

Welcome to the world of cybersecurity architecture–where innovation meets resilience, and vigilance paves the path to a safer tomorrow.

Get a Free eBook

We hope you are enjoying your recently purchased book! Your feedback is incredibly valuable to us, and to all other readers looking for great books.

If you found this book helpful or enjoyable, we would truly appreciate it, if you could take a moment to leave a short review with a 5 star rating on Amazon. It helps us grow, and lets other readers discover our books.

As a thank you, we would love to send you a free digital copy of this book, and a **30%** discount code on your next cart value on our official websites:

www.orangeava.com

www.orangeava.in (For Indian Subcontinent)

☑ **Here's how:**

Leave a review for the book on Amazon.

Take a screenshot of your review, and send an email to **info@orangeava.com** (it can be just the confirmation screen).

Once, we receive your screenshot, we will send you the digital file, within 24 hours.

Thank you so much for your support – it means a lot to us!

Colored Images

Please follow the links or scan the QR codes to download the ***Images*** of the book:

You can find code bundles of our books on our official Github Repository. Go to the following link to and QR code to explore the further:

https://github.com/orgs/ava-orange-education/repositories

Please follow the link to download the Colored Images of the book:
https://rebrand.ly/2748da

In case there's an update to the code, it will be updated on the existing GitHub repository.

Errata

We take immense pride in our work at **Orange Education Pvt Ltd,** and follow best practices to ensure the accuracy of our content to provide an indulging reading experience to our subscribers. Our readers are our mirrors, and we use their inputs to reflect and improve upon human errors, if any, that may have occurred during the publishing processes involved. To let us maintain the quality and help us reach out to any readers who might be having difficulties due to any unforeseen errors, please write to us at :

errata@orangeava.com

Your support, suggestions, and feedback are highly appreciated.

DID YOU KNOW

Did you know that Orange Education Pvt Ltd offers eBook versions of every book published, with PDF and ePub files available? You can upgrade to the eBook version at **www.orangeava.com** and as a print book customer, you are entitled to a discount on the eBook copy. Get in touch with us at: **info@orangeava.com** for more details.

At **www.orangeava.com**, you can also read a collection of free technical articles, sign up for a range of free newsletters, and receive exclusive discounts and offers on AVA™ Books and eBooks.

PIRACY

If you come across any illegal copies of our works in any form on the internet, we would be grateful if you would provide us with the location address or website name. Please contact us at **info@orangeava.com** with a link to the material.

ARE YOU INTERESTED IN AUTHORING WITH US?

If there is a topic that you have expertise in, and you are interested in either writing or contributing to a book, please write to us at **business@orangeava.com**. We are on a journey to help developers and tech professionals to gain insights on the present technological advancements and innovations happening across the globe and build a community that believes Knowledge is best acquired by sharing and learning with others. Please reach out to us to learn what our audience demands and how you can be part of this educational reform. We also welcome ideas from tech experts and help them build learning and development content for their domains.

REVIEWS

Please leave a review. Once you have read and used this book, why not leave a review on the site that you purchased it from? Potential readers can then see and use your unbiased opinion to make purchase decisions. We at Orange Education would love to know what you think about our products, and our authors can learn from your feedback. Thank you!

For more information about Orange Education, please visit **www.orangeava.com**.

Table of Contents

1. Zero Trust Frameworks and Best Practices Simplified **1**

Introduction 1

Structure 2

Role of Cybersecurity Architect 2

Introduction to Best Practices 4

Explanation of Best Practices 4

Usage of Best Practices by Cybersecurity Architect 5

Scenario: A Financial Institution Implementing Best Practices 6

Zero Trust RaMP Initiatives 7

Microsoft Cybersecurity Reference Architecture (MCRA) 7

Microsoft Cloud Security Benchmark (MCSB) 8

Cloud Adoption Framework (CAF) 8

Well-Architected Framework (WAF) 8

Main Objectives of Zero Trust Deployment 8

Application Areas of Zero Trust Deployment 11

Zero Trust Security: Enhancing Visibility and Automation 12

Securing Identity with Zero Trust Technology 13

Securing Network with Zero Trust Model 13

Securing Infrastructure with Zero Trust Technology 14

Securing Data with Zero Trust Technology 15

Securing Endpoint with Zero Trust Technology 15

Conclusion 15

Multiple Choice Questions 16

Answers 17

2. Cloud Blueprint-Conforming Solutions **18**

Introduction 18

Structure 19

Strategic Approaches to Enhancing Security 19

Cloud Adoption Framework 20

Key Components of the Cloud Adoption Framework ... 20

Business Scenario for Cloud Adoption Framework ... 25

Cloud Adoption Framework Secure Methodology ... 27

Azure Landing Zone ... 28

Business Scenario: Enterprise Migration and Transformation with Azure Landing Zones ... 29

Well-Architected Framework ... 31

Conclusion ... 32

Multiple Choice Questions ... 33

Answers ... 34

3. Microsoft Security Framework-Compliant Solutions ... **35**

Introduction ... 35

Structure ... 35

Microsoft Cybersecurity Reference Architecture ... 36

Key Components of MCRA ... 36

Microsoft Cloud Security Benchmark ... 37

Key Components of MCSB ... 39

Business Scenario: Implementing Microsoft Cybersecurity Reference Architecture ... 40

Business Scenario: Implementing Microsoft Cloud Security Benchmark ... 42

Capabilities and Controls of MCSB ... 46

Conclusion ... 49

Multiple Choice Questions ... 49

Answers ... 51

4. Cybersecurity Threat Resilience Design ... **52**

Introduction ... 52

Structure ... 52

Understanding Common Cyberthreats and Attack Patterns ... 53

Guarding Against Cyber Threats: From Phishing to Zero-Days ... 54

Strengthening Cybersecurity with MITRE ATT&CK and Attack Chain Modeling ... 55

Building Business Resilience ... 56

Case Study: Building Business Resilience in Cybersecurity ... 57

Defending Against Ransomware Attacks: Strategies and Real-Life Insights ... 59

Enhancing Data Security Through Comprehensive Backup Configurations ... 61

Scenario: Enhancing Data Security Through Comprehensive Backup Configurations ... 61

Secure Systems with Azure: Automating Patch Management for Enhanced Reliability ... 63

Case Study: Secure Systems with Azure - Automating Patch Management for Enhanced Reliability ... 64

Conclusion ... 66

Multiple Choice Questions ... 67

Answers ... 68

5. Compliance-Driven Solution Architecture ... 69

Introduction ... 69

Structure ... 69

Understanding Regulatory Compliance in Today's Dynamic Landscape ... 70

Navigating the Regulatory Maze: The Crucial Role of Compliance in Today's Dynamic Business Landscape ... 70

Securing Compliance: Transforming Regulations into Robust Cyber Defenses ... 72

Role of Regulatory Compliance in Today's Dynamic Landscape ... 75

Navigating the Regulatory Landscape: The Vital Role of Compliance in Today's Dynamic Business Environment ... 76

Microsoft Cloud Compliance Program (CMCP): Navigating Regulatory Landscapes ... 78

Microsoft Priva and Azure Policy: Real-time Solutions for Privacy and Compliance ... 79

Securing Infrastructure: A Guide to Compliance with Microsoft Defender for Cloud ... 80

Conclusion ... 81

Multiple Choice Questions (MCQs)....81
Answers....83
6. Identity and Access Control Design....84
Introduction....84
Structure....84
Streamlining Access: Microsoft Entra ID Case Study in Multinational Corporation's Cloud Journey....85
Streamlining Access: Microsoft Entra ID in Hybrid and Multi-Cloud Environments....86
Hybrid Cloud Environment....86
Secure Collaboration: Microsoft Entra ID B2B Case Study in Global E-commerce....88
Real-Time Scenario: Safeguarding Collaboration in Global E-commerce....89
Tomorrow's Security: Modern Authentication Strategies....91
Problem Statement....91
Solution: Designing Modern Authentication and Authorization Strategies....92
Zero Trust Cybersecurity: Aligned Access Policies in Finance....93
Business Scenario: Zero Trust in Action for Cybersecurity in a Multinational Financial Institution....95
Implementation of Zero Trust with Conditional Access Policies....95
Managing Security in Financial Cybersecurity....97
FortifyBank Cybersecurity Breach Response....97
Conclusion....99
Multiple Choice Questions....99
Answers....101
7. Designing Access Security for High-Privilege Users....102
Introduction....102
Structure....103
Protecting Digital Assets: Privileged Access Management....103
Enterprise Access Model Implementation....104

Business Scenario: XYZ Corporation 104
Identity Governance Solutions in Finance 106
Securing Tenant Administration in Shared Infrastructures 108
Cloud Infrastructure Entitlement Management: E-commerce Case Study 110
Tailored Entitlement Management for Multi-Cloud 111
Conclusion 113
Multiple Choice Questions 114
Answers 115

8. Security Operations Design 116
Introduction 116
Structure 116
Strategizing Cybersecurity Defenses: A Brief Overview 117
Crafting Security Operations in Hybrid and Multi-Cloud: Real-Time Business Case 119
Maximizing Efficiency with Unified Operations 121
Unified Operations: Definition and Example 121
Unified Operations Decomposed: A Comprehensive Examination 121
Securing Business Operations: Centralized Logging and Auditing Design 123
Crafting SIEM Solutions: Orchestrating Cybersecurity 125
Designing Solutions for Detection and Response: A Real-Time Scenario 128
Orchestrating Cybersecurity Excellence: Designing a SOAR Solution 130
Safeguarding Cyber Frontiers: Designing Effective Security Workflows 133
Fortifying Digital Ramparts: Designing Comprehensive Threat Detection Coverage 136
Case Study: Securing a Global Financial Institution 136
Conclusion 139
Multiple Choice Questions 139

Answers 140

9. Microsoft 365 Security Design 141

Introduction 141

Structure 141

Microsoft 365 Security Blueprint 141

Exchange Online 142

SharePoint Online 142

OneDrive for Business 142

Microsoft Teams 142

Microsoft 365 Security: Defender for Office 365 143

Office 365 Security Journey: EOP to Defender 144

XYZ Corporation's Microsoft 365 Security Case Study 145

Business Scenario: XYZ Corporation 145

Designing a Microsoft Defender XDR Solution: A Real-Time Scenario 146

Scenario: GlobalTech Innovations 147

Design Configurations and Operational Practices for Microsoft 365: A Business Scenario 149

Scenario: TechSolutions Inc. 149

Conclusion 151

Multiple Choice Questions 151

Answers 152

10. Application Security Design 153

Introduction 153

Structure 153

Securing Applications in the DevOps Era: A Case Study 154

Background 154

Challenges 154

Implementation of Secure Coding Practices 155

Authentication and Authorization Mechanisms 155

Continuous Security Assessments 155

DevOps Security Integration 155

Case Study Results 155

Design and Implementing Standards to Secure Application Development: A Comprehensive Approach 156

Business Scenario 156

Designing Security Standards 157

Implementation of Security Standards 157

Benefits and Future Considerations 158

Evaluating the Security Posture of Existing Application Portfolios: A Strategic Imperative 158

Business Case Study 158

Significance of Evaluating Security Posture 159

Methodology for Security Posture Evaluation 160

Outcomes and Future Roadmap 160

Evaluating Application Threats with Threat Modeling: A Proactive Security Approach 161

Case Study 161

Significance of Threat Modeling 161

Implementation of Threat Modeling at SecureFin 162

Outcomes and Future Considerations 163

Overview of Microsoft Threat Modeling Tool 163

Microsoft Threat Modeling Tool (MTMT): An Overview 164

Real-time Business Scenario 164

Outcomes and Future Considerations 165

Evaluate Application Threats with Threat Modeling 166

Business Scenario 166

Implementation of Threat Modeling at TechMart 167

Outcomes and Future Considerations 168

Designing a Security Lifecycle Strategy for Applications: A Proactive Approach for Business Resilience 169

Business Scenario 169

Cost-Efficient Security Measures 169

Designing the Security Lifecycle Strategy for SecureBank 170

Outcomes and Future Considerations 171

Safeguarding Digital Ecosystems in Real-time Scenarios 171

Real-time Business Scenario 172

Outcomes and Future Considerations 173

Designing a Robust Solution for API Management and Security: Empowering Business Innovation 174

Business Scenario 174

Key Considerations in Designing the Solution: API Lifecycle Management 174

Outcomes and Future Considerations 175

Designing a Solution for Secure Access to Applications: Navigating the Digital Frontier 176

Real-time Business Scenario 176

Key Considerations in Designing the Solution: Identity and Access Management (IAM) 176

Outcomes and Future Considerations 177

Conclusion 178

Multiple Choice Questions 178

Answers 179

11. Data Protection Strategy Development 180

Introduction 180

Structure 180

Securing Digital Information in a Growing Landscape 180

Securing Data: A Dual Focus on Protecting Data at Rest and in Transit 182

Designing a Data Discovery and Classification Solution with Microsoft Purview 183

Business Scenario 183

Benefits 184

Navigating Data Governance: The Importance of Data Maps in a Retail Scenario 185

Real-Time Scenario 185

Benefits 186

Designing a Comprehensive Data Protection Solution 186

Business Scenario 187

Benefits 189

Designing a Data Protection Solution: A Case Study 190

Business Scenario 190

Designing Security for Azure Storage: Real-time Examples 192

Designing a Comprehensive Security Solution: Microsoft Defender for SQL and Microsoft Defender for Storage 195

Business Scenario 195

Conclusion 198

Multiple Choice Questions 198

Answers 199

12. Security Specifications for Cloud Services 200

Introduction 200

Structure 201

Introduction to Security for SaaS, PaaS, and IaaS 201

SaaS 201

PaaS 202

IaaS 203

Security Baselines for SaaS, PaaS, and IaaS Services 203

SaaS 203

PaaS 204

IaaS 205

Specify Security Requirements for Web Workloads 206

Business Scenario 207

Key Security Requirements for Web Workloads 207

Specify Security Requirements for Containers and Container Orchestration 213

Business Scenario 213

Security Requirements for Containers 213

Security Requirements for Container Orchestration 217

Conclusion 223

13. Hybrid and Multi-Cloud Security Framework 224

Introduction 224

Structure 224

Introduction to Hybrid Cloud Management 225

Understanding Hybrid Cloud 225

Benefits of Hybrid Cloud Management 226

Challenges and Considerations 226

Multicloud Management: Navigating Complexity for Agility 227

Understanding Multicloud Management 227

Benefits of Multicloud Management 227

Challenges and Considerations of Multicloud Management 228

Evaluating Security with Microsoft Cloud Benchmark: A Business Priority 229

Understanding Microsoft Cloud Security Benchmark 229

Business Scenario: Global Financial Services Firm 229

Benefits of Using Microsoft Cloud Security Benchmark: Comprehensive Guidance 230

Security Control: Posture and Vulnerability Management – A Case Study 231

Business Scenario: Multinational Technology Corporation 231

Challenges Faced 231

Implementation of Posture and Vulnerability Management: Comprehensive Security Assessment 232

Results and Benefits 233

Integrated Posture Management and Workload Protection: Strategic Priority 234

Business Scenario: Global Financial Institution 234

Comprehensive Posture Management: Integrated Protection 235

Benefits and Outcomes 236

Securing Cloud Applications: A Real-time Scenario 237

Business Scenario: Dynamic Technology Company 237

Securing Cloud Applications: Real-time Measures Implemented 238

Benefits and Outcomes 240

Improving Your Security Posture: A Business Scenario....241
Business Scenario: Multinational Finance Corporation....241
Improving Security Posture: Real-time Measures Implemented....242
Benefits and Outcomes:....243
Protecting Cloud Workloads: A Real-time Scenario....244
Business Scenario: Innovative Technology Company....245
Protecting Cloud Workloads: Real-time Measures Implemented....245
Benefits and Outcomes:....247
Defender for Cloud Planning and Operations: A Real-time Scenario....248
Business Scenario: Multinational Corporation in the Financial Sector....248
Defender for Cloud Planning and Operations: Real-time Measures Implemented....249
Benefits and Outcomes:....250
Evaluating Security Posture with Microsoft Defender for Cloud: A Real-time Case Study....251
Business Scenario: Global E-commerce Corporation....252
Microsoft Defender for Cloud Implementation: Real-time Measures Unified Security Dashboard....252
Real-time Scenario....253
Benefits and Outcomes:....254
Business Scenario....255
Attack Path Analysis Implementation: Real-time Measures....256
Benefits and Outcomes:....257
Posture Evaluation with Microsoft Defender for Cloud Secure Score: A Business Scenario....259
Business Scenario: Global Technology Enterprise....259
Posture Evaluation with Microsoft Defender for Cloud Secure Score: Real-time Measures....260
Benefits and Outcomes:....261
Designing Cloud Workload Protection with Microsoft Defender for Cloud: A Business Scenario....262

Business Scenario: Innovative Healthcare Organization.....263
Designing Cloud Workload Protection with Microsoft Defender for Cloud: Real-time Measures.....263
Benefits and Outcomes:.....265
Database Workload Protections: Safeguarding Critical Data in Real-Time Scenarios.....266
Business Scenario: Financial Institution Database Security.....266
Database Workload Protections: Real-Time Measures.....267
Benefits and Outcomes:.....269
Integrating Hybrid and Multicloud Environments with Azure Arc: A Business Scenario.....270
Business Scenario: Global Manufacturing Enterprise.....270
Integrating with Azure Arc: Real-Time Measures.....271
Benefits and Outcomes:.....272
Designing a Solution for External Attack Surface Management: Safeguarding Business Assets in Real-Time.....273
Business Scenario: Global Financial Institution.....274
Designing the Solution for External Attack Surface Management: Real-Time Measures.....274
Benefits and Outcomes:.....276
Conclusion.....277
Multiple Choice Questions.....277
Answers.....278
14. Secure Endpoint Solution Design.....279
Introduction.....279
Structure.....279
Introduction to Endpoint Security.....280
Security Control: Endpoint security.....281
Strengthening Cybersecurity Defenses: Leveraging Endpoint Detection and Response (EDR) for Business Resilience.....282
Safeguarding Business Assets: The Imperative of Deploying Modern Anti-Malware Software.....283

Cybersecurity Vigilance: The Crucial Role of Regular Anti-Malware Updates in Business Defense 284

Fortifying the Digital Fortress: Specifying Server Security Requirements in a Real-World Context 285

Navigating Cyber Waters: Strengthening Network Security in a Real-World Setting 286

Orchestrating Cyber Vigilance: The Crucial Role of Logging and Monitoring in a Corporate Landscape 287

Gatekeepers of Security: Navigating Identity and Access Control in a Real-World Context 288

Safeguarding Confidentiality: A Dive into Data Protection in a Real-World Scenario 289

Strengthening Cyber Resilience: Navigating Vulnerability Management in a Real-World Setting 290

Orchestrating Security Harmony: Inventory and Asset Management in a Real-World Scenario 292

Fortifying Digital Defenses: Secure Configuration in a Real-World Scenario 293

Sentinel Protectors: Malware Defense Strategies in a Real-World Scenario 294

Harmonizing Security: Strategic Specification of Requirements for Mobile Devices and Clients in a Global Corporation 295

Scenario Overview 295

Seamless Integration: Leveraging Existing and New Devices in a Business Environment 297

Safeguarding Sensitive Data: A Case Study on Least-Privileged Access in a Financial Institution 298

Conclusion 300

Multiple Choice Questions 300

Answers 301

15. Secure Network Design 302

Introduction 302

Structure 302

Safeguarding Digital Frontiers: Secure Network Design Imperative 302

Strategic Network Segmentation: Cybersecurity Enhancement 303
Scenario Overview 303
Secure Digital Highways: Network Security Group Traffic Filtering 304
Scenario Overview 305
Design Solutions for Traffic Filtering with Network Security Groups 305
Safeguarding Enterprise Integrity: Network Posture Management 306
Scenario Overview 306
Strengthening Financial Fortresses: A Guide to Network Posture Management at SecureBank Corp 307
Network Monitoring: Business Resilience Vigilance 308
Scenario Overview 308
SwiftGuard: Elevating E-Commerce Stability with Advanced Network Monitoring 308
Conclusion 310
Multiple Choice Questions 310
Answers 311
Index 312

CHAPTER 1
Zero Trust Frameworks and Best Practices Simplified

Introduction

Ensuring the security of sensitive data and systems has become paramount in today's world. *Zero Trust Frameworks and Best Practices Simplified* presents a comprehensive guide to one of the most cutting-edge paradigms in cybersecurity. In this book, we will embark on a journey through the multifaceted world of Zero Trust, exploring its critical components and unveiling practical strategies for its successful implementation.

The opening topic, *Role of Cybersecurity Architect*, sheds light on the pivotal role played by cybersecurity architects in shaping and safeguarding modern digital ecosystems. It delves into their responsibilities and key decision-making processes within the Zero Trust framework.

Our exploration continues with *Introduction to Best Practices*, which lays the foundation for understanding the core principles of Zero Trust. This topic elucidates the fundamental concepts and provides an overview of the best practices that underpin a successful Zero Trust strategy.

Subsequently, we transition into *Usage of Best Practices by Cybersecurity Architects*, delving deeper into the practical application of these strategies by cybersecurity architects. Real-world scenarios and case studies demonstrate how best practices can be implemented to fortify digital environments.

Zero Trust RaMP Initiatives takes center stage, offering an in-depth analysis of the Zero Trust framework's key initiatives, highlighting the critical RaMP (Risk, Access, Micro-Segmentation, and Privilege) components that are central to its success.

Our journey then shifts to the *Main Objectives of Zero Trust Deployment*, where we explore the overarching goals and objectives that organizations aim to achieve when adopting a Zero Trust security model. These objectives serve as a roadmap for effective implementation.

Finally, *Application Areas of Zero Trust Deployment* uncovers the diverse domains where Zero Trust can be deployed for enhanced security. From network security to cloud environments and beyond, this chapter showcases the versatility of the Zero Trust approach.

Throughout this chapter, we aim to provide an informative, engaging, and insightful exploration of Zero Trust, equipping cybersecurity architects and professionals with the knowledge and tools necessary to bolster security measures in an ever-changing digital world.

Structure

In this chapter, we will cover the following topics:

- Role of Cybersecurity Architect
- Introduction to Best Practices
- Usage of Best Practices by Cybersecurity Architect
- Zero Trust RaMP Initiatives
- Main Objectives of Zero Trust Deployment
- Application Areas of Zero Trust Deployment

Role of Cybersecurity Architect

Cybersecurity architects play a critical role in designing and implementing a robust and secure cybersecurity infrastructure for organizations. Their responsibilities involve creating a strategic plan to safeguard digital assets, mitigate cyber threats, and ensure compliance with security regulations. Cybersecurity Architect interacts with technical leadership,technical managers, and security practitioners in generating the security architecture for the organization.

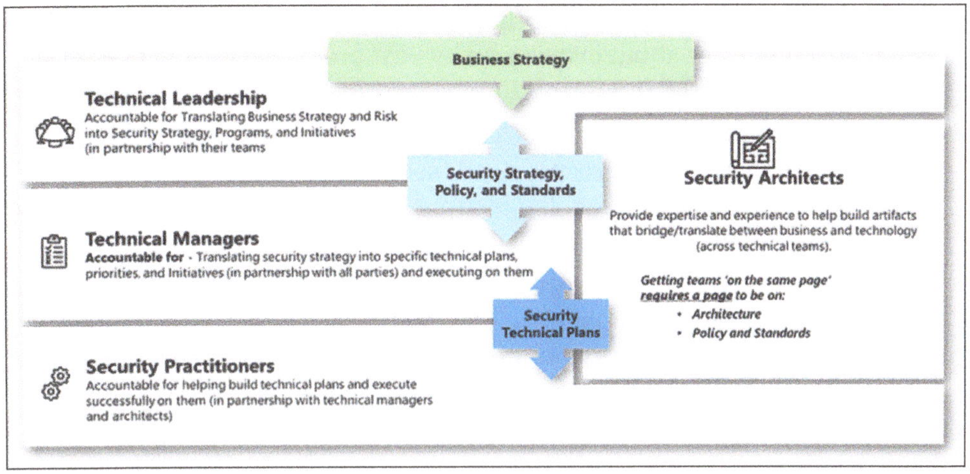

Figure 1.1: *Role Cybersecurity Architect* (*Source*: SC-100: Design solutions that align with security best practices and priorities - Training | Microsoft Learn)

Here is an explanation of their role:

- **Risk Assessment and Analysis:** Cybersecurity architects assess an organization's digital assets and identify potential vulnerabilities and threats. They evaluate the potential impact of security breaches and help prioritize risks based on their severity.
- **Security Strategy Development**: These professionals develop a comprehensive cybersecurity strategy tailored to the organization's specific needs and goals. This strategy includes defining security policies, procedures, and guidelines to protect against a wide range of threats.
- **Architecture Design**: Cybersecurity architects design the organization's security architecture, which includes network security, data protection, access controls, and other security measures. They ensure that all components work together seamlessly to provide defense-in-depth.
- **Technology Evaluation**: They research, evaluate, and recommend cybersecurity technologies, tools, and solutions that align with the organization's security objectives. This may involve selecting firewalls, intrusion detection systems, encryption methods, and more.
- **Compliance Management**: Cybersecurity architects ensure that the organization complies with relevant cybersecurity regulations, industry standards, and best practices. They design security measures that help meet compliance requirements and prepare for audits.
- **Incident Response Planning**: Planning for security incidents is a crucial aspect of the role. Architects develop incident response plans, outlining procedures for identifying, containing, and mitigating security breaches. They also conduct tabletop exercises to test these plans.

- **Security Awareness and Training**: They establish training programs to educate employees about cybersecurity best practices, raising overall security awareness within the organization.
- **Monitoring and Surveillance**: Cybersecurity architects set up monitoring systems to detect and respond to security incidents in real-time. This includes intrusion detection, log analysis, and security information and event management (SIEM) solutions.
- **Collaboration:** They work closely with IT teams, network administrators, and other stakeholders to implement security measures across the organization. Effective communication and collaboration are essential to ensure that security policies are enforced consistently.
- **Adaptation and Improvement**: The cybersecurity landscape is constantly evolving. Architects stay up-to-date with emerging threats and technologies, making adjustments to security strategies and architectures to address new challenges.
- **Budgeting**: They develop and manage cybersecurity budgets, ensuring that necessary resources are allocated to maintain and enhance security measures.
- **Documentation**: Proper documentation of security policies, procedures, and configurations is essential. This documentation helps with auditing, compliance, and troubleshooting.

In summary, a cybersecurity architect is responsible for designing, implementing, and managing a comprehensive cybersecurity strategy that protects an organization's digital assets from a wide range of threats. Their role is pivotal in maintaining the confidentiality, integrity, and availability of sensitive information while ensuring compliance with relevant regulations and standards.

Introduction to Best Practices

Best practices are a set of proven and established methods, techniques, or approaches that are recognized as the most effective and efficient way to achieve a particular goal or outcome in a specific field, industry, or context. These practices are developed through years of experience, research, and continuous improvement, and they represent the highest standards of quality, safety, or performance in a given domain.

Explanation of Best Practices

Best practices serve as guidelines or benchmarks for individuals, organizations, or professionals to follow when striving for excellence or success in their respective areas. They offer a systematic and reliable way to achieve desired results while minimizing risks and errors. Here are some key characteristics and purposes of best practices:

- **Expert Consensus:** Best practices are often established based on the consensus of experts and practitioners who have extensive knowledge and experience in a particular field. They reflect the collective wisdom of those who have encountered and solved common challenges.
- **Continuous Improvement:** Best practices are not static; they evolve over time as new technologies, methodologies, or insights emerge. Continuous improvement is integral to their definition, encouraging adaptation to changing circumstances and advancements.
- **Efficiency and Effectiveness:** Best practices are designed to optimize processes, maximize efficiency, and enhance effectiveness. They aim to reduce waste, minimize errors, and achieve the desired outcome with the least number of resources.
- **Risk Mitigation:** Following best practices helps mitigate risks by incorporating proven strategies for identifying and addressing potential issues. This can be especially critical in fields like healthcare, finance, and cybersecurity, where errors can have serious consequences.
- **Standardization**: Best practices often promote standardization, making it easier to compare, assess, and replicate successful approaches across different contexts. This consistency can lead to better quality control and reliability.
- **Industry Compliance:** In some industries, adherence to specific best practices is mandated by regulations or standards to ensure safety, security, and ethical conduct. For example, healthcare organizations must follow the best practices outlined in HIPAA regulations.
- **Competitive Advantage**: Embracing best practices can provide a competitive advantage by distinguishing an individual or organization as a leader in their field. Customers and stakeholders often value companies that demonstrate a commitment to quality and excellence.
- **Continuous Learning**: Implementing best practices fosters a culture of continuous learning and improvement. It encourages individuals and organizations to stay informed about the latest developments and innovations in their field.

In essence, best practices are not rigid rules but adaptable guidelines that help individuals and organizations navigate complex challenges and achieve superior results. They are rooted in the wisdom of experience and serve as a roadmap for achieving excellence and addressing common problems efficiently and effectively.

Usage of Best Practices by Cybersecurity Architect

Cybersecurity architects play a crucial role in implementing and applying best practices to protect an organization's digital assets. Let us explore how they use best practices in a real-time business scenario:

Scenario: A Financial Institution Implementing Best Practices

Imagine a financial institution that employs a cybersecurity architect to enhance its cybersecurity posture. Here is how the cybersecurity architect uses best practices:

- **Risk Assessment:** The cybersecurity architect begins by conducting a comprehensive risk assessment. They identify potential threats and vulnerabilities, including phishing attacks, data breaches, and insider threats. They use best practices such as the NIST Cybersecurity Framework or ISO 27001 to guide this assessment.
- **Security Framework Adoption**: Based on the assessment, the architect decides to adopt the NIST Cybersecurity Framework as a best practice framework for the organization. This framework provides a structured approach to managing and reducing cybersecurity risks.
- **Access Control**: Following best practices, the architect implements strict access control policies. They enforce the principle of least privilege, ensuring that employees only have access to the systems and data necessary for their roles. This reduces the risk of unauthorized access.
- **Encryption**: Best practices dictate that sensitive data should be encrypted both in transit and at rest. The architect ensures that encryption protocols and mechanisms are in place, protecting customer financial information from unauthorized access.
- **Incident Response Plan:** Using best practices for incident response, the architect develops a comprehensive plan that outlines procedures for identifying, containing, and mitigating security incidents. This plan includes communication protocols, roles and responsibilities, and coordination with law enforcement if necessary.
- **Security Awareness Training**: The architect implements a security awareness training program for all employees. Following best practices, the program covers topics such as recognizing phishing attempts, creating strong passwords, and safeguarding sensitive information.
- **Patch Management**: Best practices recommend regular patch management to address known vulnerabilities. The architect establishes a process to ensure that all systems and software are kept up to date with security patches.
- **Vendor Risk Management**: Recognizing the importance of third-party security, the architect implements vendor risk management best practices. They assess the security practices of third-party vendors who have access to sensitive financial data.

- **Monitoring and Alerts**: The architect deploys a SIEM (Security Information and Event Management) system as a best practice to monitor network and system activity. This system generates alerts for suspicious behavior, allowing for rapid response to potential threats.
- **Regular Auditing and Testing**: Following best practices, the architect schedules regular security audits and penetration tests. These assessments help identify weaknesses and validate the effectiveness of security controls.
- **Documentation and Compliance**: Best practices emphasize maintaining detailed documentation of security policies, procedures, and configurations. The architect ensures that the organization complies with industry regulations, such as those from regulatory bodies like the SEC or FINRA.
- **Incident Response Exercise**: As part of ongoing preparedness, the architect conducts simulated incident response exercises to test the effectiveness of the response plan and the team's readiness.

In this scenario, the cybersecurity architect uses best practices as a framework for designing and implementing a comprehensive cybersecurity strategy. By doing so, they help the financial institution proactively manage risks, protect customer data, and respond effectively to potential security incidents. These best practices not only enhance security but also ensure compliance with industry regulations and build trust with customers. In the next chapters, we will discuss the best frameworks that will be useful for designing solutions.

Zero Trust RaMP Initiatives

Zero Trust RaMP stands for **Zero Trust Rapid Modernization Plan**. It is an approach that organizations adopt to quickly implement Zero Trust principles into their cybersecurity strategies. RaMP initiatives involve accelerating the adoption of Zero Trust security measures by focusing on key areas such as user authentication, device security, network segmentation, and continuous monitoring. The goal is to reduce the reliance on implicit trust and instead verify every user, device, and application attempting to access resources, whether on-premises or in the cloud.

Microsoft Cybersecurity Reference Architecture (MCRA)

Microsoft Cybersecurity Reference Architecture is a comprehensive framework provided by Microsoft to guide organizations in designing and implementing effective cybersecurity solutions using Microsoft technologies. It offers best practices, architectural guidance, and reference designs for building secure and compliant environments in various scenarios, including cloud and hybrid environments. This reference architecture helps organizations align their security strategies with Microsoft's cybersecurity capabilities and recommendations.

Microsoft Cloud Security Benchmark (MCSB)

The Microsoft Cloud Security Benchmark is a set of best practices and recommendations for securing Microsoft Azure, Microsoft 365, and other Microsoft cloud services. It provides guidance on configuring security settings, monitoring for threats, and implementing security controls to protect cloud-based resources effectively. This benchmark helps organizations assess their cloud security posture and align their configurations with industry-recognized security standards.

Cloud Adoption Framework (CAF)

The Microsoft Cloud Adoption Framework is a set of guidelines and best practices for organizations transitioning to the cloud, specifically for Microsoft Azure. It offers guidance on planning, readiness assessments, migration strategies, governance, and ongoing management of cloud resources. This framework helps organizations adopt cloud technologies in a structured and secure manner while aligning with their business objectives.

Well-Architected Framework (WAF)

The Well-Architected Framework, often associated with Amazon Web Services (AWS), provides a set of best practices for designing, building, and maintaining secure and high-performing cloud infrastructures. It covers areas such as security, reliability, performance efficiency, cost optimization, and operational excellence. The framework helps organizations ensure their cloud architectures are well-designed, secure, and aligned with their business needs.

These concepts and frameworks are essential for organizations looking to strengthen their cybersecurity posture, implement cloud technologies securely, and optimize their IT infrastructure for performance and cost-effectiveness. They provide valuable guidance and best practices to help organizations achieve their security and cloud adoption objectives.

Main Objectives of Zero Trust Deployment

Traditional cybersecurity relied on perimeter-based models, assuming trust once inside the network. Access controls were often static, providing broad permissions based on user roles. Remote access lacked the same stringent controls as on-premises, potentially exposing vulnerabilities. Monitoring and response mechanisms primarily focused on known threats, leaving room for undetected malicious activities. Data protection measures were often fragmented, with varying levels of encryption, and compliance efforts were challenging to maintain consistently.

The main objectives of Zero Trust deployment revolve around enhancing an organization's cybersecurity posture by shifting from a traditional perimeter-based security model to a more proactive and adaptive approach. Here is an explanation of the key objectives of Zero Trust:

- **Never Trust, Always Verify:** The fundamental objective of Zero Trust is to eliminate the assumption of trust, both inside and outside the network perimeter. Every user, device, application, or network segment attempting to access resources must be continuously verified and authenticated, ensuring that only authorized entities gain access.
- **Minimize Attack Surface:** Zero Trust aims to minimize the attack surface by implementing the principle of least privilege. It restricts access rights to the minimum necessary for users and devices to perform their roles, reducing the potential pathways for attackers to exploit.
- **Just-in-time-Access:** Just-In-Time (JIT) access in the Zero Trust model provides temporary, need-based access to users. It limits permissions to the minimum required for a specific task or timeframe, reducing the attack surface. This dynamic approach enhances security by ensuring users only have access when necessary, minimizing potential risks.
- **Secure Remote Access:** In today's remote and distributed work environments, Zero Trust extends security to remote access scenarios. It ensures that remote users and devices are subject to the same stringent authentication and access controls as on-premises users.
- **Continuous Monitoring:** Zero Trust mandates continuous monitoring of user, device behavior, and network activity. Leveraging advanced Security Information and Event Management (SIEM) tools, such as Azure Sentinel, organizations gain real-time insights. Additionally, Security Orchestration, Automation, and Response (SOAR) platforms, like Microsoft Azure Sentinel, enable rapid response to anomalies and suspicious activities. These tools empower proactive threat detection, response, and enhance overall cybersecurity resilience in dynamic, ever-evolving environments.
- **Data Protection:** Zero Trust extends security to data protection, ensuring that sensitive data is encrypted both in transit and at rest. Access controls and encryption mechanisms are implemented to safeguard data from unauthorized access.

Zero Trust emphasizes robust data protection by implementing comprehensive measures. Sensitive data is encrypted both in transit and at rest, ensuring confidentiality. Access controls, including the principle of least privilege, are rigorously enforced. Advanced encryption mechanisms, such as Azure Information Protection, safeguard data, thus mitigating unauthorized access risks. These measures collectively fortify data security, aligning with Zero Trust's overarching goal of securing assets across diverse environments.

- **Adaptive Security:** Zero Trust is adaptive and context-aware. Access decisions are made based on contextual factors, such as user behavior, device health, location, time of access, and the trustworthiness of the network. Access privileges can be dynamically adjusted in response to changing conditions.

  Zero Trust embraces adaptability and context-awareness in access controls. Decisions are influenced by dynamic factors: user behavior, device health, location, time of access, and network trustworthiness. Leveraging solutions like Conditional Access in Microsoft Azure, access privileges dynamically adjust in response to evolving conditions, ensuring a proactive and flexible security stance. This nuanced approach enhances overall cybersecurity resilience by tailoring access based on real-time contextual insights.

- **Compliance and Governance:** Zero Trust aligns with industry regulations and security standards. It helps organizations maintain compliance by enforcing security policies and providing audit trails for monitoring and reporting.

Zero Trust within Azure aligns seamlessly with various industry regulations and security standards. This includes compliance frameworks such as:

- **CIS (Center for Internet Security):** Zero Trust principles within Azure contribute to compliance with CIS benchmarks, providing guidelines for securing systems and data against cyber threats.
- **NIST (National Institute of Standards and Technology):** Azure's implementation of Zero Trust assists organizations in aligning with NIST's cybersecurity framework, promoting effective risk management and cybersecurity practices.
- **DSS PCI (Payment Card Industry Data Security Standard):** Azure's Zero Trust model supports compliance with PCI DSS, ensuring secure processing, storage, and transmission of payment card data.
- **Azure Security Benchmark**: Microsoft's Azure Security Benchmark, aligned with Zero Trust principles, serves as a guide for implementing security best practices within Azure, enhancing overall security posture.
- **ISO 27001:** Zero Trust in Azure aids organizations in meeting the requirements of ISO 27001, an international standard for information security management systems.

By adhering to Zero Trust principles, organizations in Azure can confidently navigate a diverse range of regulatory requirements, enforcing robust security policies and providing comprehensive audit trails for monitoring, reporting, and maintaining compliance. This alignment ensures a proactive and secure approach to cybersecurity within Azure's dynamic and evolving cloud environment.

In summary, the main objectives of Zero Trust deployment are to create a dynamic and context-aware security model that continuously verifies and adapts access controls, minimizes attack surfaces, and protects data and resources across on-premises and cloud environments. This approach enhances an organization's ability to detect and respond to security threats effectively while improving overall cybersecurity resilience.

Application Areas of Zero Trust Deployment

Zero Trust deployment has versatile application areas across various industries and scenarios. Let us explore some of these application areas with real-time examples:

- **Enterprise Network Security**
  Example: A global financial institution adopts Zero Trust principles to secure its internal network. They implement strict identity verification, micro-segmentation, and continuous monitoring to protect sensitive customer data and financial transactions. Even employees within the corporate network must continuously authenticate and prove their identity to access critical systems.
- **Remote Work and Bring Your Own Device (BYOD)**
  Example: A technology company embraces a Zero Trust approach to accommodate remote work and BYOD. Employees, whether in the office or working remotely, are required to undergo multi-factor authentication (MFA) and device health checks before accessing company resources. This ensures secure access, regardless of the location or device used.
- **Cloud Security**
  Example: A healthcare provider migrates patient records and applications to the cloud. They implement a Zero Trust architecture to protect sensitive patient data. Access to electronic health records (EHRs) is strictly controlled, with identity verification and encryption enforced, even within cloud environments like Microsoft Azure or Amazon Web Services (AWS).
- **IoT Device Security**
  Example: An industrial manufacturing plant employs Zero Trust to secure its Internet of Things (IoT) devices. Sensors and machinery within the plant are subject to continuous authentication and authorization. Any unusual behavior is flagged for investigation, preventing potential disruptions or tampering.
- **Critical Infrastructure Protection**
  Example: A government agency responsible for critical infrastructure, such as power grids or water supply systems, adopts Zero Trust to safeguard against cyber threats. They employ stringent access controls, real-time monitoring, and intrusion detection systems to protect against potential attacks on essential infrastructure components.
- **Supply Chain Security**
  Example: A multinational retail corporation implements Zero Trust to secure

its supply chain operations. Suppliers and partners accessing the company's systems and data must undergo rigorous verification processes. This ensures the integrity of the supply chain and guards against unauthorized access or data breaches.

- **Healthcare Data Security**
  Example: A healthcare provider leverages Zero Trust to protect electronic medical records (EMRs) and patient information. All users, including doctors, nurses, and administrative staff, must authenticate continuously and adhere to strict access controls. This approach safeguards patient privacy and complies with healthcare regulations like HIPAA.
- **Financial Services and Banking**
  Example: A banking institution adopts a Zero Trust model to secure online banking and financial transactions. Customers are required to use MFA and device verification for online banking access. Even trusted devices must continuously authenticate, reducing the risk of unauthorized account access.
- **E-commerce and Customer Data Protection:**
  Example: An e-commerce platform prioritizes Zero Trust for customer data protection. User accounts, payment information, and transaction records are safeguarded with strict identity verification and data encryption. This approach builds trust with customers concerned about online privacy.

These real-world examples demonstrate the diverse application areas of Zero Trust deployment. It is a versatile security framework that can be adapted to various industries and use cases, providing enhanced protection against evolving cyber threats while enabling secure access to critical resources and data.

Zero Trust Security: Enhancing Visibility and Automation

Zero trust security is a strategic approach that emphasizes the implementation of continuous visibility, automation, and orchestration across various dimensions of IT infrastructure. This includes identity, endpoints, data, applications, infrastructure, and network components.

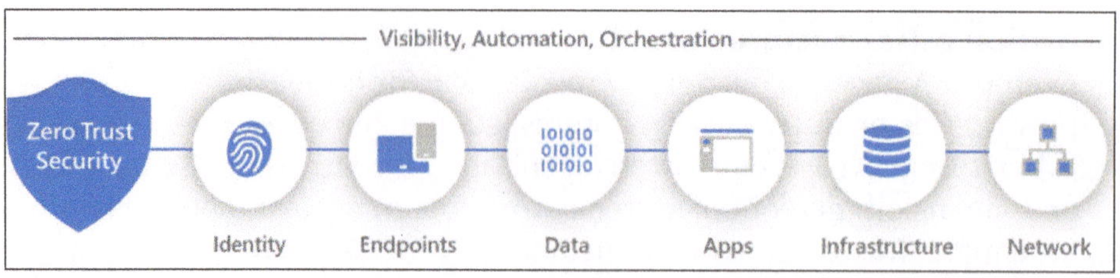

Figure 1.2: *Zero Trust Security* (Source: SC-100: Design solutions that align with security best practices and priorities - Training | Microsoft Learn)

The objective is to enhance security by assuming that no entity, whether internal or external, should be automatically trusted. Instead, access to resources and sensitive data is granted based on strict verification of identity and continuously monitored behavior, regardless of the user's location or network environment. This approach minimizes the risk of unauthorized access, lateral movement, and data breaches by implementing granular access controls, real-time threat detection, and dynamic policy enforcement.

Securing Identity with Zero Trust Technology

Securing identity with Zero Trust Technology involves a paradigm shift from traditional network security models by assuming that no one, whether inside or outside the organization, can be trusted implicitly. In a typical business problem scenario, let us consider a multinational corporation facing challenges with remote workforce security. Employees and contractors access sensitive company resources from various locations and devices, making it difficult to ensure the integrity of their identities. To address this, the organization implements Zero Trust principles. Firstly, it adopts multi-factor authentication (MFA) to verify user identities rigorously. Secondly, it employs continuous monitoring and analytics to scrutinize user behavior for anomalies, such as unusual access patterns or suspicious activity. Thirdly, the organization establishes granular access controls, only permitting users to access resources necessary for their roles. Lastly, it utilizes micro-segmentation to isolate critical assets from unauthorized access. This approach not only bolsters security but also enhances the user experience and adaptability in a dynamic business landscape.

Securing Network with Zero Trust Model

Securing a network with Zero Trust Model involves a fundamental shift in the traditional security paradigm. In this approach, trust is never assumed, and verification is required for every user, device, and application attempting to access the network resources. Imagine a business scenario where a remote employee needs access to sensitive company data. Instead of relying solely on a username and password, Zero Trust would demand multi-factor authentication and continuous monitoring of the user's behavior, ensuring that access is granted only if the user's identity and activity align with their permissions. Additionally, micro-segmentation and strict access controls are implemented to limit lateral movement within the network. Zero Trust thus mitigates risks associated with unauthorized access, insider threats, and external attacks, offering a more robust and adaptable security posture for modern businesses.

Business Problem:

Consider a multinational corporation grappling with remote workforce security challenges. Employees and contractors, accessing sensitive company resources from diverse locations and devices, pose identity and integrity concerns.

Multi-Factor Authentication (MFA):

Illustration: Each user undergoes rigorous identity verification through MFA, requiring multiple factors such as passwords and biometrics. This ensures only authenticated individuals gain access.

Continuous Monitoring and Analytics:

Illustration: Continuous monitoring scrutinizes user behavior in real-time. Advanced analytics detect anomalies like unusual access patterns or suspicious activities, triggering immediate response to potential threats.

Granular Access Controls:

Illustration: Access controls are granular, permitting users access only to resources essential for their roles. This minimizes the attack surface and reduces the risk of unauthorized access to sensitive information.

Micro-Segmentation:

Illustration: Critical assets are isolated through micro-segmentation, limiting lateral movement and preventing unauthorized access. This ensures that even if one part of the network is compromised, the damage is contained.

Outcome:

This Zero Trust approach not only enhances security but also improves the user experience. Employees and contractors can seamlessly adapt to a dynamic business landscape, accessing resources securely based on their roles. The model provides a robust, adaptable, and user-friendly solution to the complex security challenges posed by a remote workforce in a multinational setting.

Securing Infrastructure with Zero Trust Technology

Securing infrastructure with Zero Trust Technology involves fundamentally rethinking traditional network security approaches. In a hypothetical business problem scenario, consider a company that has been struggling with data breaches and unauthorized access to sensitive information. To address this challenge, they decide to implement a Zero Trust security model. The process starts with identifying and classifying critical assets and data. Next, they implement strict access controls and multi-factor authentication, ensuring that no user or device is trusted by default, regardless of their location within or outside the corporate network. Continuous monitoring and behavior analysis are crucial components, allowing the company to detect and respond to anomalies in real-time. In this Zero Trust model, trust is never assumed, and verification is required at every access point, significantly reducing the attack surface and enhancing overall security posture.

Securing Data with Zero Trust Technology

Securing data with Zero Trust Technology involves a comprehensive approach to safeguarding sensitive information in a constantly evolving threat landscape. In a hypothetical business problem scenario, imagine a healthcare organization grappling with data breaches and regulatory compliance challenges. To address this, they adopt a Zero Trust strategy. Firstly, they identify and classify their patient records and other sensitive data. They then implement encryption, access controls, and strict authentication mechanisms, ensuring that only authorized users, devices, and applications can access data, regardless of their location. Continuous monitoring and anomaly detection are crucial components, allowing them to swiftly identify and respond to any suspicious activities. With Zero Trust, trust is never assumed, and every data transaction is rigorously verified, mitigating the risk of data breaches and ensuring compliance with data protection regulations.

Securing Endpoint with Zero Trust Technology

Securing endpoints with Zero Trust Technology entails a comprehensive approach to protect devices and data, even when they are outside the corporate network. Imagine a business facing a growing number of cybersecurity threats due to remote work and an increasingly mobile workforce. To address this, they adopt a Zero Trust strategy. The process begins by ensuring that all endpoints, including laptops, smartphones, and IoT devices, are equipped with strong identity verification mechanisms like biometrics or multi-factor authentication. These endpoints are continuously monitored for suspicious activities, with real-time alerts triggered for any anomalies. Access to sensitive data and applications is granted on a need-to-know basis, and all communications, whether within or outside the network, are encrypted and closely inspected for threats. By implementing Zero Trust, this business mitigates the risks associated with unsecured endpoints, safeguarding critical assets and maintaining robust security, even in a dynamic and dispersed work environment.

Conclusion

In this chapter, we delved into the critical role of the cybersecurity architect in implementing a Zero Trust security framework. The chapter begins by introducing best practices, emphasizing their importance in bolstering security measures. It highlights how these best practices are effectively employed by cybersecurity architects to ensure comprehensive protection for an organization's digital assets.

The chapter also discusses the Zero Trust RaMP (Risk Assessment and Management Program) initiatives, showcasing their significance in building a robust security posture. The main objectives of Zero Trust deployment, which include continuous monitoring and strict access controls, are outlined as essential pillars of this security strategy. Furthermore, the chapter examines various application areas of Zero Trust deployment, underscoring its versatility in securing data, networks, and applications across diverse organizational domains. By following these best practices and principles, cybersecurity architects can pave the way for a more secure and resilient digital landscape.

In the upcoming chapter, we will explore the concept of Cloud blueprint-conforming solutions, which are tailored strategies designed to align seamlessly with the unique architecture and requirements of cloud environments. Readers can anticipate an in-depth analysis of how these solutions ensure optimal performance, scalability, and security in the cloud, offering valuable insights into harnessing the full potential of cloud technologies while adhering to industry best practices.

Multiple Choice Questions

1. Which of the following is the primary responsibility of a cybersecurity architect in an organization?
   a. Handling employee training and development
   b. Evaluating marketing strategies
   c. Developing and managing cybersecurity budgets
   d. Managing the organization's social media presence
2. Which characteristic is integral to the definition of best practices?
   a. Expert consensus
   b. Standardization
   c. Competitive advantage
   d. Rigidity in rules
3. What does the acronym RaMP stand for in the context of cybersecurity?
   a. Rapid and Managed Protection
   b. Resource Management Protocol
   c. Rapid Modernization Program
   d. Risk Assessment and Mitigation Plan
4. What is one of the primary objectives of Zero Trust deployment in an organization's cybersecurity strategy?
   a. Trusting all users and devices within the network perimeter
   b. Maximizing the attack surface to improve network flexibility

   c. Implementing static access controls for all users and devices
   d. Continuously verifying and authenticating all entities and minimizing attack surfaces

5. In which industry or scenario is the application of Zero Trust principles illustrated in the given examples?
   a. Agricultural and Farming
   b. Entertainment and Media
   c. Healthcare Data Security
   d. Automotive Manufacturing

6. In securing identity with Zero Trust Technology, which of the following measures is NOT typically part of the approach for a multinational corporation dealing with remote workforce security?
   a. Implementing multi-factor authentication (MFA)
   b. Employing continuous monitoring and analytics for user behavior
   c. Providing open access to all resources for all users
   d. Establishing granular access controls

Answers

1. c
2. a
3. c
4. d
5. c
6. c

CHAPTER 2
Cloud Blueprint-Conforming Solutions

Introduction

The ever-increasing demand for innovation, scalability, and security has led to the development of robust frameworks designed to guide organizations towards cloud success. Within this technological evolution, three notable blueprints emerge as the vanguards of cloud transformation: the Cloud Adoption Framework, the Well-Architected Framework, and Azure Landing Zone. These visionary frameworks, championed by industry leaders such as Microsoft and AWS, usher organizations into the era of cloud-centric operational excellence.

As organizations journey towards cloud adoption, these frameworks offer more than just a roadmap; they provide a comprehensive approach that encompasses strategy, compliance, security, and optimization, ensuring that the transition to the cloud is not merely a technological shift, but a strategic enabler of business objectives.

The Cloud Adoption Framework is a structured methodology that empowers organizations to align their cloud strategy with their overarching business goals. It facilitates the establishment of a strategic plan, governance, and well-considered processes, assuring that the cloud becomes a catalyst for innovation and competitiveness rather than a mere technology shift.

The Well-Architected Framework, underpins the core principles of reliability, security, performance efficiency, and cost optimization. This blueprint ensures that cloud solutions are meticulously designed and architected to meet these criteria, enhancing the overall reliability and efficiency of cloud-based applications and services.

Azure Landing Zone, on the other hand, presents a blueprint that orchestrates the swift and secure deployment of organizational cloud environments, complete with governance, compliance, and connectivity. It is a powerful enabler for organizations seeking to swiftly establish a compliant and secure foothold in the Azure cloud.

These frameworks collectively represent the industry's response to the multifaceted challenges of cloud adoption. They stand as more than guidelines; they are visionary roadmaps, drawn from the collective wisdom of cloud leaders, aimed at ensuring that organizations not only survive but thrive in the cloud era.

This exploration delves into each of these cloud blueprint-conforming solutions, highlighting their unique strengths and collective potential to revolutionize the way organizations approach and leverage cloud technologies. We will examine the principles that underlie their effectiveness, their critical roles in cloud migration, and their transformative impact on business operations. With these blueprints as companions on the journey to the cloud, organizations are better equipped to harness the full potential of cloud technologies and emerge as innovators and leaders in the digital age.

Structure

In this chapter, we will cover the following topics:

- Strategic Approaches to Enhancing Security
- Cloud Adoption Framework
- Key Components of the Cloud Adoption Framework
- Business Scenario for Cloud Adoption Framework
- Cloud Adoption Framework Secure Methodology
- Azure Landing Zone
- Business Scenario: Enterprise Migration and Transformation with Azure Landing Zones
- The Role of Azure Landing Zones
- Outcomes and Benefits
- Well -Architected Framework

Strategic Approaches to Enhancing Security

Effective security strategies are multifaceted, encompassing a variety of elements, including risk assessment, technology, and human factors. It begins with a thorough risk assessment, identifying potential threats and vulnerabilities specific to the organization or system in question. This critical first step allows for a targeted and proactive approach to security.

The role of technology cannot be understated in modern security strategy. From firewalls and encryption to intrusion detection systems and biometrics, technology is the foundation of protection. However, technology is not infallible, and that is where the human element comes into play. Security awareness and training for employees is integral to the overall strategy. Ensuring that staff are educated about the latest threats and best practices in security can prevent many breaches. A successful security strategy must also consider compliance with relevant regulations and standards, such as GDPR, HIPAA,NIST,CIS,PCI DSS, or industry-specific guidelines. Violations of these standards can lead to severe consequences, including legal actions and reputational damage.

Regularly monitoring and updating the security strategy is essential, as the threat landscape is constantly evolving. New vulnerabilities emerge, and attackers become increasingly sophisticated. Collaboration with security experts and staying informed about emerging trends is crucial for adapting the strategy to meet the evolving challenges. Security is a dynamic field, and a well-crafted strategy is the first line of defense against an ever-changing array of threats.

Cloud Adoption Framework

The Cloud Adoption Framework (CAF) is a comprehensive and strategic approach to adopting and implementing cloud technologies within an organization. It is designed to help businesses navigate the complexities of cloud adoption, align their cloud strategies with their overall business objectives, and ensure a smooth transition to the cloud.

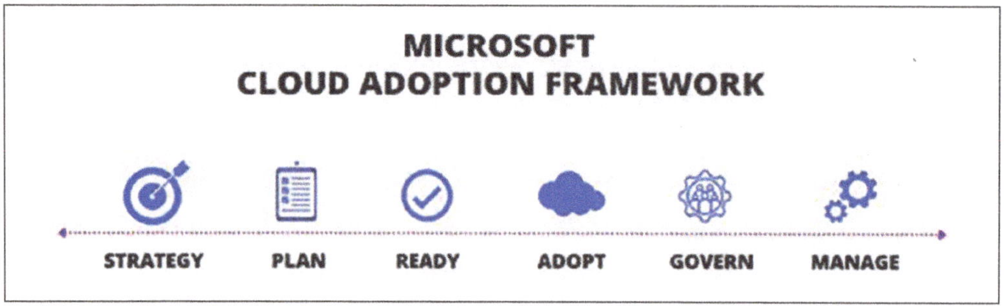

Figure 2.1: *Cloud Adoption Framework (Source:* Cloud adoption Archives - FITTS)

This framework provides a structured methodology that incorporates best practices and guidelines, facilitating a successful migration to the cloud while minimizing risks and optimizing outcomes.

Key Components of the Cloud Adoption Framework

Some of the key components are:

1. **Strategy:** CAF begins by establishing a clear and well-defined cloud strategy that aligns with the organization's goals and objectives. This involves identifying

the specific business needs, cost considerations, and expected outcomes associated with cloud adoption.

Motivations:

- **Efficiency and Agility**: Adopting cloud services allows organizations to scale resources up or down based on demand, promoting operational efficiency and agility.
- **Innovation**: Cloud facilitates the adoption of emerging technologies, fostering innovation and providing a competitive edge in the market.
- **Global Reach**: Cloud services enable organizations to expand their reach globally, serving customers and accessing resources from anywhere in the world.

Business Outcomes:

- **Improved Time-to-Market**: Cloud adoption accelerates the development and deployment of applications, reducing time-to-market for new products and services.
- **Enhanced Customer Experience**: Leveraging cloud services can lead to improved customer experiences through faster response times, increased availability, and seamless scalability.
- **Business Continuity**: Cloud strategies often include robust disaster recovery and business continuity plans, ensuring minimal disruption in case of unforeseen events.

Financial Considerations:

- **Cost Optimization**: Cloud adoption allows organizations to shift from a capital expenditure (CapEx) model to an operational expenditure (OpEx) model, optimizing costs and paying only for the resources consumed.
- **Predictable Expenses**: Cloud services often offer pay-as-you-go pricing models, providing predictability in expenses and avoiding upfront infrastructure investments.
- **ROI (Return on Investment):** Organizations evaluate the return on investment by considering the benefits gained from cloud adoption compared to the costs incurred.

Technical Considerations:

- **Scalability**: Cloud services provide the ability to scale resources dynamically, ensuring that the infrastructure can handle varying workloads effectively.
- **Security**: Implementing robust security measures is crucial, including data encryption, identity management, and compliance with industry standards and regulations.

- **Integration**: Compatibility and integration with existing systems and applications are essential to ensure a smooth transition to the cloud and optimal performance.

In summary, a well-defined cloud strategy considers the motivations behind adopting cloud services, aligns with specific business outcomes, addresses financial considerations for optimal cost management, and incorporates technical considerations to ensure a secure, scalable, and integrated cloud environment. The Cloud Adoption Framework emphasizes these elements to guide organizations in aligning their cloud strategies with overall goals and objectives.

2. **Plan:** With a solid strategy in place, CAF guides organizations in creating a detailed plan for their cloud migration. This includes a roadmap, milestones, and a comprehensive understanding of the required resources, both human and technical.

    Rationalize Your Digital Estate:

    - **Definition**: Rationalizing the digital estate involves assessing and optimizing the existing IT infrastructure, applications, and services to determine what should be migrated to the cloud, retired, or replaced.
    - **Importance**: This step ensures that organizations carry forward only the most relevant and efficient components to the cloud, reducing unnecessary complexity and costs.
    - **Considerations**: Factors like application dependencies, performance requirements, and compliance regulations are considered to make informed decisions about each element of the digital estate.

    Organizational Alignment:

    - **Definition**: Aligning the organization involves ensuring that the cloud migration plan is synchronized with business objectives, and stakeholders across the organization are aware of and support the migration efforts.
    - **Importance**: Achieving organizational alignment helps in minimizing resistance, fostering collaboration, and ensuring that cloud initiatives align with broader business goals.
    - **Considerations**: Effective communication, change management strategies, and involving key stakeholders in the decision-making process are crucial for successful organizational alignment.

    Skills Readiness Plan:

    - **Definition**: Developing a skills readiness plan involves assessing the current skill set within the organization and identifying the gaps that need to be addressed for successful cloud adoption.

- **Importance**: As cloud technologies evolve, ensuring that the workforce has the necessary skills and knowledge is critical for efficient cloud operations.
- **Considerations**: Training programs, certifications, and hiring strategies may be part of the skills readiness plan to ensure that the organization has the expertise needed for managing and optimizing cloud resources.

DevOps Cloud Adoption Plan:

- **Definition**: The DevOps cloud adoption plan outlines how development and operations teams will collaborate in a cloud environment to enhance the speed, efficiency, and reliability of software delivery.
- **Importance**: DevOps practices are essential for leveraging the full potential of the cloud, enabling continuous integration, continuous delivery (CI/CD), and automation.
- **Considerations**: This plan includes tools selection, process integration, cultural changes, and establishing feedback loops to ensure seamless collaboration between development and operations teams throughout the cloud migration journey.

In summary, these elements contribute to a comprehensive cloud migration plan under the Cloud Adoption Framework . Rationalizing the digital estate ensures a streamlined transition, organizational alignment fosters support and cooperation, a skills readiness plan ensures the workforce is equipped for the cloud, and a DevOps cloud adoption plan facilitates efficient development and operations collaboration in the cloud environment. Together, these plans form a roadmap for a successful and well-executed cloud migration.

3. **Governance:** Governance is a critical aspect of CAF, ensuring that policies, procedures, and controls are in place to manage and oversee cloud resources effectively. This helps maintain compliance, security, and cost management in the cloud environment.

   Benchmark Assessment:

   - **Definition**: A benchmark assessment involves evaluating the current state of governance practices against industry standards, regulatory requirements, and best practices.
   - **Importance**: Understanding where an organization stands in terms of governance benchmarks provides a baseline for improvement and helps identify areas that may require attention to meet compliance and security standards.
   - **Considerations:** Organizations may conduct regular benchmark assessments to track progress, identify gaps, and ensure continuous improvement in their governance practices.

Governance Foundation:

- **Definition**: The governance foundation involves establishing the fundamental policies, procedures, and controls needed to govern cloud resources effectively.
- **Importance**: A solid governance foundation provides a framework for decision-making, risk management, and resource allocation in the cloud, contributing to compliance, security, and cost-effectiveness.
- **Considerations**: This foundation may include policies related to data privacy, access controls, resource tagging, and budget management, forming the basis for more advanced governance practices.

Improve the Foundation:

- **Definition**: Continuous improvement of the governance foundation is an ongoing process of refining and optimizing policies, procedures, and controls based on evolving organizational needs, technology advancements, and lessons learned.
- **Importance**: Cloud environments are dynamic, and governance practices must adapt to changes. Continuous improvement ensures that governance remains effective in addressing new challenges and opportunities.
- **Considerations:** Regular reviews, feedback mechanisms, and staying informed about industry trends contribute to the ongoing improvement of the governance foundation, enabling organizations to stay agile and responsive to changing requirements.

In summary, governance within the Cloud Adoption Framework involves not only establishing a strong foundation for policies and controls but also continuously assessing and improving these practices. Benchmark assessments provide insights into the current state, the governance foundation sets the groundwork for effective management, and ongoing improvements ensure that governance practices remain relevant and robust in the ever-changing landscape of cloud technologies. This holistic approach contributes to maintaining compliance, enhancing security, and optimizing costs in the cloud environment.

4. **Adoption:** CAF emphasizes a phased approach to adopting cloud technologies, allowing organizations to incrementally move workloads to the cloud while ensuring minimal disruption to ongoing operations.
5. **Operations:** Once in the cloud, CAF provides guidance on how to operate, monitor, and manage cloud services efficiently. This includes ongoing optimization to control costs and improve performance.
6. **Security and Compliance:** Security is a top priority in the Cloud Adoption Framework. It assists organizations in implementing robust security measures and maintaining compliance with industry standards and regulations.

7. **Organizational Change Management:** CAF recognizes that adopting cloud technologies often necessitates a cultural shift within an organization. It offers guidance on change management, training, and building the necessary skills to adapt to the cloud.

8. **Well-Architected Framework:** CAF leverages the AWS Well-Architected Framework (or equivalent cloud provider best practices) to ensure that solutions built in the cloud are designed for reliability, security, performance efficiency, and cost optimization.

Cloud Adoption Framework is a holistic and strategic approach to cloud adoption, ensuring that organizations can harness the full potential of cloud technologies while mitigating risks and maximizing benefits. By addressing strategy, planning, governance, adoption, operations, security, compliance, change management, and architectural best practices, CAF serves as a reliable guide for organizations embarking on their cloud journey. It promotes a structured, organized, and successful transition to the cloud, ultimately enhancing an organization's ability to innovate, scale, and compete in the digital age.

Business Scenario for Cloud Adoption Framework

In a typical business scenario, the Cloud Adoption Framework is an invaluable tool for an organization looking to modernize its IT infrastructure, improve operational efficiency, and drive innovation. Let us explore a business scenario that highlights the relevance and benefits of CAF:

Scenario: A Financial Services Institution's Cloud Transformation

Background: ABC Financial Services, a well-established institution with decades of history, is facing significant challenges in today's digital-first landscape. The traditional on-premises infrastructure is becoming increasingly cumbersome and costly to maintain. To remain competitive, ABC Financial Services recognizes the need to transition to the cloud, which promises agility, scalability, and enhanced customer experiences.

The Role of CAF:

- **Strategy:** ABC Financial Services begins by developing a comprehensive cloud strategy using CAF. They identify their objectives, which include reducing operational costs, improving customer engagement, and enhancing data security.
- **Plan:** CAF helps them outline a detailed plan for their cloud migration. This plan includes a phased approach to move their core financial applications and customer-facing services to the cloud.
- **Governance:** With CAF, ABC Financial Services establishes robust governance

models, ensuring that they have proper controls in place for data protection, compliance with financial regulations, and cost management.

- **Adoption:** Following CAF's guidance, they start migrating their less critical workloads to the cloud, gaining experience and expertise while minimizing disruption. This approach ensures a smooth transition and minimizes downtime.
- **Operations:** Once their applications are in the cloud, CAF assists in optimizing and managing cloud resources efficiently. It recommends cost-saving measures, such as auto-scaling, and monitors the performance of their applications to guarantee an excellent customer experience.
- **Security and Compliance:** Given the sensitive nature of financial data, CAF helps ABC Financial Services implement stringent security measures and ensures compliance with industry regulations like GDPR and financial industry standards.
- **Organizational Change Management:** Moving to the cloud involves a shift in culture and skill sets. CAF supports ABC Financial Services in training their IT teams, adapting to cloud-native technologies, and fostering a cloud-first mindset.
- **Well-Architected Framework:** They utilize the Well-Architected Framework, recommended by CAF, to ensure their applications are built for reliability, scalability, and security, while optimizing costs.

Outcomes and Benefits:

As a result of implementing the Cloud Adoption Framework, ABC Financial Services achieves several key outcomes:

- Substantial cost savings from reduced infrastructure and maintenance costs.
- Increased agility, allowing them to quickly adapt to market changes and customer demands.
- Enhanced security and data protection, bolstering customer trust.
- Improved customer experiences through more responsive and scalable cloud-based services.
- Better compliance with industry regulations and standards.
- A more innovative and competitive position in the financial services sector.

In this business scenario, CAF serves as a strategic guide for ABC Financial Services, ensuring a successful cloud transformation that aligns with their business goals, mitigates risks, and positions them for a digitally empowered future. The framework enables them to embrace cloud technologies, drive operational excellence, and ultimately better serve their customers in the evolving financial landscape.

Cloud Adoption Framework Secure Methodology

The CAF Secure methodology is an essential component of Microsoft's CAF and focuses on ensuring the security and compliance of an organization's cloud adoption journey. It offers a comprehensive set of principles, best practices, and guidelines to help organizations build and maintain a secure and compliant cloud environment. Here is an explanation of the CAF Secure methodology:

- **Identity and Access Management (IAM):** In the CAF Secure methodology, managing identities and controlling access is fundamental. It involves implementing robust authentication and authorization mechanisms, such as multi-factor authentication (MFA) and role-based access control (RBAC). Organizations need to maintain strict control over user and application access to prevent unauthorized access to resources.
- **Data Protection:** Protecting data is of paramount importance. The CAF Secure methodology emphasizes encryption of data at rest and in transit. Organizations should classify their data and implement appropriate access controls, ensuring that sensitive information is safeguarded and compliant with industry regulations like GDPR, HIPAA, or PCI DSS.
- **Network Security:** Securing the network infrastructure is vital. This involves implementing Virtual Private Clouds (VPCs), firewalls, network security groups, and intrusion detection systems to monitor and control traffic. A Zero Trust network approach is encouraged, where trust is never assumed, and every access request is verified.
- **Threat Protection:** CAF Secure methodology advises organizations to employ advanced threat protection solutions. This includes implementing threat detection systems, security information and event management (SIEM) tools, and conducting regular security assessments to identify vulnerabilities and respond to threats swiftly.
- **Security Governance:** Establishing a strong security governance framework is crucial. It involves creating security policies, procedures, and guidelines, and defining roles and responsibilities for security teams. Organizations should ensure compliance with relevant industry standards and regulations and regularly audit and assess their security posture.
- **Compliance and Legal**: Compliance is a key aspect of the CAF Secure methodology. Organizations need to be aware of legal and compliance requirements specific to their industry and geographic location. This may include data residency, privacy regulations, and contractual agreements with cloud service providers.

- **Security Operations:** Effective security operations are essential to monitor, detect, and respond to security incidents. The CAF Secure methodology recommends implementing Security Operations Centers (SOCs) and incident response plans to address security breaches promptly.
- **Business Continuity and Disaster Recovery**: Organizations must plan for business continuity and disaster recovery in the cloud. This involves regular backup, redundancy, and failover mechanisms to ensure minimal disruption in case of unforeseen events.

The CAF Secure methodology provides organizations with a structured approach to address security concerns during their cloud adoption journey. By following these principles and best practices, organizations can significantly reduce security risks, protect sensitive data, and maintain compliance in the cloud, ultimately ensuring a secure and resilient cloud environment.

Azure Landing Zone

Azure Landing Zones are a set of best practices, guidelines, and resources provided by Microsoft Azure to help organizations establish a secure, well-architected, and compliant cloud environment. These Landing Zones serve as foundational structures that assist organizations in deploying workloads and applications on Azure with confidence, while ensuring they meet security, governance, and compliance standards.

- **Purpose:** Azure Landing Zones are designed to accelerate and streamline the process of adopting Microsoft Azure by providing a set of well-defined blueprints, design patterns, and infrastructure as code (IaC) templates. These resources help organizations build a strong foundation for their cloud workloads.
- **Core Components:**

  Azure Landing Zones consist of several core components:

  - **Design Guidelines**: They offer architectural recommendations and best practices to ensure the environment's scalability, reliability, and security. These guidelines help organizations make informed decisions regarding the structure of their Azure environment.
  - **IaC Templates:** Infrastructure as Code templates, such as Azure Resource Manager (ARM) templates or Terraform scripts, are provided to automate the deployment of Azure resources. These templates align with best practices for resource organization and security.
  - **Policies:** Azure policies, often implemented through Azure Policy and Blueprints, help enforce governance and compliance requirements. These policies can ensure that resources adhere to predefined standards and prevent configuration drift.

    - **Landing Zones for Different Needs**: Azure Landing Zones are not one-size-fits-all. Microsoft provides a variety of Landing Zones tailored to specific needs, such as:
        - **Foundational Landing Zone:** This is suitable for organizations new to Azure and looking to establish a basic environment with emphasis on security and governance.
        - **Enterprise-Scale Landing Zone**: Designed for large enterprises with complex requirements, this Landing Zone offers more advanced governance, security, and networking capabilities.
        - **Custom Landing Zones:** Organizations can create custom Landing Zones tailored to their specific business and regulatory requirements by leveraging Azure's modular approach.

- **Benefits:**

  By using Azure Landing Zones, organizations can realize several benefits:

    - **Accelerated Deployment:** Landing Zones reduce the time required to set up and configure Azure environments, enabling faster project deployment and time-to-value.
    - **Enhanced Security and Compliance:** Azure Landing Zones enforce security and compliance standards, helping organizations meet regulatory requirements and protect their data and applications.
    - **Consistency:** Organizations can ensure consistency in their Azure environments, reducing configuration errors and security vulnerabilities.
    - **Scalability:** The modular design of Landing Zones allows organizations to scale resources up or down as needed, adapting to changing business demands.

In summary, Azure Landing Zones are a valuable set of resources that facilitate the adoption of Microsoft Azure by providing best practices, design guidelines, IaC templates, and governance policies. By using Azure Landing Zones, organizations can efficiently establish a secure and well-architected cloud environment that aligns with their specific needs and requirements.

Business Scenario: Enterprise Migration and Transformation with Azure Landing Zones

Background: Imagine a large, well-established global enterprise, XYZ Corporation, with a legacy IT infrastructure distributed across multiple data centers. XYZ Corporation is keen on modernizing its operations, enhancing scalability, and improving its overall business resilience. To achieve these goals, they have chosen Microsoft Azure as their cloud platform. Azure Landing Zones play a pivotal role in this transformation journey.

The Role of Azure Landing Zones:

- **Strategy and Planning:** XYZ Corporation employs Azure Landing Zones to formulate a comprehensive cloud strategy. They assess their existing infrastructure, identify specific business objectives, and formulate a phased migration plan. This includes prioritizing workloads, data, and applications for migration to Azure.
- **Provisioning and Governance:** Azure Landing Zones allow XYZ Corporation to quickly set up standardized, compliant, and secure environments. They utilize the Azure Blueprints feature to create governance policies, compliance standards, and resource templates. This ensures that their cloud resources adhere to corporate policies and industry regulations.
- **Landing Zones:** XYZ Corporation deploys multiple Azure Landing Zones, customized to their specific needs. For instance, they set up a central Landing Zone to manage enterprise-wide policies and resource organization, while also creating project-specific Landing Zones for various business units.
- **Security and Compliance:** With the help of Azure Security Center and Azure Policy, XYZ Corporation establishes robust security controls. They continuously monitor and respond to threats and ensure compliance with data protection regulations such as GDPR or HIPAA.
- **Networking and Connectivity**: Leveraging Azure Landing Zones, they configure secure, high-performance network connections, connecting their on-premises data centers to Azure via ExpressRoute. This ensures minimal disruption to their ongoing operations.
- **Operations and Optimization:** Azure Monitor and Azure Cost Management enable XYZ Corporation to gain insights into their cloud operations. They continuously optimize resource usage, scale applications as needed, and keep costs in check.
- **Application Modernization**: As they migrate their applications to Azure, XYZ Corporation leverages services like Azure Kubernetes Service (AKS) to containerize and modernize legacy applications, improving scalability and reducing operational overhead.

Outcomes and Benefits:

By implementing Azure Landing Zones, XYZ Corporation realizes several key outcomes and benefits:

- **Cost Savings:** Efficient resource provisioning and optimization lead to substantial cost reductions in infrastructure maintenance and operations.
- **Scalability and Flexibility:** Azure's elasticity allows XYZ Corporation to scale resources on-demand, accommodating business growth and fluctuations seamlessly.

- **Improved Security**: The robust security measures in place enhance data protection and boost customer trust.
- **Regulatory Compliance:** By adhering to Azure's security and compliance standards, they ensure they meet industry-specific regulations, avoiding costly fines and reputational damage.
- **Business Resilience:** The distributed architecture and disaster recovery options offered by Azure Landing Zones improve business resilience in the face of unforeseen disruptions.
- **Innovation:** XYZ Corporation can now focus on innovation by modernizing applications, exploring AI and machine learning, and experimenting with new technologies.

In this business scenario, Azure Landing Zones serve as a crucial foundation for XYZ Corporation's cloud transformation. They facilitate a seamless migration to Azure, ensuring alignment with business objectives, compliance with industry standards, and cost-effective, secure, and scalable operations. The outcome is a modernized, innovative, and competitive enterprise ready to embrace the opportunities of the digital age.

Well-Architected Framework

The Well-Architected Framework provides a structured approach for designing and implementing secure, reliable, high-performing, and cost-effective architectures on Azure. It encompasses five pillars: reliability, cost optimization, operational excellence, performance efficiency, and security.

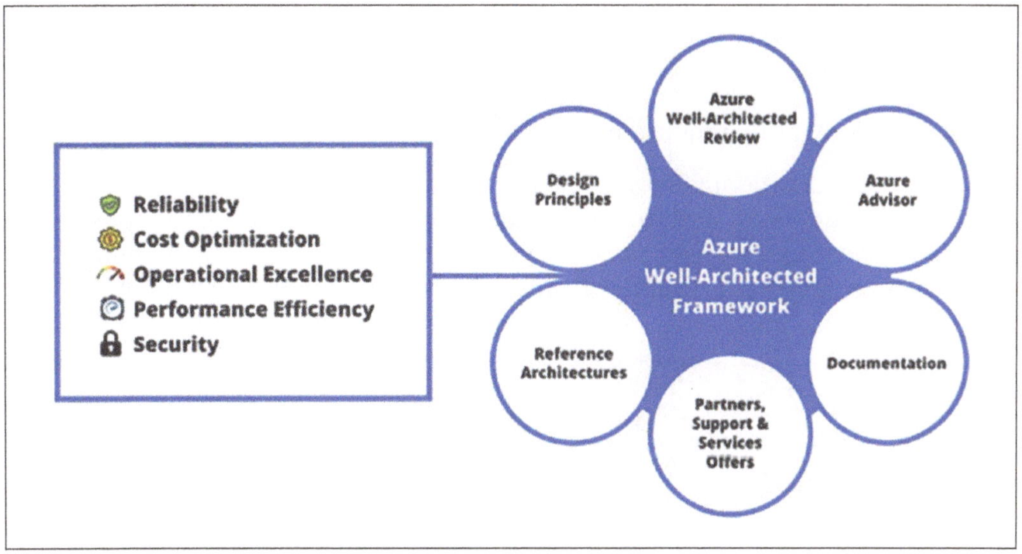

Figure 2.2: *Well-Architected Framework*

Reliability ensures systems recover from failures and continue to function as expected. By applying design principles like redundancy and fault tolerance, businesses can minimize downtime and maintain service availability. Azure Well-Architected Reviews and Azure Advisor offer insights and recommendations to enhance reliability, while reference architectures provide proven patterns for building resilient systems.

Cost optimization involves maximizing the efficiency of cloud resources to minimize expenses without sacrificing performance or reliability. Through careful planning and monitoring, organizations can leverage features like Azure Cost Management and Azure Advisor to analyze spending patterns and identify opportunities for optimization. Additionally, documentation and guidance from Azure partners help implement cost-effective solutions aligned with business goals.

Operational excellence focuses on streamlining operations to deliver business value and improve agility. By adhering to design principles such as automation and monitoring, teams can streamline workflows and enhance decision-making. Azure services like Azure Monitor and Azure DevOps facilitate continuous improvement through monitoring, logging, and automation, while Azure support and services provide expert guidance to optimize operations.

Performance efficiency aims to deliver optimal performance to meet the demands of users and workloads. Design principles such as scalability and elasticity enable systems to dynamically adapt to changing demands. Azure Well-Architected Reviews and documentation offer guidance on optimizing performance, while reference architectures provide proven patterns for achieving high performance at scale.

Security is paramount in protecting data, systems, and assets from unauthorized access, breaches, and threats. Design principles like defense in depth and least privilege help establish robust security postures. Azure services such as Azure Security Center and Azure Sentinel provide tools for threat detection, monitoring, and response. Additionally, Azure partners offer specialized expertise and solutions to address specific security requirements.

The Well-Architected Framework provides a comprehensive approach to designing and implementing cloud architectures that prioritize reliability, cost optimization, operational excellence, performance efficiency, and security. By applying design principles, leveraging Azure services and tools like Azure Well-Architected Reviews, Azure Advisor, documentation, and support services, organizations can build and maintain resilient, efficient, and secure cloud environments aligned with best practices and industry standards.

Conclusion

In the dynamic field of cloud computing, the Cloud Adoption Framework, Well-Architected Framework, and Azure Landing Zone, which are endorsed by industry leaders like Microsoft and AWS, guide organizations toward operational excellence. CAF offers a structured methodology aligning cloud strategy with business goals, going beyond migration to foster innovation. The Well-Architected Framework sets a gold standard for reliable and efficient cloud solutions, emphasizing security and cost optimization. Azure Landing Zone facilitates secure cloud deployments, ensuring swift, compliant entry into Azure. These blueprints collectively address challenges, offering visionary roadmaps for organizations to thrive in the cloud era, enabling them to harness cloud technologies for innovation and leadership. In the next chapter, we will discuss Microsoft security framework compliant solutions.

Multiple Choice Questions

1. What is the primary goal of the Cloud Adoption Framework (CAF)?
   a. Technology migration
   b. Ensuring security compliance
   c. Aligning cloud strategy with business goals
   d. Enhancing reliability and efficiency
2. Which framework emphasizes key aspects like reliability, security, performance, and cost optimization for cloud solutions?
   a. Cloud Adoption Framework
   b. Well-Architected Framework
   c. Azure Landing Zone
   d. Cloud Security Framework
3. What is the main focus of the Azure Landing Zone in cloud deployments?
   a. Technology migration
   b. Governance, compliance, and connectivity
   c. Maximizing cost savings
   d. Architectural design and best practices
4. What do the cloud blueprints, including CAF, Well-Architected Framework, and Azure Landing Zone, collectively provide to organizations?
   a. Guidelines
   b. Compliance standards

   c. Visionary roadmaps
   d. Hardware recommendations
5. How do these cloud blueprints help organizations in the digital age?
   a. By providing technological solutions
   b. By simplifying the migration process
   c. By ensuring survival in the cloud era
   d. By offering strategic guidance and tools for innovation
6. Which framework plays a key role in enhancing the efficiency and reliability of cloud-based applications and services?
   a. Cloud Adoption Framework
   b. Well-Architected Framework
   c. Azure Landing Zone
   d. Cloud Security Framework

Answers

1. c
2. b
3. b
4. c
5. d
6. b

CHAPTER 3
Microsoft Security Framework-Compliant Solutions

Introduction

Microsoft, one of the technology industry's giants, has recognized the significance of cybersecurity and has made significant strides in enhancing the security of its cloud services. To aid this endeavor, Microsoft has developed the Cybersecurity Reference Architecture and Cloud Security Benchmark. This comprehensive framework is designed to provide a structured approach to securing cloud environments and is a testament to Microsoft's commitment to safeguarding digital ecosystems.

Structure

In this chapter, we will cover the following topics :

- Microsoft Cybersecurity Reference Architecture
- Key Components of MCRA
- Microsoft Cloud Security Benchmark
- Key Features of MCSB
- Key Components of MCSB
- Business Scenario: Implementing Microsoft Cybersecurity Reference Architecture
- Scenario: XYZ Corp's Enhanced Cybersecurity
- Business Scenario: Implementing Microsoft Cloud Security Benchmark
- Capabilities and Controls of MCSB

Microsoft Cybersecurity Reference Architecture

The Microsoft Cybersecurity Reference Architecture (MCRA) is a blueprint for securing cloud environments built on Microsoft Azure, a leading cloud platform. It offers a comprehensive overview of best practices and architectural guidelines for designing secure and resilient cloud solutions. This reference architecture encompasses a wide array of topics, including identity and access management, network security, data protection, and threat detection and response.

Key Components of MCRA

- **Identity and Access Management**: This component emphasizes the importance of strong identity management practices. It promotes the use of Azure Active Directory and Multi-Factor Authentication to ensure secure access to cloud resources. Role-based access control (RBAC) is a central concept that allows organizations to define and manage user permissions effectively.

  In Microsoft's cybersecurity reference architecture, Identity and Access Management (IAM) encompasses a comprehensive suite of end-to-end security components. Azure Active Directory (AAD) forms the core, providing secure user authentication and authorization. Conditional Access policies ensure adaptive access controls based on various factors. Multi-Factor Authentication (MFA) adds an extra layer of identity verification. Azure Identity Protection detects and responds to identity-related risks. Privileged Identity Management (PIM) manages, monitors, and audits privileged access. Microsoft Defender for Identity employs advanced analytics to detect and respond to identity threats. Together, these components establish a robust IAM framework, safeguarding digital identities and ensuring secure access across Microsoft environments.

- **Network Security:** In the reference architecture, network security is a focal point. It advocates the use of virtual networks, network security groups, and Azure Firewalls to safeguard communication and data flow. Security policies and threat detection mechanisms help identify and respond to network intrusions effectively.

  Microsoft's cybersecurity reference architecture employs end-to-end security components for robust network security. It includes Azure Firewall and Virtual Network Appliances for perimeter defense. Azure Bastion ensures secure remote access, while Azure Application Gateway provides application-layer protection. Azure DDoS Protection safeguards against distributed denial-of-service attacks. Identity and Access Management (IAM) controls user access. Threat intelligence, delivered by Azure Sentinel, enhances detection and response. Additionally, the Azure Security Center monitors and assesses security posture, while the Azure Active Directory secures identity infrastructure. This comprehensive approach ensures a resilient network environment, safeguarding against various cyber threats with Microsoft's integrated security solutions.

- **Data Protection**: Data is a valuable asset, and the reference architecture addresses its protection comprehensively. Features like Azure Disk Encryption, Azure Key Vault, and Azure SQL Database Transparent Data Encryption are recommended for data security. Data classification and labeling also play a pivotal role in managing sensitive information.

  Microsoft's cybersecurity reference architecture incorporates end-to-end security components for robust data protection. Azure Information Protection encrypts and classifies data, ensuring confidentiality. Azure Security Center employs threat intelligence and analytics for advanced threat detection and response. Identity and Access Management tools, such as Azure Active Directory, ensure authorized access. Advanced Threat Protection services, including Microsoft Defender, safeguard against malware and cyber threats. Continuous monitoring and auditing, facilitated by Azure Monitor and Azure Sentinel, enhance visibility and compliance. This comprehensive approach, utilizing encryption, threat detection, access controls, and monitoring ensures a resilient data protection framework within Microsoft's cybersecurity reference architecture.

- **Threat Detection and Response:** Microsoft promotes a proactive approach to threat detection and response. Azure Security Center and Azure Sentinel are key components in identifying and **mitigating security threats.** These tools leverage machine learning and threat intelligence to provide real-time insights and recommendations.

  Microsoft's cybersecurity reference architecture employs end-to-end security components for effective threat detection and response. Azure Sentinel, a cloud-native SIEM, collects and analyzes data, enabling real-time threat detection. Azure Security Center leverages advanced analytics to identify and remediate vulnerabilities across hybrid environments. Microsoft Defender ATP offers endpoint protection, detecting and responding to sophisticated threats. Automation through Azure Logic Apps orchestrates incident response workflows. These integrated components form a cohesive defense, enhancing resilience against cyber threats with continuous monitoring, swift detection, and automated, orchestrated responses to mitigate security risks.

Microsoft Cloud Security Benchmark

The Microsoft Cloud Security Benchmark (MCSB) is an integral part of Microsoft's cybersecurity strategy. It offers prescriptive guidance on how to configure Microsoft

Azure services securely. This benchmark aligns with global security standards and provides measurable security controls to help organizations assess and enhance their cloud security posture.

Key Features of MCSB:

- **Secure Defaults**: The benchmark encourages users to configure Azure services with secure defaults to minimize vulnerabilities. It includes recommendations on settings like authentication, encryption, and access control.

  Microsoft Cloud Security Benchmark establishes security standards, and security defaults play a pivotal role. Security defaults in Azure enforce baseline security measures, simplifying protection against common threats. By automatically implementing robust settings like multi-factor authentication and risk-based conditional access, security defaults enhance overall cloud security posture. This approach aligns with the benchmark's best practices, providing a standardized foundation for organizations using Microsoft Cloud services. Security defaults serve as an out-of-the-box, proactive security solution, ensuring a secure configuration and minimizing potential vulnerabilities in line with Microsoft's recommended security baseline.

- **Continuous Monitoring**: Regular monitoring is essential for maintaining a secure cloud environment. The benchmark emphasizes the importance of continuous monitoring and provides guidelines on using Azure Security Center and Azure Monitor to stay informed about security events.

  The Microsoft Cloud Security Benchmark advocates continuous monitoring for robust cloud security. Utilizing Azure Security Center ensures ongoing visibility into cloud environments, assessing configurations against best practices. Continuous monitoring detects deviations, promptly alerting security teams to potential vulnerabilities or policy violations. By employing Azure Monitor, organizations gain real-time insights into system performance and potential threats. This proactive approach, aligned with the benchmark, fosters a dynamic security posture, enabling swift response to evolving risks, and maintaining compliance with Microsoft's recommended security standards for a resilient and well-monitored cloud infrastructure.

- **Compliance and Regulations:** For organizations subject to specific regulatory requirements, the benchmark offers guidance on aligning cloud security with compliance standards. This is especially important in industries like healthcare, finance, and government.

  The Microsoft Cloud Security Benchmark underscores compliance and regulatory adherence by aligning with industry standards. Leveraging Azure Policy and Azure Blueprints, organizations enforce specific configurations to meet regulatory requirements. Azure Compliance Manager facilitates tracking and managing compliance against multiple regulatory frameworks. Through continuous monitoring and automated assessments, it ensures a proactive stance in addressing evolving compliance needs. By integrating these benchmark-recommended practices, Microsoft empowers businesses to navigate diverse regulatory landscapes, fostering a secure cloud environment that aligns with industry standards and safeguards sensitive data in accordance with regional and global regulations.

- **Automation and DevSecOps**: Security is increasingly integrated into the DevOps process. The benchmark promotes automation and the integration of security practices into the development pipeline, ensuring that security is not an afterthought but an integral part of the development process.

  The Microsoft Cloud Security Benchmark emphasizes automation and DevSecOps for a robust security posture. Azure Policy automates policy enforcement, ensuring adherence to security standards from the start of development. Azure DevOps integrates security into the development lifecycle, promoting a DevSecOps culture. Automated workflows, facilitated by Azure Logic Apps and GitHub Actions, enable continuous integration and delivery with security checks. This approach streamlines code deployment while incorporating security measures seamlessly. By aligning with the benchmark's principles, organizations achieve an automated and collaborative security framework, fostering agility, resilience, and proactive security practices throughout the entire cloud development and operational lifecycle.

The Microsoft Cloud Security Benchmark is a comprehensive framework and set of best practices designed to enhance the security posture of organizations using Microsoft cloud services. This initiative is driven by Microsoft's commitment to providing robust security tools and guidance to help organizations protect their data, applications, and infrastructure in the cloud. MCSB is an invaluable resource for organizations seeking to maximize the security of their cloud environments.

Key Components of MCSB

- **Security Controls**: MCSB provides a comprehensive set of security controls that organizations can implement to safeguard their cloud resources. These controls cover a wide range of areas, such as identity and access management, data protection, network security, and threat detection.
- **Best Practices**: The benchmark is built on Microsoft's vast experience in cloud security and offers best practices for configuring and managing various Microsoft cloud services, including Azure, Microsoft 365, and others. These best practices are continually updated to address emerging threats and vulnerabilities.
- **Scoring and Assessment**: MCSB provides organizations with a scoring mechanism that allows them to assess their security posture and identify

areas that need improvement. This scoring system can help organizations track their progress and prioritize security enhancements.

- **Compliance and Regulations**: The benchmark aligns with various compliance standards and regulations, making it easier for organizations to meet their regulatory requirements. This is especially crucial for businesses in regulated industries, such as healthcare and finance.
- **Automation:** MCSB promotes automation by providing scripts and templates that enable organizations to streamline security configuration and monitoring tasks. Automation not only improves security but also reduces operational overhead.
- **Integration with ·Security Tools**: Microsoft has designed MCSB to work seamlessly with its security tools and services, such as Microsoft Defender and Azure Security Center. This integration allows organizations to benefit from a holistic security approach.
- **Community Involvement:** MCSB is a collaborative effort that welcomes feedback and contributions from the community. This ensures that the benchmark remains up-to-date and relevant to the evolving threat landscape.
- **Detailed Documentation**: Organizations can access detailed documentation and resources that explain the rationale behind each security control and provide step-by-step instructions for implementation.
- **Continuous Improvement**: Microsoft remains committed to continuously improving the MCSB framework, keeping it aligned with the latest security trends and technologies.

Business Scenario: Implementing Microsoft Cybersecurity Reference Architecture

In today's digital landscape, businesses are facing a growing number of cyber threats and security challenges. Protecting sensitive data, ensuring the availability of critical services, and maintaining compliance with industry regulations are paramount concerns. One effective way to address these challenges is by implementing the Microsoft Cybersecurity Reference Architecture. This architecture provides a comprehensive and well-structured framework for designing and implementing a robust cybersecurity strategy tailored to an organization's needs. Let's explore a business scenario where a company leverages the Microsoft Cybersecurity Reference Architecture to enhance its security posture:

Scenario: XYZ Corp's Enhanced Cybersecurity

XYZ Corp, a multinational manufacturing company, has been experiencing a rise in cyberattacks and data breaches over the past year. They operate in a highly competitive industry and recognize that their intellectual property and customer data are prime targets for cybercriminals. Additionally, they must comply with stringent data protection regulations to maintain their global operations.

To address these concerns, XYZ Corp decided to adopt the Microsoft Cybersecurity Reference Architecture. Here's how they go about it:

1. **Assessment and Planning:**

   XYZ Corp begins by conducting a comprehensive assessment of their current cybersecurity posture. They identify vulnerabilities and areas that require improvement.

   They establish clear business goals, such as reducing the number of security incidents, improving incident response times, and ensuring regulatory compliance.

2. **Design and Deployment:**

   Using the Microsoft Cybersecurity Reference Architecture as a blueprint, XYZ Corp designs a security infrastructure that includes Microsoft solutions like Azure Security Center, Microsoft Defender, and Azure Active Directory.

   They implement a zero trust network model, ensuring that every user and device is verified and authenticated before accessing any resources.

3. **Monitoring and Detection:**

   XYZ Corp deploys advanced threat detection and monitoring tools as recommended by the reference architecture.

   They use Azure Sentinel to collect and analyze security data from multiple sources, enabling them to proactively detect and respond to security threats.

4. **Identity and Access Management**:

   Leveraging Azure Active Directory, XYZ Corp strengthens identity and access management with features like Multi-Factor Authentication (MFA) and Conditional Access policies.

   They implement Just-In-Time (JIT) and Just-Enough-Access (JEA) principles to limit access to privileged resources.

5. **Compliance and Governance:**

   To address their compliance requirements, XYZ Corp utilizes Azure Policy and Azure Blueprint to enforce regulatory standards and track compliance.

   They also leverage Microsoft Compliance Manager to assess and report on their compliance status.

6. **Education and Training:**

   XYZ Corp invests in cybersecurity training for employees and regularly conducts security awareness programs to educate their workforce about cyber threats and safe practices.

7. **Incident Response:**

   They establish a well-defined incident response plan in accordance with the reference architecture.

   XYZ Corp conducts regular tabletop exercises to ensure that their security team is prepared to respond effectively to security incidents.

Business Scenario: Implementing Microsoft Cloud Security Benchmark

Imagine a medium-sized healthcare organization that has recently migrated its operations to Microsoft Azure to take advantage of the scalability, flexibility, and cost-efficiency of cloud computing. However, given the sensitive nature of patient data and regulatory requirements, security is of paramount concern. The organization is looking for a way to assess and enhance its cloud security posture effectively. In this scenario, they turn to the Microsoft Cloud Security Benchmark (MCSB).

Example of how MCSB is applied:

1. **Assessment and Scoring:**

   The healthcare organization starts by using the MCSB framework to assess its current security measures in the Azure environment. They go through the recommended security controls and best practices specified in the benchmark.

2. **Scoring and Gap Analysis:**

   After evaluating their security configurations against the benchmark's guidelines, they receive a security score. This score helps them identify areas where they need to make improvements. The score serves as a baseline to measure progress over time.

3. **Implementation of Security Controls:**

   The organization then begins implementing the security controls and best practices suggested by MCSB. For instance, they ensure that multi-factor authentication (MFA) is enabled for all user accounts and that data encryption is properly configured for sensitive patient records in Azure.

4. **Compliance Alignment:**

   Healthcare organizations are subject to strict regulatory requirements, such as HIPAA (Health Insurance Portability and Accountability Act). The MCSB framework offers guidance on aligning security configurations with these regulations, ensuring that the organization remains compliant.

5. **Automation and Integration:**

   The organization leverages the automation scripts and templates provided by MCSB to streamline security configuration processes. They also integrate Azure Security Center and Microsoft Defender for added threat detection and response capabilities.

6. **Ongoing Monitoring and Improvement:**

   The healthcare organization continues to monitor its security posture and compliance using the MCSB framework. They regularly review their security score and make adjustments as needed to stay resilient against emerging threats.

7. **Community and Updates:**

   The organization actively participates in the MCSB community, sharing experiences and contributing insights to the framework. They benefit from collective knowledge and stay informed about the latest security best practices and updates.

By using the MCSB, the healthcare organization effectively enhances its cloud security posture. They establish a strong foundation for securing patient data in the cloud, ensuring compliance with regulatory requirements, and protecting their reputation. The ongoing monitoring and community involvement allow them to adapt to evolving threats and maintain a proactive security stance in their Azure environment, which is critical in the healthcare industry.

The Microsoft Cloud Risk Assessment is a vital component of Microsoft's cloud security and compliance services, designed to help organizations assess and mitigate risks associated with their use of Microsoft cloud services. This tool provides comprehensive capabilities and controls that empower businesses to enhance their security posture, comply with industry regulations, and safeguard their data and resources effectively. Here, we will delve into the key capabilities and controls offered by MCRA.

Capabilities of MCRA:

- **Risk Identification and Assessment**: MCRA enables organizations to identify and assess potential risks within their Microsoft cloud environments. It offers insights into areas that may pose security, compliance, or operational risks, helping businesses prioritize their remediation efforts.
- **Data Protection**: Data is a valuable asset, and MCRA assists in evaluating the

security of data within Microsoft cloud services. It assesses controls related to data encryption, access management, and data loss prevention, helping organizations protect sensitive information effectively.

- **Identity and Access Management (IAM):** Controlling access to resources is crucial for security. MCRA evaluates IAM practices, including identity verification, multi-factor authentication, and role-based access control, ensuring that only authorized users can access resources.
- **Network Security**: Network security is vital in a cloud environment. MCRA examines network configurations, firewall rules, and network monitoring to identify potential vulnerabilities and recommend improvements.
- **Compliance and Regulations**: MCRA helps organizations assess their compliance with industry-specific regulations and standards. This is particularly valuable for businesses subject to stringent compliance requirements, such as healthcare organizations dealing with HIPAA or financial institutions following GDPR.
- **Threat Detection and Response**: MCRA evaluates threat detection and response capabilities, including the integration of Microsoft security tools like Microsoft Defender and Azure Security Center. It helps organizations enhance their ability to detect and respond to security incidents promptly.
- **Automation and Remediation**: MCRA promotes automation by providing recommendations for automating security and compliance tasks. Automation can help organizations reduce human error and respond faster to security incidents.

Controls with MCRA:

- **Security Score:** MCRA generates a security score for the organization based on various controls and best practices. This score serves as a benchmark for evaluating the overall security posture, making it easier to track improvements over time.
- **Data Encryption:** MCRA assesses the encryption of data at rest and in transit. It ensures that sensitive data is adequately protected through encryption mechanisms, reducing the risk of unauthorized access.
- **Access Management:** Proper identity and access management are crucial in preventing unauthorized access to resources. MCRA examines IAM controls, including user provisioning, access revocation, and multi-factor authentication, to ensure that only authorized users can access critical systems.
- **Data Loss Prevention (DLP):** Protecting sensitive data from accidental or intentional exposure is essential. MCRA evaluates DLP measures in place, including policies, classifications, and monitoring, to prevent data leaks.

- **Network Security:** MCRA scrutinizes network configurations, firewall rules, and intrusion detection systems to identify weaknesses in network security. It provides recommendations for securing network access and monitoring network traffic for anomalies.
- **Compliance Checks:** MCRA assists in aligning cloud configurations with industry-specific compliance standards. It ensures that organizations meet the necessary requirements and are better prepared for audits and regulatory scrutiny.
- **Threat Detection and Response:** MCRA evaluates threat detection capabilities, including the use of security tools like Microsoft Defender and Azure Security Center. It ensures that organizations have adequate systems in place to identify and respond to security incidents effectively.
- **Automation Recommendations:** MCRA provides suggestions for automating security and compliance tasks. Automation can streamline processes, reduce human error, and enhance the organization's overall security posture.
- **Best Practices Guidance**: MCRA offers best practices for each assessed control, providing organizations with a roadmap for improving their security and compliance measures. These best practices are continuously updated to address emerging threats and vulnerabilities.
- **Community Involvement:** MCRA encourages organizations to participate in a community of users who share experiences and insights. This collaborative approach ensures that the tool remains relevant and benefits from collective knowledge.
- **Ongoing Monitoring:** MCRA is not a one-time assessment; it supports ongoing monitoring and improvement. Organizations can continually track their security score, implement recommendations, and adapt to evolving security threats.

Controls within the Microsoft Cybersecurity Reference Architecture encompass a range of features and tools, with real-time examples illustrating their application:

- **Secure Score:**

  Monitoring and improving the organization's secure score in Microsoft 365, which quantifies the adherence to security best practices. Implementing multi-factor authentication can raise the secure score.

- **Data Encryption:**

  Utilizing Azure Disk Encryption to encrypt virtual machine disks, safeguarding data from unauthorized access, even if the virtual machine is compromised.

- **Access Management:**

  Implementing Azure Active Directory Identity Protection to detect and respond to identity-based risks, enhancing access management by enforcing adaptive access controls.

- **Data Loss Prevention:**

  Configuring Microsoft 365 Data Loss Prevention policies to prevent sensitive information, such as credit card numbers, from being shared inadvertently in emails or documents.

- **Network Security:**

  Employing Azure Network Security Groups to control inbound and outbound traffic to network interfaces, enhancing network security by defining allowed and denied communication.

- **Compliance Checks:**

  Utilizing Azure Policy to enforce compliance with regulatory standards, ensuring that resources deployed adhere to specific compliance requirements such as GDPR or HIPAA.

- **Threat Detection and Response:**

  Leveraging Microsoft Defender Advanced Threat Protection (ATP) to detect and respond to advanced threats in real-time, offering automated investigation and remediation capabilities.

- **Best Practices Guidance:**

  Adhering to Microsoft's best practices guidance for Azure, which includes recommendations for secure configurations and continuous improvement of security postures.

Capabilities and Controls of MCSB

The Microsoft Cloud Security Benchmark is a comprehensive framework that provides organizations with a set of capabilities and controls to enhance their security posture in the Microsoft cloud ecosystem, including Azure, Microsoft 365, and other cloud services. MCSB is designed to address the evolving threat landscape and help organizations safeguard their data, applications, and infrastructure effectively. Here, we will delve into the key capabilities and controls offered by MCSB, highlighting their significance and impact on cloud security.

One of the primary capabilities of MCSB is its ability to establish a robust security baseline for organizations operating in the Microsoft cloud environment. The benchmark offers a standardized set of security controls, best practices, and guidelines that enable organizations to configure their cloud resources securely. This standardization is crucial because it helps organizations maintain a consistent and high level of security across their cloud deployments, regardless of their scale or complexity.

MCSB's capabilities also include assessment and scoring mechanisms. Organizations can utilize the benchmark to assess their current security posture. The scoring system allows them to measure how well they align with the recommended security controls and best practices. This scoring serves as a critical tool for organizations to gauge their security effectiveness and identify areas where improvements are needed. It provides a quantitative and measurable way to track security progress and prioritize efforts to mitigate risks.

Additionally, the benchmark aligns with various compliance standards and regulations, making it a valuable resource for organizations in regulated industries. Compliance is a critical aspect of cloud security, especially for sectors like healthcare, finance, and government. MCSB's controls and best practices are designed to help organizations meet their regulatory requirements, simplifying the often complex process of demonstrating compliance.

Automation is another key capability of MCSB. The benchmark provides scripts, templates, and automation guidance to streamline the implementation of security controls. Automation not only reduces the potential for human error but also accelerates the deployment of security measures. By automating security configurations, organizations can maintain consistency, respond to security threats faster, and save time and resources.

Integration with Microsoft's suite of security tools is a fundamental aspect of MCSB's capabilities. Microsoft offers a range of security solutions, such as Azure Security Center, Microsoft Defender, and Azure Sentinel. These tools provide advanced threat detection, response, and monitoring capabilities. MCSB facilitates the integration of these security tools, ensuring that organizations have a holistic approach to security. It enables organizations to leverage the full potential of Microsoft's security ecosystem and gain deeper insights into their cloud security posture.

MCSB emphasizes the importance of continuous improvement. The cloud security landscape is dynamic, with new threats and vulnerabilities emerging regularly. Therefore, the benchmark is not a static document; it evolves to stay current with the latest security trends and technologies. This capability ensures that organizations are well-prepared to address new and evolving threats in their cloud environments.

Detailed documentation is a cornerstone of MCSB's capabilities. The benchmark provides organizations with comprehensive explanations of each security control, the rationale behind it, and step-by-step instructions for implementation. This documentation is an invaluable resource for both security professionals and IT teams. It enables them to understand not only what needs to be done but also why it's necessary, empowering them to make informed decisions about their security configurations.

A critical capability of MCSB is its community involvement. The benchmark is a collaborative initiative that welcomes feedback and contributions from the community of security professionals, organizations, and experts. This inclusive approach ensures that MCSB remains up-to-date and relevant. It benefits from the collective knowledge and experience of a wide range of users, making it a living resource that adapts to the evolving needs of the cloud security community.

Now, let's explore some of the essential security controls and best practices that MCSB offers to organizations:

- **Identity and Access Management (IAM):** MCSB provides guidance on implementing robust IAM controls, including multi-factor authentication (MFA) and role-based access control (RBAC). This helps organizations ensure that only authorized users have access to their cloud resources, reducing the risk of unauthorized access.
- **Data Protection:** The benchmark includes controls for data protection, such as encryption at rest and in transit. It guides organizations on how to secure sensitive data stored in the cloud, mitigating the risk of data breaches and exposure.
- **Network Security:** MCSB offers controls for configuring network security measures, such as firewall rules, network security groups, and virtual network segmentation. These controls help organizations protect their cloud infrastructure from network-based attacks and threats.
- **Threat Detection and Response:** Organizations can benefit from MCSB's recommendations on setting up threat detection and response capabilities. This includes configuring advanced threat protection tools like Microsoft Defender for endpoints and Azure Sentinel, enabling organizations to detect and respond to security incidents in real-time.
- **Compliance and Auditing:** The benchmark includes controls for auditing and compliance monitoring. It provides guidance on enabling audit logs and ensuring that organizations can track and report on activities within their cloud environment. This is crucial for meeting regulatory requirements and conducting security audits.
- **Patch Management**: MCSB offers best practices for managing software and security updates. Timely patching of cloud resources is essential to mitigate vulnerabilities and reduce the risk of exploitation by attackers.
- **Incident Response Planning**: The benchmark emphasizes the importance of having an incident response plan in place. Organizations can use the provided guidelines to develop and test their incident response procedures, ensuring a swift and effective response to security incidents.

Conclusion

In conclusion, Microsoft's commitment to enhancing cloud security through the Microsoft Cybersecurity Reference Architecture and the Microsoft Cloud Security Benchmark is a testament to its dedication to safeguarding digital ecosystems. These comprehensive frameworks provide organizations with the tools and guidance they need to strengthen their cloud security posture, protect sensitive data, and meet regulatory compliance standards.

MCRA offers a structured approach to securing cloud environments built on Microsoft Azure, covering essential areas like identity and access management, network security, data protection, and threat detection and response. It empowers organizations to design and implement a robust cybersecurity strategy tailored to their unique needs.

MCSB, on the other hand, sets a standardized security baseline for organizations, ensuring that they configure their cloud resources securely. It provides assessment and scoring mechanisms, aligns with compliance standards, promotes automation, integrates seamlessly with Microsoft's security tools, and encourages continuous improvement and community involvement.

Both MCRA and MCSB highlight the significance of identity and access management, data protection, network security, threat detection and response, compliance, automation, and detailed documentation. These controls and best practices are essential for organizations seeking to fortify their cloud security and maintain a proactive stance in the face of evolving threats.

In an era where cybersecurity concerns continue to grow, Microsoft's dedication to providing these invaluable resources enables organizations to stay ahead of the curve and protect their digital assets. By implementing the principles and recommendations outlined in these frameworks, businesses can ensure the confidentiality, integrity, and availability of their data, ultimately contributing to a safer and more secure digital landscape for all. In the next chapter, we will be discussing Cyberthreats, Defense Strategies, and Business Resilience.

Multiple Choice Questions

1. What is the primary purpose of the Microsoft Cybersecurity Reference Architecture (MCRA)?
   a. To provide a scoring mechanism for assessing cloud security
   b. To offer best practices for configuring Microsoft cloud services securely
   c. To promote automation in the cloud security process
   d. To provide detailed documentation for Microsoft cloud services

2. Which component of the Microsoft Cloud Security Benchmark (MCSB) focuses on aligning cloud security with compliance standards, especially in industries like healthcare and finance?
    a. Continuous Monitoring
    b. Automation and DevSecOps
    c. Secure Defaults
    d. Compliance and Regulations
3. Which of the following capabilities is offered by the Microsoft Cloud Security Benchmark (MCSB)?
    a. Best Practices Guidance
    b. Data Protection
    c. Detailed Documentation
    d. Identity and Access Management (IAM
4. What is one of the key features of the Microsoft Cybersecurity Reference Architecture (MCRA) related to network security?
    a. Recommendations for data encryption
    b. Promotion of automation and DevSecOps
    c. Advocacy of virtual networks and Azure Firewall
    d. Integration with Azure Security Center
5. Which aspect of the Microsoft Cloud Security Benchmark (MCSB) ensures that the benchmark remains up-to-date and relevant to the evolving threat landscape?
    a. Detailed Documentation
    b. Compliance and Regulations
    c. Community Involvement
    d. Automation Recommendations
6. What is the primary purpose of the security score generated by the Microsoft Cloud Risk Assessment (MCRA)?
    a. To measure the organization's alignment with recommended security controls
    b. To provide detailed documentation for security configurations

c. To facilitate automation of security tasks

d. To assess data protection measures

Answers

1. b
2. d
3. a
4. c
5. c
6. a

CHAPTER 4
Cybersecurity Threat Resilience Design

Introduction

From the deceptive intricacies of phishing to the extortionate tactics of ransomware attacks, the digital realm is fraught with challenges. Distributed Denial of Service (DDoS) attacks disrupt operations, malware infiltrates systems, and insider threats exploit internal vulnerabilities. Social engineering adds a psychological dimension, manipulating individuals into compromising security.Understanding these threats and implementing robust security measures is imperative in fortifying defenses against cyberattacks. Central to this defense is the concept of attack chain modeling–an indispensable tool in the realm of cybersecurity. This systematic approach dissects cyberattacks into sequential stages, allowing security professionals to identify weaknesses and formulate effective countermeasures. The attack chain, spanning initial reconnaissance to actions on objectives, serves as a roadmap for proactive security measures, enhancing an organization's resilience against cyber threats.

Structure

In this chapter, we will cover the following topics:

- Understanding Common Cyberthreats and Attack Patterns
- Strengthening Cybersecurity with MITRE ATT&CK and Attack Chain Modeling
- Building Business Resilience
- Defending Against Ransomware Attacks: Strategies and Real-Life Insights
- Enhancing Data Security Through Comprehensive Backup Configurations
- Secure Systems with Azure: Automating Patch Management for Enhanced Reliability

Understanding Common Cyberthreats and Attack Patterns

Common cyber threats and attack patterns are prevalent in today's digital landscape, posing significant risks to individuals, organizations, and governments. These threats encompass a range of malicious activities aimed at exploiting vulnerabilities in systems and networks. One common cyber threat is phishing, where attackers send deceptive emails or messages to trick recipients into revealing sensitive information or clicking on malicious links. Ransomware attacks have also surged, with attackers encrypting victims' data and demanding a ransom for its release. Distributed Denial of Service (DDoS) attacks overwhelm a target's servers with traffic, causing disruptions and downtime. Malware, including viruses, worms, and Trojans, continues to infect systems, steal data, or disrupt operations. Insider threats involving malicious or negligent employees can result in data breaches or security incidents. Additionally, social engineering exploits human psychology to manipulate individuals into revealing confidential information or performing actions detrimental to security. Understanding these common threats and implementing robust security measures is crucial to safeguarding against cyberattacks.

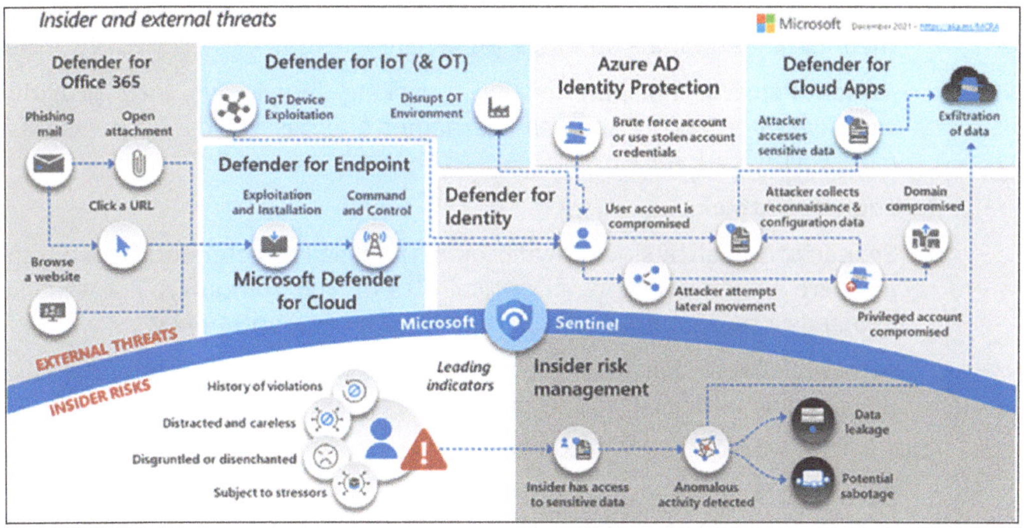

Figure 4.1: *Insider and External Threats* (*Source* : SC-100: Design solutions that align with security best practices and priorities - Training | Microsoft Learn)

Attack chain modeling is a critical concept in the field of cybersecurity, providing a systematic approach to understanding and mitigating security threats. It involves breaking down a cyberattack into a series of sequential stages or steps that an attacker follows to achieve their objective. By analyzing these stages, security professionals can identify vulnerabilities and weak points in their systems and develop effective countermeasures.

The attack chain typically includes initial reconnaissance, weaponization, delivery, exploitation, installation, command and control, and finally, actions on objectives. During each stage, the attacker may use various tactics, techniques, and procedures to advance the attack, ultimately leading to data theft, system compromise, or other malicious actions.

Understanding the attack chain allows security experts to anticipate and disrupt an attack before it reaches its final stage. It helps in the design of preventive measures and the deployment of security controls at various points in the chain. This proactive approach is crucial in enhancing an organization's security posture and minimizing the potential impact of cyberattacks. Attack chain modeling not only aids in incident response but also guides organizations in creating a more resilient defense against evolving cyber threats.

Guarding Against Cyber Threats: From Phishing to Zero-Days

- **Phishing Attack**
    - **Scenario**: Employees at a large corporation receive seemingly legitimate emails that appear to be from the IT department, asking them to update their login credentials on a fake login page.
    - **Attack Pattern**: Phishing involves tricking individuals into providing sensitive information, such as usernames and passwords, by posing as a trustworthy entity.
- **Ransomware Attack**
    - **Scenario**: A small business owner opens an email attachment that contains malware, which encrypts all critical files on the computer. The attacker demands a ransom in cryptocurrency for the decryption key.
    - **Attack Pattern**: Ransomware encrypts a user's files, rendering them inaccessible until a ransom is paid.
- **Man-in-the-Middle (MitM) Attack**
    - **Scenario:** A hacker intercepts communication between a user and a website by exploiting vulnerabilities in public Wi-Fi. The attacker can eavesdrop on sensitive information such as login credentials.
    - **Attack Pattern**: MitM attacks involve intercepting and possibly altering communication between two parties without their knowledge.
- **SQL Injection**
    - **Scenario**: An e-commerce website is vulnerable to SQL injection. An attacker manipulates the input fields to execute malicious SQL queries,

gaining unauthorized access to the database and stealing customer information.

- **Attack Pattern**: SQL injection involves injecting malicious SQL code into input fields to manipulate or access a database.

- **Denial-of-Service (DoS) Attack**
  - **Scenario**: An online service is overwhelmed with a massive volume of traffic, rendering it inaccessible to legitimate users. The service becomes slow or unresponsive.
  - **Attack Pattern**: DoS attacks aim to disrupt the normal functioning of a system by overwhelming it with excessive traffic or resource requests.
- **Malware Distribution via USB Drives**
  - **Scenario**: A company's security is compromised when an employee inserts a USB drive containing malware into a corporate computer. The malware spreads across the network, infecting multiple systems.
  - **Attack Pattern**: Malware can be distributed through removable media, exploiting vulnerabilities in systems when the infected media is connected.
- **Social Engineering Attack**
  - **Scenario**: An attacker calls an employee, posing as IT support, and convinces them to reveal sensitive information or perform actions like transferring funds to a fraudulent account.
  - **Attack Pattern**: Social engineering involves manipulating individuals to divulge confidential information or take specific actions.
- **Zero-Day Exploits**
  - **Scenario**: A hacker discovers and exploits a previously unknown vulnerability in a widely used software application before the developer can release a patch.
  - **Attack Pattern**: Zero-day exploits target vulnerabilities that are unknown to the software vendor or the public, giving attackers an edge until a patch is developed and deployed.

Strengthening Cybersecurity with MITRE ATT&CK and Attack Chain Modeling

The MITRE ATT&CK (Adversarial Tactics, Techniques, and Common Knowledge) framework plays a pivotal role in the context of understanding and addressing cyber threats and attack patterns, particularly in the framework of attack chain modeling.

MITRE ATT&CK is a comprehensive knowledge base that provides detailed insights into the tactics and techniques used by adversaries at various stages of an attack. This framework categorizes threat actor behavior, providing a structured approach for organizations to analyze, detect, and respond to cyberattacks.

Attack chain modeling and MITRE ATT&CK are closely intertwined. While attack chain modeling breaks down a cyberattack into sequential stages, MITRE ATT&CK defines the specific tactics and techniques commonly employed by attackers within each of these stages. For example, within the attack chain's initial reconnaissance phase, MITRE ATT&CK outlines techniques such as spear-phishing, which align with the broader threat actor tactics of gaining initial access.

By leveraging MITRE ATT&CK in conjunction with attack chain modeling, organizations can identify the tactics and techniques that adversaries might employ, allowing them to proactively design and implement security measures at each stage of the attack chain. This alignment enhances an organization's ability to detect and respond to threats effectively. It also helps in building a threat-informed defense strategy that focuses on the actual methods attackers use, rather than solely relying on known indicators of compromise.

MITRE ATT&CK's continuous updates and wealth of knowledge ensure that security professionals remain well-informed about emerging cyber threats and evolving attack patterns. This dynamic framework enables organizations to adapt their security posture to stay ahead of adversaries and mitigate the risks associated with today's ever-evolving threat landscape. In summary, MITRE ATT&CK and attack chain modeling complement each other by providing a comprehensive understanding of how attacks are executed and guiding the development of robust security measures to counter cyber threats effectively.

Building Business Resilience

Business resilience refers to an organization's ability to withstand and adapt to various challenges, disruptions, and unexpected changes while maintaining essential operations and services. It encompasses a comprehensive and proactive approach to risk management and crisis preparedness, ensuring that a business can continue to function effectively even in the face of adversity.

Building cybersecurity business resilience is essential in today's digital landscape, and a practical real-time example is the SolarWinds cyberattack in 2020. Many organizations responded effectively to this breach, showcasing the importance of cybersecurity resilience.

One crucial step in building resilience is continuous monitoring and threat detection. Companies that had robust security measures in place, such as intrusion detection systems and security information and event management (SIEM) solutions, could detect the breach early on. By identifying the attack swiftly, they mitigated potential damage.

Additionally, having an incident response plan was vital. Organizations with well-defined response protocols could contain the breach, analyze its impact, and quickly recover. This minimized downtime and prevented significant data loss.

The SolarWinds incident also highlighted the importance of supply chain security. Organizations learned to assess and strengthen their third-party vendors' cybersecurity measures, reducing their vulnerability to similar attacks.

Moreover, employee training and awareness were key elements. Many successful organizations invested in educating their workforce about cybersecurity best practices. This helped employees recognize phishing attempts and other social engineering tactics used by threat actors.

In summary, the SolarWinds cyberattack demonstrated that building cybersecurity business resilience involves continuous monitoring, robust incident response plans, supply chain security, and employee training. The ability to detect and respond to threats effectively is crucial in maintaining business operations and protecting sensitive data, ensuring that an organization remains resilient even in the face of sophisticated cyberattacks.

Case Study: Building Business Resilience in Cybersecurity

Background:

XYZ Corporation, a global manufacturing company, faced a significant cybersecurity breach that resulted in the compromise of sensitive customer data and intellectual property. The incident prompted the leadership team to recognize the critical need for building business resilience in the face of escalating cyber threats.

Challenge:

The cybersecurity breach had severe consequences, including reputational damage, financial losses, and legal repercussions. The challenge was not only to recover from the immediate impact but also to fortify the organization against future cyber threats. XYZ Corporation needed to establish a robust cybersecurity framework to ensure the confidentiality, integrity, and availability of its digital assets.

Objectives:

- Strengthen the cybersecurity posture to prevent future attacks.
- Develop a comprehensive incident response plan for quick and effective mitigation.

- Foster a culture of cybersecurity awareness and best practices among employees.
- Enhance collaboration with external cybersecurity experts and industry peers.

Strategy and Implementation:

- **Cybersecurity Assessment:**

  Conducted a thorough assessment of existing cybersecurity measures, identifying vulnerabilities, and benchmarking against industry best practices.

- **Security Framework Implementation:**

  Deployed a multi-layered security framework, including firewalls, intrusion detection systems, and advanced endpoint protection to secure the organization's network infrastructure.

- **Incident Response Plan:**

  Developed a detailed incident response plan outlining roles, responsibilities, and communication strategies in the event of a cybersecurity incident. Conducted regular drills to ensure the team's readiness.

- **Employee Training and Awareness:**

  Implemented a comprehensive cybersecurity training program for all employees, covering topics such as phishing awareness, secure password management, and recognizing social engineering tactics.

- **Vendor and Supply Chain Security:**

  Strengthened cybersecurity measures for third-party vendors and supply chain partners, ensuring that security standards aligned with XYZ Corporation's requirements.

- **Collaboration with Cybersecurity Experts:**

  Established partnerships with cybersecurity experts and organizations to stay informed about the latest threats, vulnerabilities, and mitigation strategies.

- **Continuous Monitoring and Improvement:**

  Implemented continuous monitoring of the IT infrastructure for anomalous activities and conducted regular penetration testing to identify and address potential weaknesses.

  Results:

- **Zero Incidents Since Implementation:**

  Following the comprehensive cybersecurity measures, XYZ Corporation experienced zero successful cyber incidents, indicating the effectiveness of the security framework and incident response plan.

- **Improved Employee Awareness:**

  Employees became more vigilant and proactive in identifying potential security threats, resulting in a significant decrease in successful phishing attempts.

- **Enhanced Reputation and Customer Trust:**

  The organization's commitment to cybersecurity and resilience efforts was well-received by customers and stakeholders, rebuilding trust and confidence.

- **Industry Recognition:**

  XYZ Corporation received industry recognition for its cybersecurity practices, contributing to a positive public image and attracting top talent in the field.

By strategically addressing cybersecurity vulnerabilities and proactively building resilience, XYZ Corporation successfully transformed its cybersecurity posture. The organization not only mitigated immediate risks but also positioned itself as a leader in cybersecurity, ensuring the long-term protection of its digital assets and maintaining trust among customers and stakeholders. This case study highlights the importance of a holistic approach to building business resilience in cybersecurity, encompassing technology, people, and processes.

Defending Against Ransomware Attacks: Strategies and Real-Life Insights

A ransomware attack is a type of malicious cyberattack in which an attacker encrypts a victim's data or files and demands a ransom, usually in cryptocurrency, in exchange for a decryption key that can restore access to the data. Ransomware attacks are often financially motivated, and the primary goal is to extort money from individuals, organizations, or businesses.

The attack typically starts with the victim unknowingly downloading or opening a malicious file or link, often delivered through phishing emails or compromised websites. Once the ransomware infiltrates the victim's system, it begins encrypting files, making them inaccessible.

After the encryption is complete, the attacker presents a ransom note, informing the victim of the attack and providing instructions on how to pay the ransom. In some cases, the ransomware may display a countdown timer, threatening to permanently delete the encrypted data if the ransom is not paid within a specified time frame.

Ransomware attacks can have severe consequences, including the loss of sensitive data, operational disruptions, and financial losses. While paying the ransom may result in the decryption of the files, it is generally discouraged, as it does not guarantee that the attacker will provide the decryption key, and it encourages further criminal activity.

Preventing ransomware attacks involves various measures, such as regular data backups, robust cybersecurity practices, employee training to recognize phishing attempts, and keeping software and systems up to date to patch known vulnerabilities. Ransomware protection is crucial in defending against this pervasive cyber threat.

Figure 4.2: *Ransomware Protection* (Source: SC-100: Design solutions that align with security best practices and priorities - Training | Microsoft Learn)

Ransomware protection is a critical cybersecurity practice aimed at preventing and mitigating the impact of ransomware attacks, where malicious actors encrypt an organization's data and demand a ransom for its release. A practical, real-time example of effective ransomware protection can be illustrated through the response of the city of New Orleans to a ransomware attack in December 2019.

The city of New Orleans experienced a ransomware attack that disrupted its government operations and services. In response, several ransomware protection measures were employed:

- **Regular Backups**: One fundamental protection strategy is maintaining up-to-date and offline backups of critical data. New Orleans had backup systems in place, allowing them to restore essential services without paying the ransom.
- **Incident Response Plan**: The city had an incident response plan that was quickly activated. It involved isolating affected systems, notifying law enforcement, and initiating forensic analysis to determine the extent of the attack.
- **Employee Training**: Ensuring that employees are aware of ransomware threats and practicing safe online behavior is essential. New Orleans invested in training to educate its workforce on recognizing phishing attempts and suspicious activities.
- **Patch Management**: Regularly updating and patching software and systems is crucial to address vulnerabilities that ransomware exploits. New Orleans focused on timely patching to reduce potential entry points for attackers.
- **Multi-Layered Security**: Implementing a multi-layered security approach with firewalls, intrusion detection systems, and endpoint security solutions helped detect and prevent ransomware.

By effectively employing these ransomware protection measures, the city of New

Orleans managed to recover without succumbing to the ransom demand. This real-time example demonstrates the significance of proactive ransomware protection practices, which enable organizations to withstand and recover from such attacks, ultimately reducing their impact and ensuring business continuity.

Enhancing Data Security Through Comprehensive Backup Configurations

Configuring secure backup and restore processes is paramount in safeguarding critical data and ensuring the resilience of digital assets. A robust backup strategy involves defining clear policies, including the frequency of backups, storage locations, and access controls. Employing encryption mechanisms, both in transit and at rest, adds an extra layer of protection against unauthorized access. It is imperative to regularly test the backup and restore procedures to verify their effectiveness and identify potential vulnerabilities. Additionally, implementing multi-factor authentication and strict access controls for individuals involved in the backup and restore processes helps to prevent unauthorized changes or deletions. Regular audits and monitoring of backup activities contribute to maintaining the integrity and security of the backup infrastructure. By adhering to these configurations, organizations can fortify their data protection measures and ensure a reliable foundation for business continuity in the face of unforeseen events or cyber threats.

Scenario: Enhancing Data Security Through Comprehensive Backup Configurations

Background:

ABC Financial Services, a prominent financial institution, recently experienced a security incident that involved a ransomware attack. The attack resulted in the encryption of critical financial data, causing operational disruptions and potential data loss. In response to this incident, ABC Financial Services recognized the urgent need to enhance data security through comprehensive backup configurations.

Challenge:

The ransomware attack highlighted the vulnerabilities in ABC Financial Services' data protection strategy. The organization realized that relying solely on traditional backup practices was insufficient, and there was a need for a more robust and proactive approach to safeguarding sensitive financial information.

Objectives:

- **Implement Comprehensive Backup Strategy:**

  Develop and implement a comprehensive backup strategy that includes regular backups of critical data, covering both on-premises and cloud-based systems.

- **Ensure Redundancy and Accessibility:**

  Ensure redundancy by having multiple backup copies stored in geographically diverse locations to prevent a single point of failure. Prioritize accessibility for quick data recovery in case of an incident.

- **Encryption and Access Controls:**

  Integrate encryption measures into the backup configurations to protect data at rest and during transmission. Implement strict access controls to limit the number of individuals with permission to modify or delete backups.

- **Regular Testing and Validation:**

  Conduct regular testing and validation of backup systems to ensure their effectiveness. Simulate various scenarios, including ransomware attacks, to evaluate the organization's ability to recover data swiftly.

- **Incident Response Plan Integration:**

  Integrate the backup strategy into the overall incident response plan, defining clear roles and responsibilities for IT and security teams in the event of a data security incident.

- **Employee Training:**

  Provide comprehensive training to employees on data security best practices, emphasizing their role in maintaining the integrity of data backups. Educate them on recognizing phishing attempts and other threats that could compromise data.

Implementation:

ABC Financial Services engaged a team of cybersecurity experts to assess its current backup configurations and implement the necessary enhancements:

- **Backup Infrastructure Upgrade:**

  Upgraded the backup infrastructure to support more frequent and comprehensive backups, ensuring that critical data is captured regularly.

- **Cloud-Based Redundancy:**

  Implemented a cloud-based backup solution for redundancy, allowing for seamless data recovery in case of on-premises system failures.

- **Encryption and Access Controls:**

  Introduced end-to-end encryption for data in transit and at rest within the backup systems. Implemented strict access controls and multi-factor authentication to prevent unauthorized access.

- **Regular Testing and Simulation:**

  Conducted regular drills and simulations to test the organization's ability to recover data from backups efficiently. Identified and addressed any weaknesses in the backup and recovery processes.

- **Employee Awareness Programs:**

  Launched employee awareness programs to educate staff about the importance of data security, emphasizing their role in maintaining the integrity of backup configurations.

Results:

- **Resilient Data Recovery:**

  ABC Financial Services achieved a more resilient data recovery capability, significantly reducing downtime in the event of a data security incident.

- **Improved Data Integrity:**

  The enhanced backup configurations ensured the integrity of critical financial data, preventing data loss and preserving business continuity.

- **Heightened Security Posture:**

  The organization's overall security posture improved, with a greater focus on proactive measures to prevent and mitigate potential threats.

- **Confidence and Trust:**

  Stakeholders, including customers and regulatory bodies, gained confidence in ABC Financial Services' commitment to data security, rebuilding trust after the previous ransomware incident.

This scenario demonstrates how a financial institution can proactively enhance its data security through comprehensive backup configurations, mitigating the impact of potential ransomware attacks and ensuring the integrity and availability of critical financial data.

Secure Systems with Azure: Automating Patch Management for Enhanced Reliability

In Azure Automation, Update Management plays a crucial role in maintaining the health and security of systems by automating the patching process for various resources.

This feature enables users to assess the update status of virtual machines, ensuring that they are up to date with the latest security patches and software updates. By centralizing update management through Azure Automation, administrators gain a comprehensive view of the update compliance across their entire infrastructure. This not only enhances security but also contributes to system reliability and performance. The solution facilitates flexible scheduling, allowing updates to be applied during specified maintenance windows to minimize disruptions. Through Update Management, Azure Automation provides a streamlined and efficient way to keep systems current, reducing vulnerabilities and promoting a robust and secure computing environment.

Case Study: Secure Systems with Azure - Automating Patch Management for Enhanced Reliability

Background:

XYZ Enterprises, a multinational corporation, faced challenges with manual patch management for its extensive IT infrastructure. The company's systems were vulnerable to security breaches due to delays in applying critical updates, leading to potential data breaches and operational disruptions. In response, XYZ Enterprises sought to enhance its cybersecurity posture by leveraging Azure's capabilities to automate patch management.

Challenge:

- **Manual Patching Inefficiencies:**

  XYZ Enterprises' IT team struggled with the manual process of tracking and applying patches across a diverse range of systems, resulting in delays and increased exposure to security vulnerabilities.

- **Security Risks and Compliance Concerns:**

  The organization faced heightened security risks and compliance concerns due to outdated systems and a lack of timely patching, putting sensitive data at risk and potentially violating regulatory requirements.

- **Operational Disruptions:**

  Frequent operational disruptions occurred when manual patching processes led to system downtimes. This negatively impacted productivity and eroded user confidence in the reliability of the company's IT infrastructure.

Objectives:

- **Automate Patch Management:**

  Implement an automated patch management solution leveraging Azure services to streamline the identification, testing, and deployment of patches across the organization's systems.

- **Ensure Compliance and Security:**

  Enhance compliance with industry regulations and improve overall cybersecurity by ensuring that systems are promptly patched to address known vulnerabilities.

- **Minimize Downtime:**

  Minimize system downtime by automating the patching process during non-business hours, ensuring that critical updates are applied without disrupting essential operations.

Solution:

XYZ Enterprises collaborated with Azure experts to implement a comprehensive patch management solution:

- **Azure Update Management:**

  Leveraged Azure Update Management to automate the assessment, deployment, and tracking of patches across on-premises and multi-cloud environments. This centralized solution allowed the IT team to monitor patch compliance in real-time.

- **Customized Patching Schedules:**

  Configured customized patching schedules based on the organization's operational needs. Critical patches were automatically deployed during non-business hours to minimize disruptions.

- **Integration with Azure Security Center:**

  Integrated Azure Security Center to continuously assess the security posture of the organization's systems. This integration provided actionable insights and recommendations for improving overall security.

- **Comprehensive Reporting and Auditing:**

  Implemented robust reporting and auditing features to track patch compliance, assess vulnerabilities, and generate reports for compliance audits. This ensured transparency and accountability in the patch management process.

Results:

- **Timely Patching and Increased Security:**

  Automated patch management through Azure resulted in the timely application of critical updates, reducing the organization's exposure to known vulnerabilities and enhancing overall cybersecurity.

- **Minimized Downtime and Improved Reliability:**

  Scheduled patch deployments during non-business hours minimized system downtime, improving the reliability of the IT infrastructure and maintaining seamless operations.

- **Enhanced Compliance:**

  Azure's patch management solution ensured that XYZ Enterprises remained compliant with industry regulations and standards, mitigating potential legal and regulatory risks.

- **Streamlined IT Operations:**

  The automated patching process streamlined IT operations, allowing the IT team to focus on strategic initiatives rather than manual, time-consuming patch management tasks.

By embracing Azure's automated patch management capabilities, XYZ Enterprises transformed its cybersecurity posture, minimized operational disruptions, and enhanced overall system reliability. This case study highlights the effectiveness of leveraging cloud-based solutions, specifically Azure, to automate critical security processes and strengthen an organization's defense against cyber threats.

Conclusion

In conclusion, the digital age presents unprecedented cybersecurity challenges, marked by prevalent cyber threats like phishing and ransomware. Combating these threats requires a proactive approach, with the integration of attack chain modeling and the MITRE ATT&CK framework proving effective. Business resilience, exemplified by responses to events like the SolarWinds cyberattack, involves continuous monitoring, robust incident response plans, supply chain security, and employee training. The fight against ransomware demands a multifaceted strategy, including regular backups, cybersecurity best practices, and employee training. Data security is enhanced through comprehensive backup configurations, defined policies, encryption, and multi-factor authentication. Cloud services, exemplified by Azure Automation, streamline patching processes, bolstering system security, reliability, and performance. In this evolving landscape, the synthesis of proactive strategies, frameworks, and real-world insights is crucial for successful cybersecurity navigation. Organizations must remain vigilant, adaptive, and collaborative to protect digital assets in an interconnected world. The next chapter will delve into Compliance-Driven Solution Architecture.

Multiple Choice Questions

1. What is the primary purpose of attack chain modeling in cybersecurity?
    a. To launch cyberattacks
    b. To identify vulnerabilities and formulate countermeasures
    c. To encourage phishing attempts
    d. To compromise security intentionally
2. How does MITRE ATT&CK complement attack chain modeling in addressing cyber threats?
    a. By launching cyberattacks
    b. By defining specific tactics and techniques used by attackers at various stages
    c. By ignoring vulnerabilities
    d. By minimizing security measures
3. What is the primary goal of ransomware attacks?
    a. To enhance cybersecurity awareness
    b. Financial motivation through extortion
    c. To provide decryption keys for free
    d. To promote ethical hacking
4. How did the city of New Orleans effectively respond to a ransomware attack in 2019?
    a. By paying the ransom
    b. By ignoring the attack
    c. By employing ransomware protection measures
    d. By blaming third-party vendors
5. What does securing compliance involve in the context of cybersecurity?
    a. Ignoring regulatory frameworks
    b. Aligning technological measures with regulatory stipulations

c. Minimizing data protection efforts

d. Prioritizing speed over security

Answers

1. b
2. b
3. b
4. c
5. b

CHAPTER 5
Compliance-Driven Solution Architecture

Introduction

Compliance encompasses the adherence to laws, regulations, and standards mandated by governing bodies to ensure ethical operations within legal boundaries. Compliance plays a pivotal role in safeguarding stakeholders' interests, building consumer trust, and mitigating risks. For a tangible illustration, consider a financial institution navigating stringent regulations on data privacy, anti-money laundering (AML), and customer protection. Non-compliance not only exposes the institution to legal consequences but also jeopardizes its reputation and customer trust. In this dynamic environment, a comprehensive understanding of regulatory compliance is imperative for businesses seeking sustainable growth.

Structure

In this chapter, we will cover the following topics:

- Understanding Regulatory Compliance in Today's Dynamic Landscape
- Securing Compliance: Transforming Regulations into Robust Cyber Defenses
- Role of Regulatory Compliance in Today's Dynamic Landscape
- Microsoft Cloud Compliance Program (CMCP): Navigating Regulatory Landscapes
- Microsoft Priva and Azure Policy: Real-time Solutions for Privacy and Compliance
- Securing Infrastructure: A Guide to Compliance with Microsoft Defender for Cloud

Understanding Regulatory Compliance in Today's Dynamic Landscape

Regulatory compliance is a critical aspect for businesses operating in today's complex and dynamic environment. Regulatory compliance refers to the adherence to laws, regulations, and standards set forth by governing bodies to ensure that organizations operate ethically, transparently, and within legal boundaries. In the contemporary business landscape, compliance plays a pivotal role in safeguarding the interests of stakeholders, fostering trust among consumers, and mitigating potential risks. To illustrate the significance of regulatory compliance in a practical business scenario, consider a financial institution that must comply with strict regulations imposed by financial authorities. This includes requirements related to data privacy, anti-money laundering (AML), and customer protection. Failure to comply with these regulations not only exposes the institution to legal repercussions but also jeopardizes its reputation and customer trust. Therefore, a comprehensive understanding of regulatory compliance is indispensable for businesses seeking sustainable growth and longevity in today's highly regulated markets.

Navigating the Regulatory Maze: The Crucial Role of Compliance in Today's Dynamic Business Landscape

Business Scenario:

ABC Financial Solutions, a global financial institution, operates in a dynamic landscape where regulatory requirements are constantly evolving. In recent years, the financial industry has witnessed a surge in regulatory changes, including stricter data protection measures, increased scrutiny of financial transactions, and more robust cybersecurity standards.

Challenge:

ABC Financial Solutions faces the challenge of navigating through the complexities of ever-changing regulatory landscapes. Compliance with various regulations, such as GDPR, PCI DSS, and regional financial compliance standards, has become paramount to maintaining trust among clients and stakeholders while avoiding legal and financial repercussions.

Objectives:

- **Adapt to Regulatory Changes:**

  Stay abreast of the latest regulatory updates and adapt business practices to ensure compliance with evolving standards.

- **Minimize Legal and Financial Risks:**

  Mitigate legal and financial risks by proactively addressing compliance requirements, avoiding penalties, and maintaining a strong reputation in the industry.

- **Safeguard Customer Trust:**

  Demonstrate a commitment to data protection, financial transparency, and ethical business practices to build and maintain trust among clients and stakeholders.

- **Efficient Compliance Management:**

  Implement an efficient compliance management system that can dynamically adjust to regulatory changes, ensuring timely adherence to new requirements without disrupting business operations.

Solution:

ABC Financial Solutions strategizes to address the challenges of regulatory compliance:

- **Compliance Monitoring and Reporting:**

  Utilize advanced compliance monitoring tools to continuously track changes in regulations and generate real-time reports. This enables the organization to stay proactive in meeting new compliance requirements.

- **Cross-Functional Compliance Teams:**

  Establish cross-functional teams comprising legal, IT, finance, and operations professionals to collaborate on interpreting and implementing regulatory changes across different aspects of the business.

- **Regular Compliance Training:**

  Conduct regular training sessions to educate employees about the importance of compliance, providing them with the knowledge and tools needed to adhere to evolving regulations in their day-to-day activities.

- **Investment in Technology:**

  Invest in cutting-edge technology solutions that automate compliance processes, enabling the organization to efficiently manage and adapt to changing regulatory landscapes.

Results:

- **Timely Adherence to Regulations:**

  ABC Financial Solutions achieves timely adherence to new regulations, avoiding legal consequences and maintaining a reputation for reliability and trustworthiness.

- **Proactive Risk Mitigation:**

  By proactively addressing compliance requirements, the organization mitigates legal and financial risks associated with non-compliance, ensuring long-term sustainability in the market.

- **Enhanced Customer Trust:**

  Demonstrating a commitment to compliance and data protection builds and enhances customer trust. Clients feel confident that their financial information is secure and handled with the utmost care.

- **Operational Efficiency:**

  The implementation of technology-driven compliance solutions streamlines processes, enhancing overall operational efficiency and freeing up resources to focus on strategic business objectives.

By embracing a proactive approach to compliance management, the company not only meets legal requirements but also safeguards its reputation, fosters customer trust, and positions itself as a reliable player in the ever-evolving financial industry.

Securing Compliance: Transforming Regulations into Robust Cyber Defenses

In the contemporary landscape of cybersecurity, the translation of compliance requirements into effective security solutions is a critical imperative for organizations aiming to fortify their digital infrastructure. Compliance standards, whether mandated by regulatory bodies or industry-specific authorities, serve as benchmarks to ensure the confidentiality, integrity, and availability of sensitive information. Translating these requirements into a robust security solution involves a meticulous process of aligning technological measures with the stipulations of the regulatory frameworks. For instance, in the healthcare sector, the Health Insurance Portability and Accountability Act (HIPAA) necessitates stringent measures to protect patient data. An organization operating within the scope of HIPAA compliance must implement encryption protocols, access controls, and regular security audits to safeguard patient information effectively. Similarly, the General Data Protection Regulation (GDPR) in the European Union emphasizes the protection of personal data. To translate GDPR compliance requirements into a security solution, organizations often deploy mechanisms such as anonymization of data, data encryption, and transparent privacy policies. Real-time examples showcase the effectiveness of such translations; the financial industry, bound by regulations like PCI DSS, employs secure payment gateways, encryption, and tokenization to protect sensitive cardholder information during electronic transactions. In summary, the translation of compliance requirements into security solutions is not only a legal obligation but also a strategic imperative that enhances data protection, mitigates risks, and builds trust with stakeholders.

Scenario:

XYZ Healthcare, a leading healthcare provider, operates in an industry where data privacy and regulatory compliance are of utmost importance. With the increasing number of cyber threats targeting sensitive patient information, XYZ Healthcare faces the critical challenge of aligning its cybersecurity measures with evolving healthcare regulations.

Challenge:

Recent updates to healthcare regulations have introduced stricter requirements for protecting patient data, imposing hefty fines for non-compliance. XYZ Healthcare must navigate this intricate landscape, balancing the need for cutting-edge cybersecurity with adherence to regulatory standards.

Objectives:

- **Align Cybersecurity with Regulations:**

  Ensure that XYZ Healthcare's cybersecurity framework aligns seamlessly with the latest healthcare regulations, such as the Health Insurance Portability and Accountability Act (HIPAA) and other regional data protection laws.

- **Data Encryption and Access Controls:**

  Implement robust data encryption measures and access controls to safeguard patient records and sensitive healthcare information, addressing specific requirements outlined in the regulatory framework.

- **Regular Compliance Audits:**

  Conduct regular internal compliance audits to assess the effectiveness of cybersecurity measures, identify potential gaps, and proactively address any issues before they lead to regulatory violations.

- **Incident Response Preparedness:**

  Develop and test a comprehensive incident response plan that not only aligns with regulatory guidelines but also ensures swift and effective responses to potential data breaches or cyber incidents.

Solution:

XYZ Healthcare takes a proactive approach to secure compliance and transforming regulations into robust cyber defenses:

- **Cybersecurity Framework Enhancement:**
  Collaborate with cybersecurity experts to enhance the organization's cybersecurity framework, aligning it with the specific requirements of healthcare regulations. This includes implementing advanced threat detection, network segmentation, and endpoint protection.
- **Data Encryption and Access Controls:**
  Deploy state-of-the-art encryption technologies and access controls to safeguard patient data, ensuring that only authorized personnel have access to sensitive healthcare information. This involves regular training for employees on data handling best practices.
- **Regular Compliance Audits:**
  Conduct periodic compliance audits, leveraging both internal and external expertise to assess the effectiveness of cybersecurity measures. The audits include vulnerability assessments, penetration testing, and a review of policies and procedures.
- **Incident Response Simulation:**
  Conduct regular simulations of potential cybersecurity incidents, involving key stakeholders and response teams. This ensures that the incident response plan is well-understood and can be executed effectively in a real-time scenario.

Results:

- **Adherence to Regulatory Standards:**
  XYZ Healthcare achieves seamless alignment with healthcare regulations, ensuring that its cybersecurity measures meet or exceed the stipulated standards. This minimizes the risk of regulatory penalties and legal consequences.
- **Heightened Data Security:**
  The implementation of advanced encryption and access controls results in heightened data security, providing patients with assurance that their sensitive healthcare information is well-protected.
- **Proactive Risk Mitigation:**
  Regular compliance audits and incident response simulations enable XYZ Healthcare to proactively identify and mitigate potential risks, strengthening the organization's overall cybersecurity posture.
- **Strengthened Reputation:**
  By transforming regulatory compliance into robust cyber defenses, XYZ

Healthcare builds a reputation as a trustworthy and secure healthcare provider. This fosters patient confidence and enhances the organization's standing in the healthcare industry.

Summary

XYZ Healthcare successfully transforms the challenge of securing compliance into an opportunity to bolster its cybersecurity defenses. By aligning with regulatory standards, implementing advanced technologies, and conducting regular audits, the organization not only meets legal requirements but also fortifies itself against evolving cyber threats in the dynamic healthcare landscape.

Role of Regulatory Compliance in Today's Dynamic Landscape

Addressing compliance requirements with Microsoft Purview involves a systematic approach to ensure data governance and regulatory adherence. First and foremost, organizations need to initiate the process by identifying the specific compliance requirements applicable to their industry or region. This could involve regulations related to data privacy, security, or industry-specific standards. Once these requirements are clearly defined, the next step is to leverage Microsoft Purview's comprehensive data discovery capabilities. Through advanced scanning and classification tools, Purview enables organizations to locate and categorize sensitive data across various repositories, including on-premises and cloud environments.

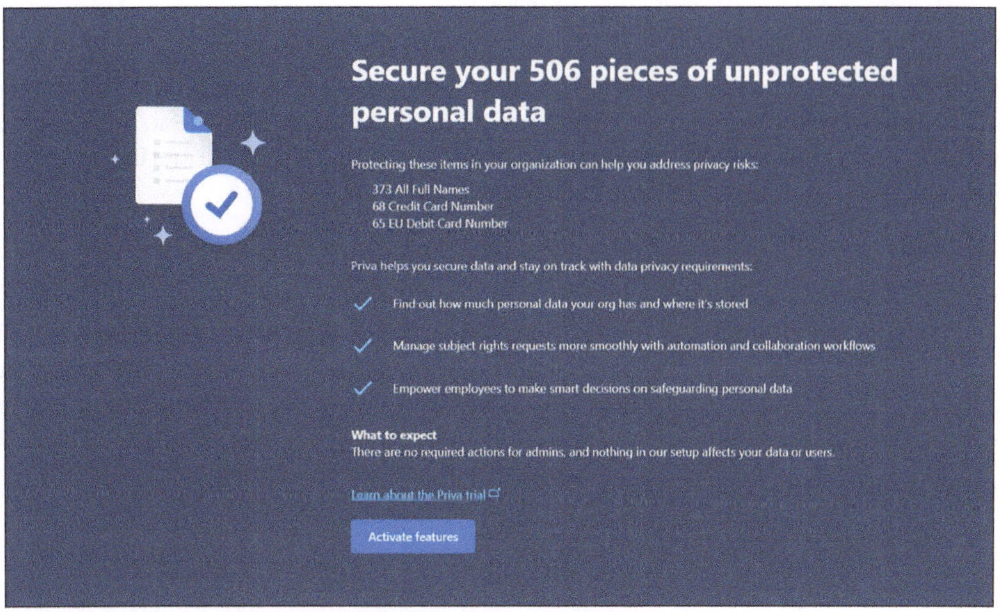

Figure 5.1: *Microsoft Purview*

Following the data discovery phase, organizations can utilize a purview to establish and enforce data policies. This involves defining rules and access controls to ensure that sensitive information is handled and shared in accordance with compliance standards. Microsoft Purview's policy management features provide a centralized mechanism to monitor and control data throughout its lifecycle.

Moreover, Microsoft Purview facilitates ongoing compliance monitoring and reporting. Organizations can set up regular scans and assessments to identify any deviations from established compliance policies. The platform generates detailed reports and dashboards, offering insights into the organization's overall compliance posture. This step is crucial for proactively addressing potential compliance issues and demonstrating a commitment to regulatory standards during audits.

Altogether, Microsoft Purview offers a comprehensive solution to address compliance requirements in a step-by-step manner, starting from identifying regulations, discovering sensitive data, and establishing and enforcing policies, to continuous monitoring and reporting. This holistic approach not only helps organizations meet regulatory obligations but also enhances overall data governance and security.

Navigating the Regulatory Landscape: The Vital Role of Compliance in Today's Dynamic Business Environment

Let us analyze the concept with Business Scenario:

Background:

ABC Tech Solutions, a rapidly growing technology company, operates in a dynamic global market characterized by continuous technological advancements and evolving regulatory frameworks. The organization faces the challenge of adhering to diverse compliance standards while staying agile and innovative.

Challenge:

ABC Tech Solutions encounters a multifaceted challenge – managing compliance with an array of regulations such as GDPR, CCPA, and industry-specific standards. The dynamic nature of the business landscape requires the company to balance innovation with a robust compliance framework, ensuring legal adherence while fostering technological advancements.

Objectives:

- **Multinational Regulatory Alignment:**

  Navigate and align with diverse international and regional regulations to ensure compliance across various markets where ABC Tech Solutions operates.

- **Innovation Without Compromise:**

  Foster a culture of innovation while maintaining compliance, ensuring that the company remains at the forefront of technological advancements without compromising legal and ethical standards.

- **Data Privacy and Security:**

  Prioritize data privacy and security, especially in an era where customer trust is pivotal. Implement measures to protect customer data in accordance with global data protection regulations.

- **Agile Compliance Management:**

  Develop an agile compliance management system capable of adapting to frequent regulatory changes, ensuring the company's ability to respond promptly to new requirements.

Solution:

ABC Tech Solutions strategizes to address the challenges posed by the dynamic regulatory landscape:

- **Compliance Intelligence Teams:**

  Establish specialized teams responsible for monitoring and interpreting changes in global regulations, providing real-time insights to relevant departments to facilitate prompt adjustments in business processes.

- **Innovation and Compliance Committees:**

  Form cross-functional committees that include legal, IT, and innovation experts. These committees assess the impact of proposed innovations on compliance and provide recommendations to ensure a harmonious balance.

- **Data Protection by Design:**

  Implement a "Privacy by Design" approach in product development, integrating data protection measures into the core of new technologies and solutions to proactively address privacy concerns.

- **Continuous Compliance Training:**

  Conduct ongoing compliance training for employees at all levels, fostering awareness and understanding of the importance of regulatory adherence in day-to-day operations.

Results:

- **Global Regulatory Adherence:**

  ABC Tech Solutions successfully aligns with diverse global regulations, ensuring that its products and services comply with legal standards in each market, thereby mitigating the risk of legal consequences.

- **Innovation and Compliance Synergy:**

  The establishment of innovation and compliance committees facilitates a seamless synergy between technological advancements and regulatory adherence, allowing the company to stay competitive while ensuring ethical business practices.

- **Enhanced Data Protection:**

  The "Privacy by Design" approach results in enhanced data protection measures, strengthening customer trust and loyalty while mitigating the risk of data breaches and associated legal challenges.

- **Agile Response to Changes:**

  The agile compliance management system enables ABC Tech Solutions to respond swiftly to regulatory changes, ensuring that the company remains adaptable and compliant in the face of an ever-evolving regulatory landscape.

In today's dynamic business landscape, the role of regulatory compliance is critical for companies like ABC Tech Solutions. By proactively addressing the challenges posed by diverse regulations, the company not only ensures legal adherence but also fosters innovation, maintains customer trust, and positions itself as a responsible and forward-thinking player in the technology industry.

Microsoft Cloud Compliance Program (CMCP): Navigating Regulatory Landscapes

Regulatory compliance is pivotal for safeguarding sensitive information. Organizations must align with industry-specific or regional regulations to ensure data protection, privacy, and overall cybersecurity resilience.

Securing Compliance: Transforming Regulations into Robust Cyber Defenses:

Achieving compliance involves transforming regulatory requirements into robust cyber defenses. This includes implementing security measures, data protection protocols, and access controls. Microsoft Cloud Compliance Program (CMCP) offers a structured framework to navigate and address diverse compliance challenges.

Microsoft Priva and Azure Policy: Real-time Solutions for Privacy and Compliance:

Microsoft Priva and Azure Policy play integral roles in ensuring real-time privacy and compliance. Microsoft Priva facilitates data subject requests and consent management, while Azure Policy allows organizations to define and enforce compliance standards across their Azure environment.

In summary, the Microsoft Cloud Compliance Program (CMCP) provides organizations with a robust framework to navigate and implement regulatory requirements. Leveraging tools like Microsoft Priva, Azure Policy, and Microsoft Defender for Cloud, businesses can fortify their cybersecurity defenses and stay compliant in an ever-evolving regulatory landscape. For comprehensive details on Microsoft's compliance offerings, visit the Microsoft Trust Center.

Microsoft Priva and Azure Policy: Real-time Solutions for Privacy and Compliance

Addressing privacy requirements with Microsoft Priva is a strategic imperative for businesses navigating the intricate landscape of data protection. Consider a multinational e-commerce corporation as a real-time business scenario. With an extensive customer base, this company handles a vast amount of personal information, including customer names, addresses, and payment details. In this context, compliance with privacy regulations, such as the General Data Protection Regulation (GDPR) is paramount. Microsoft Priva comes into play by providing a robust framework for managing and safeguarding sensitive data.

To start, the organization utilizes Priva's data discovery capabilities to locate and classify personal data within its databases and storage systems. This proactive identification process ensures a comprehensive understanding of the data landscape, a crucial step in meeting privacy compliance requirements. Subsequently, the company leverages Priva's data governance features to implement and enforce privacy policies. These policies define how personal information is collected, processed, and stored, aligning with the principles outlined in GDPR.

Moreover, Microsoft Priva's dynamic data masking and encryption functionalities add an extra layer of protection to sensitive information. This is particularly essential when certain personnel within the organization require access to customer data for legitimate purposes. The platform's granular control mechanisms allow the company to balance data accessibility with stringent privacy measures.

In real-time, Microsoft Priva's continuous monitoring capabilities provide the organization with insights into potential privacy risks. Automated alerts and reporting mechanisms help the company swiftly address any deviations from privacy policies, ensuring ongoing compliance. This proactive approach not only mitigates the risk of regulatory penalties but also fortifies customer trust by demonstrating a commitment to safeguarding their personal information. Thus, Microsoft Priva emerges as a pivotal tool for businesses seeking to navigate the intricate terrain of privacy requirements in a data-driven world.

Effectively addressing security and compliance requirements is paramount for businesses, and Azure Policy provides a robust solution to achieve this in a real-time business context. Take, for instance, a multinational corporation managing sensitive customer data across its global operations. In compliance with data protection regulations, the organization employs Azure Policy to enforce stringent access controls and encryption standards. Through Azure Policy's centralized management, the company can define and implement policies consistently across its diverse Azure resources, spanning virtual machines, databases, and cloud storage.

For instance, the corporation can establish policies specifying that all Azure virtual machines must have encryption at rest enabled and that access to specific data repositories should adhere to the principle of least privilege. Azure Policy's real-time monitoring capabilities continuously assess the compliance of these resources, automatically flagging any deviations from the established policies. This ensures that the organization can promptly identify and address potential security risks or compliance gaps, reducing the likelihood of data breaches and regulatory penalties.

Moreover, Azure Policy provides a unified dashboard for comprehensive visibility into the compliance posture of the entire Azure infrastructure. This real-time monitoring and reporting capability not only streamlines audit processes but also empowers the organization to demonstrate its commitment to security and compliance during regulatory assessments.

In conclusion, Azure Policy serves as a critical tool for businesses to address security and compliance requirements in real-time. The aforementioned multinational corporation's use case exemplifies how Azure Policy can be pivotal in maintaining a secure and compliant cloud environment, ultimately safeguarding sensitive data and fostering trust among customers and regulatory bodies alike.

Securing Infrastructure: A Guide to Compliance with Microsoft Defender for Cloud

Assessing infrastructure compliance with Microsoft Defender for Cloud (MDC) involves a comprehensive process tailored to diverse regulatory environments. Organizations initiate the evaluation by identifying specific compliance standards pertinent to their industry or regulatory framework. These may encompass data protection, access controls, and other security protocols. Once defined, Microsoft Defender for Cloud's scanning capabilities are harnessed to conduct a meticulous examination of the infrastructure, pinpointing vulnerabilities, misconfigurations, and potential security risks.

Post-scanning, organizations leverage Defender for Cloud to enforce security policies. This involves configuring the platform to align with defined compliance standards, implementing robust access controls, and ensuring the infrastructure meets necessary security benchmarks. The centralized dashboard in Microsoft Defender for Cloud streamlines policy management, simplifying the monitoring and control of security configurations.

Continuous monitoring is paramount in evaluating infrastructure compliance. Defender for Cloud provides real-time visibility into the security posture, enabling prompt detection and response to any deviations from compliance standards. The platform generates alerts and reports, offering insights into potential security incidents or areas requiring attention.

In summary, the process of evaluating infrastructure compliance with Microsoft Defender for Cloud entails defining standards, scanning for vulnerabilities, enforcing security policies, and implementing continuous monitoring. This systematic approach not only ensures adherence to regulatory requirements but also enhances the overall security posture of the organization's digital infrastructure.

Conclusion

In conclusion, the discussed compliance-driven solution architecture emphasizes the critical role of regulatory adherence, data protection, and security in the modern business landscape. Highlighting examples from diverse industries, including finance, healthcare, and e-commerce, the integration of Microsoft Purview, Priva, Azure Policy, and Defender for Cloud offers a comprehensive approach to real-time compliance management. Microsoft Purview facilitates data discovery and continuous monitoring, while Priva addresses privacy requirements through proactive data governance. Azure Policy, crucial for managing sensitive data in the cloud, ensures centralized policy management and real-time monitoring. Real-world examples showcase its effectiveness in maintaining a secure and compliant cloud environment. The structured process outlined with Microsoft Defender for Cloud emphasizes defining compliance standards, thorough scans, policy enforcement, and continuous monitoring enhancing overall security posture. This compliance-driven architecture not only meets legal obligations but also serves as a strategic imperative for sustainable growth and trust in a dynamic regulatory and cyber threat landscape. The next chapter will delve into the role of identity and access management.

Multiple Choice Questions (MCQs)

1. What is the primary role of regulatory compliance in today's business landscape?

    a. Enhancing profit margins

    b. Ensuring ethical operations within legal boundaries

   c. Expanding market share
   d. Minimizing innovation risks
2. Why is compliance crucial for a financial institution dealing with data privacy, anti-money laundering (AML), and customer protection?
   a. To maximize profits
   b. To avoid legal consequences and safeguard reputation
   c. To reduce customer trust
   d. To encourage risky financial practices
3. What does the translation of compliance requirements into security solutions involve in the cybersecurity landscape?
   a. Ignoring regulatory frameworks
   b. Aligning technological measures with regulatory stipulations
   c. Minimizing data protection efforts
   d. Prioritizing speed over security
4. How does Microsoft Purview contribute to addressing compliance requirements?
   a. By ignoring data discovery capabilities
   b. By avoiding policy enforcement
   c. Through comprehensive data discovery and ongoing monitoring
   d. By compromising data security
5. What is the role of Azure Policy in a multinational corporation managing sensitive customer data across its global operations?
   a. To ignore compliance standards
   b. To enforce stringent access controls and encryption standards
   c. To prioritize data breaches
   d. To limit visibility into compliance posture

Answers

1. b
2. b
3. b
4. c
5. b

CHAPTER 6
Identity and Access Control Design

Introduction

Identity and Access Management (IAM) plays a pivotal role in contemporary cybersecurity, providing a robust framework for organizations to manage and control users' access to their digital resources. IAM is fundamentally concerned with authenticating the identities of users and ensuring that they have appropriate levels of access to systems, applications, and data. By implementing IAM solutions, businesses can enforce the principle of least privilege, granting users the minimum access necessary for their roles. This not only enhances security but also mitigates the risk of unauthorized access and potential data breaches. IAM systems typically involve authentication mechanisms like multi-factor authentication (MFA) to bolster security measures. Moreover, IAM facilitates the efficient management of user identities throughout their lifecycle, from onboarding to offboarding, ensuring that access permissions are adjusted in real-time based on changes in job roles or responsibilities. In today's dynamic and interconnected digital landscape, a well-implemented IAM strategy is essential for safeguarding sensitive information, meeting compliance requirements, and building a secure foundation for overall organizational cybersecurity.

Structure

In this chapter, we will cover the following topics:

- Streamlining Access: Microsoft Entra ID Case Study in Multinational Corporation's Cloud Journey
- Streamlining Access: Microsoft Entra ID in Hybrid and Multi-Cloud Environments
- Real-Time Scenario: Safeguarding Collaboration in Global E-commerce
- Secure Collaboration: Microsoft Entra ID B2B Case Study in Global E-commerce

- Tomorrow's Security: Modern Authentication Strategies
- Zero Trust Cybersecurity: Aligned Access Policies in Finance
- Business Scenario: Zero Trust in Action for Cybersecurity in a Multinational Financial Institution
- Managing Security in Financial Cybersecurity
- FortifyBank Cybersecurity Breach Response

Streamlining Access: Microsoft Entra ID Case Study in Multinational Corporation's Cloud Journey

Multinational corporations rely heavily on cloud technology for their operations. However, managing access to these cloud resources efficiently and securely can be a daunting task. This is where Microsoft Entra ID steps in as a solution that simplifies the process.

Entra ID offers a unified approach to access management, allowing employees to seamlessly navigate cloud resources with a single set of credentials. This not only enhances productivity but also reduces the burden on IT teams by streamlining authentication protocols.

Moreover, Entra ID's adaptability ensures compliance with various regulatory frameworks, no matter where the corporation operates. Whether it's GDPR in Europe or CCPA in California, Entra ID helps multinational corporations navigate the complex landscape of data privacy laws effortlessly.

Let's consider a real-world example: XYZ Corp, a multinational corporation with offices across different continents. Before implementing Entra ID, XYZ Corp struggled with managing access to its cloud-based resources, leading to inefficiencies and security concerns.

However, with Entra ID in place, XYZ Corp experienced a significant improvement. Employees could now access cloud resources with ease, boosting productivity and collaboration across the organization. Additionally, Entra ID's compliance features ensured that XYZ Corp remained in line with relevant regulations, mitigating legal risks and ensuring data security.

Microsoft Entra ID is a game-changer for multinational corporations embarking on their cloud journey. By simplifying access management, ensuring compliance, and enhancing collaboration, Entra ID enables corporations to harness the full potential of cloud technology in today's digital world.

Streamlining Access: Microsoft Entra ID in Hybrid and Multi-Cloud Environments

In a real-time scenario, let's consider a multinational corporation (MNC) that operates across various geographical locations and has adopted a hybrid cloud infrastructure. The company has diverse business units, each utilizing different cloud providers for specific applications and services. As part of its digital transformation journey, the MNC faces challenges in unifying access to resources hosted both on-premises and in the cloud.

To address these challenges, the organization has decided to leverage Microsoft Entra ID (Active Directory) to optimize access across its hybrid and multi-cloud environments.

Hybrid Cloud Environment

On-premises legacy applications and sensitive data are still integral to the organization's operations.

The company has migrated certain workloads to the Azure cloud to benefit from scalability and flexibility.

Users, including employees and partners, need seamless access to resources both on-premises and in the Azure cloud.

Challenges Faced:

- Users experience friction in accessing resources, as separate credentials are required for on-premises and cloud-based applications.
- Inconsistent access policies lead to potential security vulnerabilities and difficulties in enforcing compliance standards.
- The organization lacks a centralized identity management system, causing delays in provisioning and de-provisioning user access.

Integration of Microsoft Entra ID:

- The MNC decides to implement Microsoft Entra ID as the central identity and access management solution.
- Microsoft Entra ID is configured to integrate with the existing on-premises Active Directory, providing a seamless experience for users with single sign-on (SSO) capabilities.
- Multi-factor authentication (MFA) is enforced to enhance security, especially for accessing critical resources.

Multi-Cloud Expansion:

- Recognizing the need for flexibility, the organization expands its infrastructure to a multi-cloud environment, incorporating services from multiple cloud providers, such as AWS and Google Cloud.

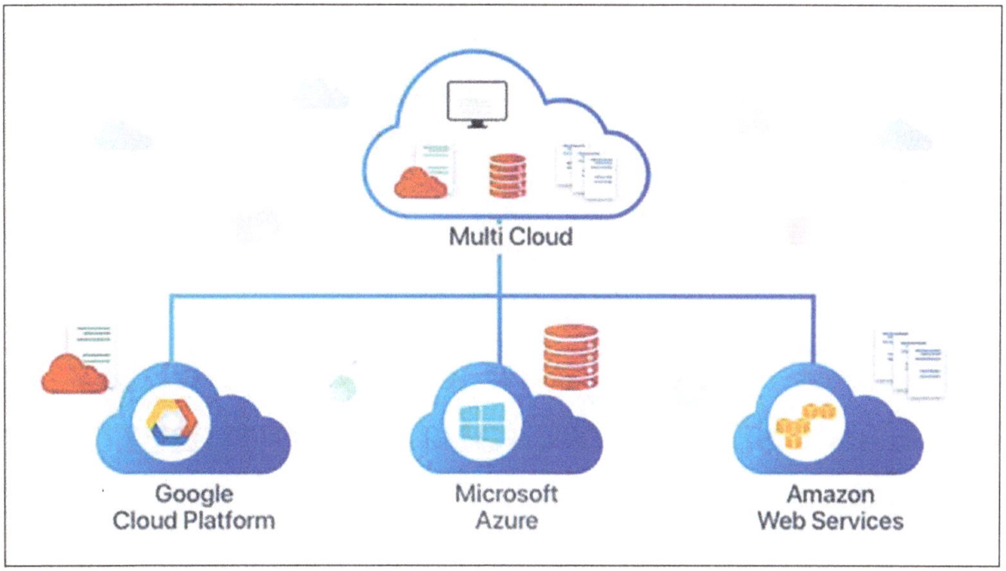

Figure 6.1: *Multi-Cloud Environment* (*Source* : What is Multi-Cloud and Hybrid Cloud | Use-Cases (xenonstack.com))

- Microsoft Entra ID's compatibility with various identity standards allows for seamless integration with other cloud platforms, ensuring a cohesive access strategy.

Identity Federation and Single Sign-On:

- Identity federation protocols are implemented to enable users to access resources across different clouds without the need for separate sets of credentials.
- Single sign-on is extended to include not only Azure but also other cloud platforms, enhancing user experience and reducing the risk of password-related security issues.

Conditional Access Policies:

- The organization leverages Microsoft Entra ID's conditional access policies to enhance security.
- Policies are configured based on contextual factors such as user location, device health, and the sensitivity of the accessed data, ensuring that access controls dynamically adapt to the changing risk landscape.

Results and Benefits:

- Users now experience a unified access experience, seamlessly navigating resources across on-premises and multiple cloud environments.
- Security is strengthened with consistent access policies and the enforcement of multi-factor authentication.
- The organization achieves operational efficiency with centralized identity management, enabling real-time adjustments to user access permissions based on changes in roles or responsibilities.

This real-time scenario illustrates how Microsoft Entra ID plays a pivotal role in optimizing access for a multinational corporation operating in a hybrid and multi-cloud landscape, addressing challenges and enhancing security across diverse cloud realms.

Secure Collaboration: Microsoft Entra ID B2B Case Study in Global E-commerce

In the contemporary business landscape, designing a robust solution for external identities is paramount for organizations engaging with partners, customers, and other external stakeholders. Let's consider a business scenario to illustrate the importance and implementation of such a solution.

Imagine a global e-commerce enterprise that collaborates with numerous vendors, partners, and customers across various regions. As the company expands its digital ecosystem, the need arises for a secure and streamlined solution for managing external identities. This entails providing seamless access to the e-commerce platform for external parties while ensuring stringent security measures.

To address this challenge, the organization decided to design a comprehensive solution leveraging Azure Active Directory B2B (Business-to-Business) capabilities. Microsoft Entra ID B2B allows the e-commerce enterprise to invite external users to access its resources without the need for them to create new credentials. This eliminates the inconvenience of managing separate accounts for external collaborators and simplifies the onboarding process.

The solution involves the creation of a secure and user-friendly portal where external partners and vendors can authenticate their identities using their existing credentials from their respective organizations. Microsoft Entra ID B2B supports a wide range of identity providers, ensuring flexibility and inclusivity for external parties. Multi-factor authentication (MFA) can be enforced to add an extra layer of security, safeguarding against unauthorized access.

Furthermore, the organization implements role-based access controls (RBAC) through

Microsoft Entra ID B2B, allowing precise definition and enforcement of permissions based on the specific needs and roles of external users. This ensures that each external identity has access only to the resources necessary for collaboration, enhancing security and compliance.

The solution also incorporates Microsoft Entra ID B2B's reporting and monitoring features, enabling the organization to track external user activities, detect anomalies, and respond promptly to potential security incidents. Regular audits and assessments provide insights into the overall security posture and help in maintaining compliance with industry regulations.

In summary, by designing a solution for external identities using Microsoft Entra ID B2B, the e-commerce enterprise successfully addresses the challenges of managing access for external collaborators. This not only streamlines collaboration processes but also reinforces security measures, building trust with external partners and customers. The implementation of such a solution exemplifies a strategic approach to identity management in a globalized business environment.

Real-Time Scenario: Safeguarding Collaboration in Global E-commerce

Let us explore how seamless access management with Microsoft Entra ID fosters secure collaboration across global e-commerce platforms in real-time scenario

Company Profile:

ABC E-commerce, a multinational giant in the online retail sector, operates in various countries and engages in diverse collaborations with external partners, including suppliers, distributors, and marketing agencies. The company recognizes the crucial importance of securing these collaborations and streamlining external identity management to ensure sustained success and safeguard sensitive data.

Current Challenges:

- **Diverse External Partnerships:**

  ABC E-commerce collaborates with a multitude of external partners, each requiring access to specific resources within the company's ecosystem. Managing the diverse network of users has become complex and challenging.

- **Security Concerns:**

  The increasing exchange of sensitive data and proprietary information in collaborations raises security concerns. The existing methods of managing external user access are proving inadequate, and the company is keen on enhancing its security measures.

- **Operational Inefficiency:**
  The manual onboarding and offboarding processes for external partners are causing inefficiencies and delays. ABC E-commerce recognizes the need for a more streamlined solution to enhance operational efficiency.

Implementation of Microsoft Entra ID B2B:

In response to these challenges, ABC E-commerce has decided to implement Microsoft Entra ID B2B as a comprehensive solution for external identity management.

- **Collaborator Onboarding**
  Microsoft Entra ID B2B simplifies the onboarding process for external partners. Invited users can now seamlessly access necessary resources without the need for creating separate accounts, significantly improving the user experience.
- **Security Enhancements**
  Multi-factor authentication (MFA) is enforced to fortify security. External collaborators accessing critical information now undergo additional identity verification steps, reducing the risk of unauthorized access and potential data breaches.
- **Unified Access Control**
  Microsoft Entra ID B2B allows for centralized access control, enabling ABC E-commerce to define and enforce access policies consistently across all external collaborators. This not only ensures compliance with security standards but also mitigates the risk of unauthorized access.
- **Efficient Offboarding**
  Streamlined de-provisioning processes facilitated by Microsoft Entra ID B2B ensure the prompt removal of access for external collaborators when partnerships conclude. This minimizes the risk of lingering security threats post-collaboration.

Real-Time Results:

- **Enhanced Security:**

  The implementation of Microsoft Entra ID B2B has significantly strengthened the security of external collaboration channels. MFA and unified access controls have reduced the risk of unauthorized access, providing a more secure environment for sensitive data.
- **Streamlined Operations:**

  ABC E-commerce is experiencing increased operational efficiency with automated onboarding and offboarding processes. The reduced administrative overhead allows the company to make swift adjustments to access permissions, aligning with dynamic business requirements.

- **Improved User Experience:**

  External partners now enjoy a seamless and user-friendly access experience, fostering positive collaborations and strengthening business relationships. The enhanced user experience contributes to improved partner satisfaction.

- **Scalability:**

  Microsoft Entra ID B2B's scalability has allowed ABC E-commerce to effortlessly accommodate a growing network of external partners. This adaptability proves crucial to the ever-evolving and dynamic nature of the global e-commerce industry.

The real-time scenario at ABC E-commerce illustrates how the implementation of Microsoft Entra ID B2B is safeguarding collaboration, fortifying security, and streamlining external identity management. By addressing existing challenges, the company is establishing a secure and efficient collaboration environment, ensuring its continued success in the global e-commerce landscape.

Tomorrow's Security: Modern Authentication Strategies

Traditional methods of user verification and access control often prove inadequate in meeting the dynamic challenges posed by evolving cyber threats and diverse user expectations. To tackle these issues effectively, organizations need to adopt innovative approaches that incorporate cutting-edge technologies. A robust solution involves the integration of OAuth 2.0 and OpenID Connect for secure authentication, providing a foundation for delegated authorization and the ability to obtain user profile information without compromising credentials. Complementing this, role-based access control (RBAC) ensures granular and tailored authorization policies, allowing organizations to define and enforce access permissions based on users' roles. Adaptive authentication mechanisms add an extra layer of sophistication by dynamically adjusting security requirements based on contextual factors, including user behavior, device characteristics, and geolocation. By centralizing identity management and embracing these modern strategies, organizations not only bolster their security posture but also pave the way for scalable, user-friendly access controls in the rapidly evolving digital landscape. Let us discuss a problem statement associated with the current discussion.

Problem Statement

Organizations face challenges in accommodating diverse user needs, securing sensitive data, and adapting to the dynamic nature of contemporary technology. The need for a modern authentication and authorization strategy is apparent in scenarios where traditional methods struggle to keep pace with the evolving threat landscape and user expectations.

Solution: Designing Modern Authentication and Authorization Strategies

To address these challenges, organizations must adopt modern authentication and authorization strategies that leverage advanced technologies and adaptive approaches. A comprehensive solution involves the integration of OAuth 2.0, OpenID Connect, and role-based access control (RBAC) to establish a robust framework.

OAuth 2.0 for Secure Authentication:

- Implement OAuth 2.0 as the foundation for secure authentication. This protocol facilitates delegated authorization, allowing applications to obtain limited access to resources on behalf of a user without exposing their credentials.
- Leverage OAuth 2.0's support for various authentication methods, including social identity providers and multi-factor authentication (MFA), enhancing user authentication security.
- Integrate OpenID Connect for the identity layer on top of OAuth 2.0, providing user authentication and obtaining basic user profile information.

Role-Based Access Control (RBAC) for Authorization:

- Employ RBAC to define and enforce access right based on roles, ensuring that users have the necessary permissions for their specific responsibilities.

***Figure* 6.2**: *Role-Based Access Control*

- Implement fine-grained access controls within applications and services, restricting access to sensitive data based on user roles.
- Regularly review and update role assignments to align with changes in organizational structure and responsibilities.

Adaptive Authentication for Dynamic Security:

- Integrate adaptive authentication mechanisms that assess risk factors, such as user behavior, device characteristics, and geolocation, to dynamically adjust authentication requirements.
- Implement contextual access policies that adapt based on the user's location, the device used, and the sensitivity of the requested resources.
- Utilize machine learning algorithms to analyze patterns and anomalies, enhancing the system's ability to detect and prevent unauthorized access.

Centralized Identity Management:

- Establish a centralized identity management system that consolidates user identities across applications and services.
- Integrate with identity providers that support modern standards, ensuring compatibility and interoperability across diverse platforms.
- Implement secure user authentication workflows, such as single sign-on (SSO), to enhance user experience without compromising security.

By designing and implementing these modern authentication and authorization strategies, organizations can create a resilient security framework that adapts to the evolving needs of users and the dynamic nature of the digital landscape. This approach not only enhances security but also provides a foundation for scalable and user-friendly access control in the modern era of digital business.

Zero Trust Cybersecurity: Aligned Access Policies in Finance

Zero Trust is a security concept that operates on the premise of not automatically trusting any entity – whether it's users, devices, networks, or applications – inside or outside the network perimeter.

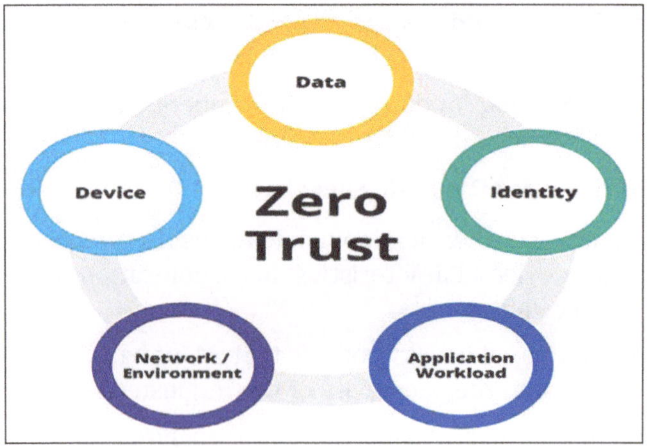

Figure 6.3: *Zero Trust Concept*

In terms of identity, it means authenticating and authorizing every user and device trying to access resources, regardless of their location or whether they are inside or outside the corporate network. For data, Zero Trust involves encrypting data both in transit and at rest, and controlling access to it based on policies that consider factors like user identity, location, and the sensitivity of the data itself. With devices, Zero Trust means treating every device as untrusted until proven otherwise, enforcing policies that require devices to meet certain security standards before granting access to corporate resources. In terms of network security, Zero Trust involves segmenting the network into smaller, more manageable parts and implementing strict access controls and inspection mechanisms to prevent lateral movement and unauthorized access. Finally, for applications and workloads, Zero Trust requires implementing granular access controls, using techniques like micro-segmentation and least privilege access, and continuously monitoring and verifying the behavior of applications and workloads to detect and respond to any suspicious activities.

Consider a real-time scenario where a multinational financial institution adopts this strategic alignment to safeguard its sensitive data. In this context, the organization implements a Zero Trust model, fundamentally distrusting every user and device attempting to access its network. By aligning conditional access policies with Zero Trust, the institution enforces stringent controls that dynamically evaluate user and device attributes before granting access to critical systems. For instance, when an employee attempts to access financial transaction data remotely, conditional access policies are configured to examine factors, such as the user's location, device health, and the sensitivity of the data being accessed. If any anomaly is detected, access is denied or additional authentication steps, such as multi-factor authentication, are triggered. This approach ensures that access decisions are contextual and responsive to the real-time risk landscape, effectively mitigating the potential impact of compromised credentials or unauthorized access attempts. The alignment of conditional access with Zero Trust not only fortifies the organization's security posture but also instils a proactive and adaptive approach to cybersecurity in an era marked by persistent and sophisticated threats.

Business Scenario: Zero Trust in Action for Cybersecurity in a Multinational Financial Institution

Introduction:

In the complex and highly regulated landscape of multinational financial institutions, cybersecurity is a top priority. Our business scenario unfolds in the headquarters of a leading global financial institution with a vast network of branches and a diverse portfolio of financial services. The institution is committed to embracing a Zero Trust security model to safeguard sensitive financial data and customer information and maintain regulatory compliance.

Challenges Faced:

- **Diverse Network of Users:**

  The financial institution has a diverse workforce, including employees, contractors, and partners, accessing critical financial systems and sensitive data from various locations and devices.

- **Growing Cyber Threat Landscape:**

  The institution faces an escalating cyber threat landscape, with sophisticated attacks targeting financial institutions globally. Traditional security measures are proving insufficient to combat the evolving nature of cyber threats.

- **Regulatory Compliance Pressure:**

  Compliance with stringent financial regulations is paramount. The institution must ensure that cybersecurity measures align with regulatory requirements to avoid legal consequences and maintain the trust of clients and stakeholders.

Implementation of Zero Trust with Conditional Access Policies

To address these challenges, the financial institution decides to implement a Zero Trust security model, focusing on conditional access policies.

- **Identity Verification:**

  Every user attempting to access the institution's systems, regardless of their location or device, must undergo thorough identity verification. Multi-factor authentication (MFA) is enforced as a standard practice.

- **Context-Aware Access Policies:**

  Conditional access policies are crafted based on contextual factors such as user roles, location, device health, and the sensitivity of the accessed financial data. This ensures that access controls dynamically adapt to the changing risk landscape.

- **Device Trustworthiness:**

  The institution implements measures to assess the trustworthiness of devices seeking access. Only devices that meet predefined security standards, including up-to-date software and antivirus protection, are granted access.

- **Continuous Monitoring:**

  Real-time monitoring of user activities and system access is implemented. Any suspicious behavior triggers immediate responses, including temporary access restrictions and alerts for further investigation.

Results and Benefits:

- **Enhanced Security Posture:**

  The implementation of Zero Trust, coupled with aligned conditional access policies, significantly enhances the institution's overall security posture. Unauthorized access attempts are minimized, reducing the risk of data breaches.

- **Regulatory Compliance:**

  The financial institution meets and exceeds regulatory cybersecurity requirements. The continuous monitoring and robust access controls ensure compliance with financial regulations, safeguarding the institution from legal repercussions.

- **Adaptive Access Control:**

  Conditional access policies allow the institution to provide adaptive access control, granting or restricting access based on the real-time risk assessment of users, devices, and accessed data. This adaptability is crucial in the dynamic financial sector.

- **User Productivity:**

  While enforcing stringent security measures, the institution ensures a seamless user experience. Employees can access the necessary financial systems and data efficiently, promoting productivity without compromising security.

This business scenario showcases how a multinational financial institution can strengthen its cybersecurity posture by implementing Zero Trust principles and aligning conditional access policies. By prioritizing identity verification, context-aware access controls, and continuous monitoring, the institution achieves a robust security framework that not only safeguards sensitive financial assets but also ensures compliance with regulatory standards in the ever-evolving threat landscape of the financial sector.

Managing Security in Financial Cybersecurity

Designing an effective solution to manage secrets, keys, and certificates is crucial for organizations safeguarding sensitive information and ensuring the integrity of their digital infrastructure. Consider a real-world scenario where a financial institution is tasked with securing its online banking platform. In this context, the organization employs a comprehensive solution that integrates with a Key Management Service (KMS) to manage cryptographic keys securely. The system ensures that sensitive data, such as customer financial information and transaction details, is encrypted and decrypted only by authorized entities using robust cryptographic keys. To manage secrets, the organization implements a centralized secrets management platform, such as HashiCorp Vault, to securely store and control access to sensitive information, such as API keys and passwords, used in various applications and services. Additionally, a robust certificate management system is integrated to handle the lifecycle of digital certificates, ensuring that SSL/TLS communications remain encrypted and secure. This holistic solution not only addresses the immediate security needs of the online banking platform but also establishes a scalable and resilient framework for managing secrets, keys, and certificates across the organization's broader digital ecosystem.

FortifyBank Cybersecurity Breach Response

Scenario:

FortifyBank, a leading financial institution, has been at the forefront of embracing digital transformation to provide seamless and secure financial services to its customers. As part of this initiative, the bank implemented a robust cybersecurity strategy titled "Securing the Digital Fort: A Comprehensive Approach to Managing Secrets, Keys, and Certificates in Financial Cybersecurity."

One day, the bank's cybersecurity team received an alert about a potential security breach in their systems. It appears that unauthorized access has been gained, and there is a risk of sensitive financial data being compromised. The incident response team quickly swings into action to assess the situation and contain the potential damage.

Here's how the scenario unfolds:

1. **Incident Discovery**
    a. The bank's security monitoring system detects unusual activity in the network.
    b. An alert is triggered when an unauthorized user attempts to access a critical server housing sensitive financial information.
2. **Initial Investigation**
    a. The incident response team, comprising cybersecurity experts, begins the initial investigation to determine the extent of the breach.
    b. They discover that the attacker has exploited a vulnerability to gain access to the server.
3. **Securing the Digital Fort Protocol Activated**
    a. The cybersecurity team refers to the bank's comprehensive cybersecurity strategy, "Securing the Digital Fort."
    b. They immediately focus on managing secrets, keys, and certificates to prevent further unauthorized access and potential data exfiltration.
4. **Secrets and Keys Rotation**
    a. The team initiates an emergency secrets and keys rotation process to invalidate compromised credentials.
    b. Automated tools are employed to ensure a swift rotation without disrupting critical banking services.
5. **Certificate Renewal and Validation**
    a. The security team reviews the certificates in use across the bank's systems.
    b. They identify and renew compromised or potentially compromised certificates to maintain a secure communication infrastructure.
6. **Collaboration with Law Enforcement**
    a. The bank's cybersecurity team collaborates with law enforcement agencies to trace the origin of the attack and gather evidence for potential legal actions.

7. **Communication and Transparency**
   a. FortifyBank communicates transparently with its customers about the incident, assuring them that immediate actions are taken to secure their data.
   b. The bank provides guidelines for customers to enhance their own cyber-security measures, such as updating passwords and enabling multi-factor authentication.
8. **Post-Incident Analysis:**
   a. After containing the breach, the incident response team conducts a thorough post-incident analysis.
   b. Lessons learned are documented to strengthen the bank's cybersecurity posture further.

By following the "Securing the Digital Fort" strategy, FortifyBank effectively mitigates the cybersecurity breach, secures its digital assets, and reinforces customer trust in its commitment to data security.

Conclusion

In conclusion, the essays emphasize the critical role of identity and access management (IAM) in cybersecurity, showcasing its significance in securing digital frontiers, optimizing access across cloud realms, safeguarding collaboration with external entities, implementing modern authentication and authorization strategies, applying Zero Trust principles, and managing secrets, keys, and certificates. These narratives underscore the importance of adopting robust solutions tailored to specific challenges, whether in multinational corporations, global e-commerce enterprises, or financial institutions. The common thread across these discussions is the recognition that effective cybersecurity requires strategic, adaptive, and comprehensive approaches to identity management, access control, and data protection in our rapidly evolving digital landscape. In the next chapter, we will discuss designing access security for high-privilege users.

Multiple Choice Questions

1. What is the primary purpose of Identity and Access Control Design in cyber-security?
   a. Enhancing network speed
   b. Simplifying data storage

   c. Ensuring secure user authentication and authorization
   d. Optimizing hardware performance

2. What is Multi-Factor Authentication (MFA) used for in Identity and Access Control Design?
   a. Single-layer password protection
   b. Adding an extra layer of security by requiring multiple forms of identification
   c. Speeding up user login processes
   d. Reducing the need for strong passwords

3. In the context of Identity and Access Management (IAM), what does the principle of "Least Privilege" mean?
   a. Providing maximum access to all users
   b. Assigning only the necessary access rights for a user's specific role
   c. Granting full administrative rights to all employees
   d. Allowing users to choose their access privileges

4. What is the purpose of Single Sign-On (SSO) in Identity and Access Control Design?
   a. Allowing users to sign in with multiple credentials
   b. Simplifying the login process by requiring multiple credentials
   c. Requiring users to sign in separately for each application
   d. Enabling users to sign in once and access multiple connected applications

5. How does Role-Based Access Control (RBAC) contribute to Identity and Access Control Design?
   a. It limits access based on the user's physical location
   b. It assigns access rights based on a user's role within an organization
   c. It focuses on biometric authentication methods
   d. It allows unrestricted access to all users

Answers

1. c
2. b
3. b
4. d
5. b

CHAPTER 7
Designing Access Security for High-Privilege Users

Introduction

Amidst the complex web of potential threats, managing and controlling privileged access emerges as a pivotal element in fortifying an organization's digital assets. Privileged access, granted to users or systems with elevated permissions, allows for the manipulation of crucial data, settings, and infrastructure within an IT environment.

Yet, this power comes with inherent risks. Improperly managed privileged access opens the door to unauthorized entry, leading to data breaches, system compromises, and the perilous exposure of an entire organization to cyber threats. Addressing these challenges, Privileged Access Management (PAM) steps into the cybersecurity arena, focusing on securing, controlling, and monitoring access within organizations. PAM achieves this through the implementation of policies and tools that restrict privileged access solely to those who genuinely require it for their roles.

The fundamental principles of Privileged Access Management include adhering to the Least Privilege Principle, ensuring secure authentication with robust mechanisms like multi-factor authentication, continuous monitoring and auditing of privileged access activities, meticulous session management, automated provisioning and de-provisioning processes, and secure password management practices.

As organizations increasingly rely on intricate IT infrastructures and cloud-based services, the significance of privileged access management becomes more apparent. A robust PAM strategy not only enhances security but also aligns seamlessly with regulatory compliance requirements, ensuring the integrity, confidentiality, and availability of sensitive information.

Structure

In this chapter, we will cover the following topics:

- Protecting Digital Assets: Privileged Access Management
- Enterprise Access Model Implementation
- Identity Governance Solutions in Finance
- Securing Tenant Administration in Shared Infrastructures
- Cloud Infrastructure Entitlement Management: E-commerce Case Study
- Tailored Entitlement Management for Multi-Cloud

Protecting Digital Assets: Privileged Access Management

One of the key elements in securing an organization's digital assets is managing and controlling privileged access. Privileged access refers to elevated permissions granted to users or systems, enabling them to access and manipulate critical data, settings, or infrastructure within an IT environment.

Privileged access is a double-edged sword. While it empowers authorized individuals or entities to perform necessary tasks and maintain systems, it also poses a significant risk, if not properly managed. Unauthorized access to privileged accounts can lead to data breaches, system compromises, and even the exposure of an entire organization to cyber threats.

Privileged Access Management (PAM) is the discipline and set of technologies designed to address these challenges. PAM focuses on securing, controlling, and monitoring access within an organization by implementing policies and tools that limit privileged access to only those who genuinely need it for their roles.

The core principles of Privileged Access Management include:

- **Least Privilege Principle:** Users should be given the minimum level of access or permissions necessary to perform their tasks. This reduces the attack surface and limits potential damage in case of a security incident.
- **Secure Authentication:** Implementing robust authentication mechanisms, such as multi-factor authentication (MFA), ensures that only authorized individuals can access privileged accounts.
- **Monitoring and Auditing:** Continuous monitoring of privileged access activities is crucial for detecting and responding to potential security incidents. Detailed audit logs help organizations understand who accessed what and when.

- **Session Management:** Controlling and monitoring active sessions is vital to prevent misuse of privileged access. This involves monitoring live sessions, terminating inactive sessions, and ensuring that access is granted on a temporary basis when possible.
- **Automated Provisioning and Deprovisioning:** Efficient management of privileged access involves automated processes for granting access when needed and revoking it promptly when no longer required. This reduces the risk associated with forgotten or abandoned privileged accounts.
- **Password Management:** Implementing secure password practices, such as regular rotation and storage in a secure vault, helps prevent unauthorized access through compromised credentials.

As organizations increasingly rely on complex IT infrastructures and cloud-based services, the importance of privileged access management becomes more evident. A robust PAM strategy not only enhances security but also aligns with regulatory compliance requirements, safeguarding the integrity, confidentiality, and availability of sensitive information.

In conclusion, this introduction to Privileged Access Management underscores its critical role in contemporary cybersecurity. As organizations navigate the digital landscape, implementing effective PAM practices is essential for mitigating the risks associated with privileged access and ensuring a robust defense against cyber threats.

Enterprise Access Model Implementation

The enterprise access model is a framework that outlines how users within an organization can access its resources, systems, and data. It encompasses various policies, procedures, and technologies to ensure that access is secure, efficient, and aligned with business objectives. Let's illustrate the concept of the enterprise access model through a business scenario.

Business Scenario: XYZ Corporation

XYZ Corporation is a multinational company with offices spread across different geographical locations. The company operates in various sectors, including manufacturing, sales, and research and development. To streamline its operations and enhance collaboration, XYZ Corporation has implemented an enterprise access model.

Key Components of the Enterprise Access Model:

Role-Based Access Control (RBAC):

- **Scenario:** In XYZ Corporation, employees have different roles based on their departments and responsibilities. For example, there are roles such as Sales Representative, Production Manager, and Research Scientist.

- **Implementation:** RBAC is employed to ensure that each employee receives access permissions based on their specific role. Sales representatives have access to customer databases, production managers can control manufacturing systems, and research scientists can access R&D resources.

Single Sign-On (SSO):

- **Scenario:** XYZ Corporation uses multiple applications and systems for daily operations, including customer relationship management (CRM) software, manufacturing control systems, and research collaboration platforms.
- **Implementation:** SSO is implemented to enable employees to log in once and gain access to all authorized systems without needing to enter credentials repeatedly. This improves user experience and reduces the risk associated with multiple passwords.

Mobile Device Management (MDM):

- **Scenario:** Many employees at XYZ Corporation frequently travel or work remotely. The company provides smartphones and tablets for employees to access corporate resources on the go.
- **Implementation:** MDM is employed to ensure that mobile devices are securely configured, and encrypted, and have necessary security policies in place. This allows employees to access corporate email, applications, and data from their mobile devices securely.

Privileged Access Management (PAM):

- **Scenario:** XYZ Corporation has a dedicated IT team responsible for managing and maintaining critical infrastructure and systems.
- **Implementation:** PAM is implemented to control and monitor access to privileged accounts within the IT team. Only authorized personnel have access to server configurations, database settings, and other critical systems to prevent unauthorized changes.

Network Segmentation:

- **Scenario:** XYZ Corporation wants to enhance security by separating its different business units and restricting access to sensitive information.
- **Implementation:** Network segmentation is employed to create isolated segments for each business unit. This ensures that employees only have access to the resources and data relevant to their specific business functions, reducing the risk of unauthorized access to sensitive information.

In summary, the enterprise access model at XYZ Corporation is a comprehensive framework that leverages RBAC, SSO, MDM, PAM, and network segmentation to ensure secure, efficient, and controlled access to resources. This model not only enhances security but also aligns with the organization's business needs and facilitates collaboration across different departments and geographical locations.

Identity Governance Solutions in Finance

Designing identity governance solutions is a critical undertaking for organizations seeking to manage and secure access to their digital resources. Identity governance involves defining and implementing policies, processes, and technologies to ensure that the right individuals have the appropriate access to systems, applications, and data. One illustrative case study is the implementation of identity governance at a global financial institution. Faced with increasingly complex regulatory requirements and the need to safeguard sensitive financial information, the organization adopted a comprehensive identity governance solution. The system incorporated automated identity provisioning, role-based access controls, and continuous monitoring of user activities. This approach streamlined user access management, reduced the risk of unauthorized access, and facilitated compliance with industry regulations. The case study underscores the significance of a well-designed identity governance solution in not only bolstering security but also in addressing regulatory challenges within the dynamic landscape of the financial sector. Let us examine the case study for identity governance solutions in the healthcare sector.

Executive Summary:

As the healthcare sector increasingly relies on digital technologies to streamline processes and improve patient care, the importance of robust identity governance solutions cannot be overstated. This case study delves into the challenges faced by healthcare organizations in managing identities, access, and permissions, and how the implementation of advanced Identity Governance Solutions (IGS) has significantly enhanced security, compliance, and operational efficiency.

Background:

Healthcare organizations are prime targets for cyber threats due to the vast amounts of sensitive patient data they handle. With the proliferation of electronic health records (EHRs) and interconnected systems, the need for a comprehensive identity governance strategy has become critical. This case study focuses on a leading healthcare provider that recognized the growing threats and decided to address them proactively through the deployment of advanced Identity Governance Solutions.

Objectives:

- **Enhanced Security:** The primary goal was to strengthen the security posture of the healthcare organization by implementing a robust identity governance framework. This involved securing access to sensitive data, applications, and systems.

- **Regulatory Compliance:** Ensuring compliance with healthcare regulations such as HIPAA (Health Insurance Portability and Accountability Act) was paramount. The organization aimed to implement identity governance solutions that not only met current compliance requirements but also anticipated future regulatory changes.
- **Operational Efficiency**: Streamlining identity and access management processes was identified as a key objective to improve operational efficiency. The organization sought to reduce the risk of unauthorized access while ensuring that authorized personnel could seamlessly perform their duties.

Implementation:

The healthcare provider collaborated with a leading identity governance solutions provider to tailor a comprehensive solution to their specific needs. The implementation process included:

- **Identity Lifecycle Management:** Automated processes for onboarding, offboarding, and role changes to ensure that access permissions were always aligned with the current status of employees.
- **Role-Based Access Control (RBAC):** Implementation of RBAC to define and manage user permissions based on job roles, reducing the risk of excessive access and unauthorized actions.
- **Real-Time Monitoring and Alerts:** Deployment of real-time monitoring tools to detect and respond to suspicious activities promptly. Automated alerts were configured to notify security teams of any anomalous behavior.
- **Multi-Factor Authentication (MFA):** Integration of MFA to add an extra layer of security, requiring users to verify their identity through multiple means before accessing sensitive information.

Results:

- **Security Improvements:** The healthcare organization experienced a significant reduction in security incidents related to unauthorized access. The implementation of IGS helped in preventing data breaches and mitigating potential threats.
- **Compliance Adherence:** The organization achieved and maintained compliance with healthcare regulations. Regular audits were conducted to ensure that the identity governance solutions were aligned with the evolving regulatory landscape.
- **Operational Streamlining:** Identity and access management processes became more efficient, leading to time and cost savings. The automation of onboarding and offboarding processes reduced administrative overhead and minimized the risk of human errors.

- **User Satisfaction:** Authorized personnel appreciated the seamless and secure access to the systems and data necessary for their roles. The positive impact on user experience contributed to a more productive and engaged workforce.

The successful implementation of identity governance solutions in the healthcare sector not only addressed the immediate challenges of security and compliance but also positioned the organization for future advancements. The case study illustrates how a proactive approach to identity governance can safeguard sensitive healthcare data, enhance operational efficiency, and provide a foundation for a secure digital future in the ever-evolving landscape of healthcare technology.

Securing Tenant Administration in Shared Infrastructures

Creating a solution to secure tenant administration is paramount for businesses managing multiple tenants within a shared infrastructure. Consider a scenario where a cloud service provider (CSP) hosts various tenants on its platform, each representing a distinct organization with its data and applications. To address the challenge of securing tenant administration, the CSP implements a robust solution. The design includes a multi-layered authentication system for administrators, employing techniques such as biometric authentication and multi-factor authentication (MFA). Role-based access controls (RBAC) are implemented to ensure that administrators only have access to the specific resources necessary for their responsibilities. Additionally, the solution incorporates encryption protocols to safeguard sensitive tenant data during transmission and storage. Regular security audits and monitoring mechanisms are established to detect and respond to any suspicious activities promptly. This comprehensive approach not only fortifies tenant administration against potential breaches but also instills confidence in the tenant organizations, assuring them that their data and operations are under stringent security measures. Let us explore the case study for securing tenant administration in shared infrastructures.

Executive Summary:

This case study explores the challenges faced by organizations managing shared infrastructures and the strategic implementation of security measures to fortify tenant administration. In an era of cloud computing and shared resources, the focus is on a forward-thinking company that recognizes the critical need to enhance security in shared environments. By adopting a strategic approach, the organization successfully strengthened tenant administration, mitigated risks, and paved the way for a more secure and collaborative future

Background:

Shared infrastructures and cloud-based services have become integral to modern business operations, offering flexibility and scalability. However, this trend introduces new security concerns, especially in multi-tenant environments where multiple users and organizations share the same infrastructure. This case study focuses on a dynamic company facing these challenges head-on, with a commitment to securing tenant administration in shared infrastructures.

Objectives:

- **Enhanced Security**: The primary goal was to fortify tenant administration to safeguard sensitive data and applications. The organization aimed to create a robust security framework that could withstand evolving cyber threats.
- **Tenant Isolation:** Ensuring strict isolation between tenants to prevent unauthorized access and data leakage. The objective was to establish a secure environment where each tenant could operate independently without compromising others' security.
- **Compliance Adherence:** Meeting regulatory requirements and industry standards were key objectives. The organization sought to implement security measures that not only met current compliance needs but also anticipated future regulatory changes.

Implementation:

The organization collaborated with cybersecurity experts and deployed a strategic security plan, including:

- **Micro-Segmentation:** Implementing micro-segmentation to create isolated zones within the shared infrastructure. This enhanced network security by restricting lateral movement and limiting the impact of security breaches.
- **Role-Based Access Control (RBAC):** Developing and implementing RBAC policies to define and manage user permissions based on roles. This ensured that each tenant had access only to the resources necessary for their operations.
- **Encryption and Data Protection:** Deploying encryption measures to protect data at rest and in transit. This included implementing strong encryption algorithms and securing communication channels to prevent unauthorized access to sensitive information.
- **Continuous Monitoring and Threat Detection:** Employing real-time monitoring tools and threat detection systems to identify and respond to security incidents promptly. Automated alerts were configured to notify security teams of any suspicious activities.

Results:

- **Improved Security Posture:** The organization experienced a notable improvement in its overall security posture. The implementation of micro-segmentation and RBAC significantly reduced the risk of unauthorized access and potential security breaches.

- **Tenant Isolation:** The strict enforcement of isolation between tenants ensured that each entity operated within its secure boundaries. This not only prevented data leakage but also instilled confidence in tenants regarding the security of shared infrastructures.
- **Compliance Assurance:** The implemented security measures helped the organization maintain compliance with regulatory requirements. Regular audits and assessments were conducted to validate adherence to industry standards.
- **Proactive Threat Response:** The organization demonstrated a proactive approach to security with the implementation of continuous monitoring and threat detection. Security teams were able to respond swiftly to potential threats, minimizing the impact on tenant administration.

By adopting a strategic approach to securing tenant administration in shared infrastructures, the organization not only addressed current security challenges but also positioned itself for future advancements. This case study illustrates how a proactive and comprehensive security strategy can fortify shared environments, fostering collaboration, and trust among tenants while mitigating the evolving risks associated with shared infrastructures. The lessons learned provide valuable insights for organizations navigating the complex landscape of cloud-based services and shared resources.

Cloud Infrastructure Entitlement Management: E-commerce Case Study

Developing a solution for Cloud Infrastructure Entitlement Management (CIEM) is critical in ensuring the secure and efficient administration of cloud resources. Consider a scenario where a rapidly growing e-commerce company has transitioned its operations to a cloud-based infrastructure. Facing challenges in managing access permissions and preventing unauthorized resource usage, the company has decided to implement a robust CIEM solution. The designed solution involves the implementation of automated entitlement reviews, leveraging machine learning algorithms to analyze user activities and adjust access privileges accordingly. Role-based access controls (RBAC) are integrated to define and manage permissions based on job roles and responsibilities. The solution also includes continuous monitoring of user entitlements, and generating real-time alerts for any suspicious or unauthorized access attempts. To enhance transparency and compliance, the CIEM solution provides detailed audit logs and reporting mechanisms. With this comprehensive approach, the e-commerce company not only ensures the security of its cloud infrastructure but also optimizes resource utilization, ultimately contributing to the efficiency and success of its digital operations.

Tailored Entitlement Management for Multi-Cloud

In response to the growing complexity of cloud infrastructures and the escalating challenge of managing access entitlements, organizations face a pressing real-life problem. Consider a multinational corporation that has adopted a multi-cloud strategy to host its applications and data. With diverse teams working on different projects, the organization encounters difficulties in effectively managing and securing entitlements across its expansive cloud environment. The lack of a centralized system leads to potential security vulnerabilities, as it becomes challenging to track and control user access permissions consistently. To address this issue, there is a critical need for a tailored Cloud Infrastructure Entitlement Management (CIEM) solution. This solution must provide a unified platform for defining, enforcing, and monitoring entitlements across various cloud services, ensuring that users have appropriate access levels aligned with their roles and responsibilities. Additionally, it should offer real-time visibility of entitlement changes, automate entitlement reviews, and integrate with existing identity management systems to streamline administration. Designing an effective CIEM solution for this real-life problem is essential for mitigating security risks, enhancing operational efficiency, and maintaining compliance within the dynamic landscape of cloud-based operations. Let us discuss a case study regarding entitlement management in a multi-cloud environment.

Executive Summary:

This case study delves into the challenges faced by organizations operating in multi-cloud environments and the strategic implementation of a tailored solution for entitlement management. As cloud adoption accelerates, ensuring secure access to resources across various cloud platforms becomes paramount. This case study focuses on a pioneering company that recognized the need for a comprehensive entitlement management approach, resulting in strengthened security, streamlined operations, and enhanced governance in its multi-cloud ecosystem.

Background:

As organizations increasingly leverage multiple cloud providers to meet diverse business needs, managing access entitlements across these environments becomes complex. Security, compliance, and operational efficiency are critical considerations in multi-cloud environments. This case study centers on a forward-thinking organization that proactively addressed these challenges by implementing a tailored solution for entitlement management.

Objectives:

- **Enhanced Security:** The primary goal was to fortify the security of the organization's multi-cloud environment by implementing robust entitlement management practices. This involved securing access to resources, applications, and data across different cloud platforms.
- **Streamlined Operations:** The organization aimed to streamline entitlement management processes, reducing administrative overhead and ensuring efficient provisioning and de-provisioning of user access. This was crucial for maintaining agility in the rapidly evolving cloud landscape.
- **Governance and Compliance:** Establishing a governance framework to monitor and enforce compliance with internal policies and industry regulations. The objective was to ensure that access privileges aligned with business requirements and regulatory standards.

Implementation:

The organization collaborated with cloud security experts to design and implement a tailored solution for entitlement management, including:

- **Centralized Identity Management:** Implementing a centralized identity management system that served as the authoritative source for user identities and access entitlements. This ensured consistency and accuracy in entitlement assignments across the multi-cloud environment.
- **Role-Based Entitlements:** Developing and implementing role-based entitlement models to categorize and assign access privileges based on job roles. This streamlined the process of granting and revoking access and aligning permissions with specific job responsibilities.
- **Automated Provisioning and Deprovisioning:** Integrating automated workflows for user provisioning and deprovisioning across cloud platforms. This not only enhanced operational efficiency but also reduced the risk of unauthorized access due to delayed deprovisioning.
- **Continuous Monitoring and Auditing:** Deploying continuous monitoring and auditing tools to track user activities, detect anomalies, and generate audit trails. This facilitated real-time visibility into entitlement management processes and supported compliance efforts.

Results:

- **Enhanced Security Posture:** The organization experienced a significant improvement in its overall security posture. The implementation of centralized identity management and role-based entitlements minimized the risk of unauthorized access and potential security breaches.

- **Operational Efficiency**: Automated provisioning and deprovisioning processes resulted in streamlined operations. The organization achieved faster onboarding of users and reduced the time and effort required for access management tasks.
- **Governance and Compliance Adherence:** The tailored solution ensured strong governance by providing visibility into entitlement assignments and enforcing compliance with internal policies and external regulations. This contributed to a culture of accountability and transparency.
- **Scalability and Flexibility:** The implemented entitlement management solution proved scalable and adaptable to the dynamic nature of the multi-cloud environment. As the organization expanded its cloud footprint, the solution seamlessly accommodated new cloud services and providers.

By crafting a tailored solution for entitlement management in their multi-cloud environment, the organization successfully navigated the complexities of securing access across diverse cloud platforms. This case study highlights the importance of a strategic and customized approach to entitlement management in the evolving landscape of multi-cloud adoption. The lessons learned provide valuable insights for organizations seeking to safeguard their cloud environments while maintaining operational agility and compliance.

Conclusion

In conclusion, the exploration of privileged access management, enterprise access models, identity governance solutions, and cloud infrastructure entitlement management collectively reinforces the indispensable role of robust cybersecurity measures in today's digital landscape. As organizations continue to grapple with the evolving challenges posed by cyber threats, it is evident that a proactive and strategic approach is essential.

Privileged access, being a critical aspect of cybersecurity, demands meticulous attention and a comprehensive Privileged Access Management (PAM) strategy. By adhering to principles such as least privilege, secure authentication, monitoring, and automation, organizations can fortify their defenses against potential breaches and ensure the integrity of sensitive information.

The enterprise access model, as exemplified by XYZ Corporation, demonstrates how aligning access controls with business needs can enhance security and promote collaboration across diverse departments and geographical locations. Through Role-Based Access Control (RBAC), Single Sign-On (SSO), Mobile Device Management (MDM), Privileged Access Management (PAM), and Network Segmentation, organizations can create a secure, efficient, and controlled access framework.

The case studies on identity governance solutions in the financial sector, securing tenant administration in shared infrastructures, Cloud Infrastructure Entitlement Management (CIEM) for dynamic e-commerce operations, and crafting tailored solutions for entitlement management in multi-cloud environments underscore the adaptability and innovation required to address specific challenges in diverse contexts.

As we look at the future, the imperative to fortify cybersecurity measures remains paramount. The dynamic nature of cyber threats necessitates ongoing vigilance, continuous improvement, and strategic investments in cutting-edge technologies. Organizations must not only secure their digital assets but also optimize efficiency in the administration of access privileges, whether in financial institutions, shared cloud environments, or rapidly expanding e-commerce operations.

In essence, the journey to a secure digital future involves not only implementing proven cybersecurity practices but also tailoring solutions to meet the unique demands of each organizational context. By doing so, we can collectively elevate security standards, foster innovation, and navigate the evolving landscape of cybersecurity with confidence and resilience. In the next chapter, we will be discussing about the design of security operations.

Multiple Choice Questions

1. What is Privileged Access Management (PAM)?
    a. Personal Access Module
    b. Public Access Measure
    c. Privileged Access Management
    d. Protected Account Method
2. Which principle suggests that users should be given the minimum level of access necessary to perform their tasks?
    a. Maximum Privilege Principle
    b. Optimal Access Principle
    c. Least Privilege Principle
    d. Access Control Principle
3. What is the primary focus of Single Sign-On (SSO) in the enterprise access model?
    a. Managing privileged accounts
    b. Streamlining user experience

   c. Controlling network segmentation
   d. Implementing role-based access controls
4. In the context of Cloud Infrastructure Entitlement Management (CIEM), what does RBAC stand for?
   a. Robust Business Application Controls
   b. Role-Based Access Controls
   c. Resource-Based Authorization Controls
   d. Remote Backup and Control
5. What is the purpose of automated entitlement reviews in CIEM?
   a. To create new access permissions
   b. To streamline user access management
   c. To analyze user activities and adjust access privileges
   d. To conduct security audits

Answers

1. c
2. c
3. b
4. b
5. c

CHAPTER 8
Security Operations Design

Introduction

Security Operations, often abbreviated as SecOps, is a crucial component of an organization's cybersecurity strategy. It encompasses the processes and technologies used to safeguard an organization's IT infrastructure, data, and systems from cyber threats. The primary goal of SecOps is to detect, respond to, and mitigate security incidents promptly to minimize potential damage.

SecOps involves collaboration between security teams and IT operations to create a proactive and integrated approach to cybersecurity. This collaboration ensures a faster response to emerging threats and vulnerabilities. Security analysts in SecOps monitor and analyze security alerts generated by various tools and systems, aiming to identify potential security incidents.

Key activities in SecOps include continuous monitoring of network traffic, log analysis, vulnerability assessments, and incident response planning. Automation plays a vital role in SecOps, streamlining routine tasks and allowing security teams to focus on more complex issues.

Effective SecOps implementation requires staying updated on the latest cyber threats, employing advanced technologies such as Security Information and Event Management (SIEM) systems, and fostering a culture of security awareness within the organization. By adopting SecOps principles, organizations can enhance their overall cybersecurity posture, ensuring a proactive defense against the evolving landscape of cyber threats.

Structure

In this chapter, we will cover the following topics:

- Strategizing Cybersecurity Defenses: A Brief Overview
- Crafting Security Operations in Hybrid and Multi-Cloud: Real-Time Business Case

- Securing Business Operations: Centralized Logging and Auditing Design
- Crafting SIEM Solutions: Orchestrating Cybersecurity
- Designing Solutions for Detection and Response: A Real-Time Scenario

Strategizing Cybersecurity Defenses: A Brief Overview

Security Operations (SecOps) is a critical aspect of an organization's cybersecurity posture, aiming to protect its IT infrastructure, data, and systems from evolving cyber threats. A robust SecOps strategy involves a combination of processes, technologies, and collaboration between security and IT teams.

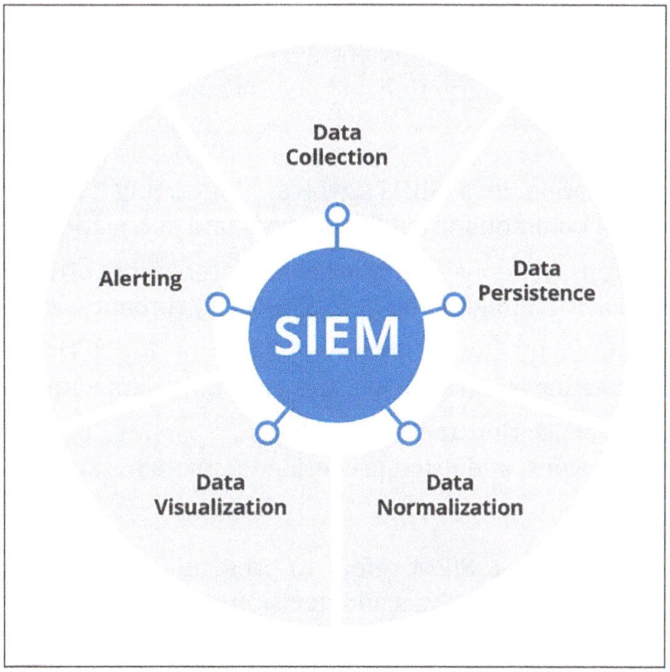

Figure 8.1: *Security Operations Strategy*

Let's break down each aspect in terms of a Security Information and Event Management (SIEM) system:

Data Collection:

- SIEM systems collect data from various sources such as network devices, security appliances, servers, endpoints, and applications.
- Sources can include firewall logs, intrusion detection/prevention system logs, antivirus logs, authentication logs, and more.

- Collection methods may involve agents installed on endpoints, syslog for network devices, APIs for cloud services, and database connectors for applications.
- Data collection should be comprehensive to ensure all relevant security events are captured for analysis.

Data Persistence:

- Data persistence in a SIEM involves storing collected data securely and efficiently for analysis and long-term storage.
- It typically involves a combination of databases, such as relational databases, NoSQL databases, or data lakes.
- SIEM systems often use indexing and compression techniques to optimize storage and retrieval performance.
- Data persistence also includes ensuring the integrity and confidentiality of stored data through encryption and access controls.

Data Normalization:

- Data normalization in a SIEM involves converting raw data from various sources into a common format for analysis and correlation.
- This process ensures consistency in how different types of data are represented, making it easier to analyze and detect security threats.
- Normalization may involve mapping different log formats to a standard schema, extracting relevant fields, and enriching data with additional context.
- Common normalization techniques include parsing log messages, applying regular expressions, and using predefined parsers for known log formats.

Data Visualization:

- Data visualization in a SIEM refers to presenting security data in a visually intuitive format to aid analysis and decision-making.
- Visualization techniques include charts, graphs, timelines, heatmaps, and dashboards.
- Visualization tools allow security analysts to identify patterns, anomalies, and trends in the data more effectively.
- Interactive features such as drill-downs and filtering enhance the usability of visualizations for exploring and investigating security incidents.

Real-Time Example:

Consider a financial institution implementing SecOps to protect customer data and financial assets. The organization employs advanced threat detection tools that continuously monitor network traffic and user activities. In real-time, the system detects an anomaly indicating a potential malware intrusion

The SecOps team, consisting of security analysts and IT professionals, collaborates to investigate the incident promptly. Automation tools assist in isolating the affected system and gathering relevant data for analysis. The incident response plan is activated, outlining the steps to contain and eradicate the malware

Simultaneously, the organization's SIEM system (Security Information and Event Management) correlates data from various sources, providing a comprehensive view of the incident. This real-time visibility enables the SecOps team to make informed decisions and implement remedial measures swiftly

The collaboration between security and IT operations ensures that the incident is not only contained but also used as an opportunity to enhance security measures and update the organization's overall cybersecurity strategy.

A well-crafted SecOps strategy, exemplified by proactive monitoring, collaboration, incident response planning, vulnerability assessments, and automation, is vital for organizations seeking to fortify their defenses against the dynamic landscape of cyber threats.

Crafting Security Operations in Hybrid and Multi-Cloud: Real-Time Business Case

Consider a multinational corporation with a hybrid and multi-cloud infrastructure spanning multiple cloud service providers (CSPs) such as AWS, Azure, and Google Cloud. This organization faces the challenge of securing diverse workloads and data distributed across on-premises servers and various cloud environments.

- **Continuous Monitoring and Visibility:**

  In a real-time scenario, the organization implements continuous monitoring solutions that provide visibility into all activities across its hybrid and multi-cloud architecture. This involves leveraging Security Information and Event Management (SIEM) tools capable of aggregating and correlating logs and events from diverse sources. The organization gains real-time insights into user activities, system changes, and potential security incidents across the entire infrastructure.

- **Cloud-Native Security Tools:**

  Recognizing the unique security requirements of each cloud environment, the organization integrates cloud-native security tools provided by individual CSPs. For example, AWS CloudTrail, Azure Security Center, and Google Cloud

Security Command Center offer tailored capabilities to monitor, detect, and respond to security threats specific to each platform. This approach ensures a customized and effective security posture in each cloud domain.

- **Automation and Orchestration:**

  Given the complexity of a hybrid and multi-cloud setup, the organization implements automation and orchestration in its SecOps strategy. Automated response mechanisms, such as incident triage and remediation workflows, help accelerate response times and minimize human error. This automation is designed to adapt to the diverse APIs and environments present in the hybrid cloud architecture.

- **Threat Intelligence Integration:**

  To enhance threat detection capabilities, the organization integrates threat intelligence feeds into its SecOps processes. By staying informed about emerging threats and attack patterns, security teams can proactively adjust security controls and policies. This integration is crucial in the rapidly changing landscape of cybersecurity, allowing the organization to fortify its defenses against new and evolving threats.

- **Compliance and Governance:**

  In a multinational setting, compliance with regional and industry-specific regulations is paramount. The organization designs SecOps capabilities that ensure continuous compliance monitoring across all cloud environments. This includes implementing controls for data residency, encryption, and access management to meet diverse regulatory requirements.

- **Cross-Platform Incident Response:**

  In the event of a security incident, the organization's SecOps teams follow a well-defined incident response plan that spans across the hybrid and multi-cloud infrastructure. This plan outlines the coordinated efforts required to contain, eradicate, and recover from the incident, considering the intricacies of working across multiple cloud providers.

Designing effective Security Operations capabilities in hybrid and multi-cloud environments is critical for organizations embracing digital transformation. By incorporating continuous monitoring, cloud-native security tools, automation, threat intelligence, and compliance measures, businesses can navigate the complexities of a diverse cloud landscape while ensuring the security, resilience, and compliance of their operations. This approach not only safeguards against current threats but also positions the organization to adapt to future cybersecurity challenges in the evolving cloud ecosystem.

Maximizing Efficiency with Unified Operations

In real-time scenarios, businesses leverage unified operations to understand and minimize costs. By integrating processes, organizations streamline workflows, and are able to reduce redundant tasks and operational expenses. For instance, if a retail company centralizes inventory management, it enhances efficiency and minimizes excess stock costs. Unified operations not only optimize resource utilization but also enable data-driven decision-making, fostering a cost-conscious and agile business environment.

Unified Operations: Definition and Example

Unified operations refer to the integration and coordination of various business processes, systems, and data to create a cohesive and streamlined operational environment. This approach aims to eliminate silos, enhance efficiency, and provide a holistic view of organizational activities.

For instance, in a manufacturing setting, unified operations might involve integrating production planning, inventory management, and supply chain logistics into a centralized system. This integration allows real-time visibility into inventory levels, production schedules, and distribution channels. By breaking down departmental barriers and fostering collaboration, unified operations improve overall organizational performance, reduce redundancy, and enable more informed decision-making. The result is a synchronized and efficient operational model that responds adeptly to changing business demands and maximizes resources.

Unified Operations Decomposed: A Comprehensive Examination

Unified operations, at its core, involve the integration and synchronization of various business processes to create a harmonized and efficient operational environment. Decomposing this concept unveils the intricate elements that contribute to its effectiveness.

- **Integration of Processes:**

  Unified operations necessitate the integration of disparate business processes. This involves breaking down silos that often exist between departments, ensuring that activities across various functions are interconnected. For example, in a retail setting, this integration may involve linking inventory management with sales and customer relationship management systems to create a seamless end-to-end process.

- **Data Centralization:**

  Centralizing data is a key aspect of unified operations. This entails aggregating information from different sources and systems into a centralized repository. In a financial institution, for instance, this could involve consolidating customer data, transaction records, and risk assessments into a unified database. Centralization enables real-time access to critical information, fostering data-driven decision-making.

- **Cross-Functional Collaboration:**

  Unified operations promote collaboration among different functional areas within an organization. Rather than working in isolation, departments collaborate to achieve shared objectives. In a technology company, for instance, cross-functional collaboration might involve the joint efforts of product development, marketing, and customer support teams to launch and support a new product.

- **Technological Integration:**

  Technological integration is a cornerstone of unified operations. It involves implementing and integrating technologies that facilitate seamless communication and data flow. In a manufacturing setting, this could mean adopting an Enterprise Resource Planning (ERP) system that integrates production planning, inventory management, and order processing, providing a unified platform for managing all aspects of operations.

- **Streamlined Workflows:**

  Unified operations seek to streamline workflows, thus eliminating redundancies and optimizing processes. In a healthcare organization, for example, unified operations might involve streamlining patient care processes by integrating electronic health records, appointment scheduling, and billing systems. This not only improves operational efficiency but also enhances the overall patient experience.

- **Real-Time Visibility:**

  Real-time visibility is a critical attribute of unified operations. It enables organizations to have a comprehensive, up-to-the-minute view of their operations. In a logistics company, real-time visibility might involve tracking shipments, managing inventory levels, and monitoring transportation routes simultaneously. This visibility allows for quick decision-making and response to changing circumstances.

- **Continuous Improvement:**

  Unified operations are not static; they involve a commitment to continuous improvement. Organizations adopting this approach regularly assess and refine their processes. For instance, in a service-oriented business, continuous improvement might involve analyzing customer feedback, identifying areas for enhancement, and implementing changes to deliver an even better customer experience.

- **Employee Empowerment:**

  Unified operations empower employees by providing them with the tools and information needed to perform their roles effectively. In a banking environment, for instance, employee empowerment might involve giving customer service representatives access to unified customer profiles, enabling them to address customer inquiries comprehensively.

The decomposition of unified operations reveals a strategic and holistic approach to managing organizational processes. By integrating processes, centralizing data, fostering cross-functional collaboration, embracing technological integration, streamlining workflows, ensuring real-time visibility, committing to continuous improvement, and empowering employees, organizations can create a unified operational model that is agile, efficient, and responsive to the complexities of the modern business landscape.

Securing Business Operations: Centralized Logging and Auditing Design

The design and implementation of centralized logging and auditing systems play a pivotal role in fortifying an organization's defenses and ensuring regulatory compliance. This strategic approach involves the consolidation of logs and auditing processes across an entire infrastructure, providing a unified view of activities, enhancing security, and enabling swift response to potential threats.

- **Business Scenario:**

  Consider a multinational financial institution operating in a complex regulatory environment. This organization processes a vast number of transactions daily, manages sensitive customer data, and must adhere to strict compliance standards. With numerous branches, online services, and backend systems, the institution faces the challenge of maintaining a secure environment while demonstrating compliance with regulatory requirements.

- **Centralized Logging:**

  The implementation of centralized logging begins with aggregating logs from diverse sources across the organization's infrastructure. In our financial institution scenario, this encompasses logs from servers, network devices, databases, and application systems. These logs contain valuable information about user activities, system events, and potential security incidents.

A centralized logging system collects, normalizes, and stores these logs in a centralized repository. This repository acts as a single source of truth, providing security analysts with real-time visibility into the organization's digital activities. In our scenario, this unified logging approach allows the institution to track user access, monitor transactional patterns, and detect anomalies that might indicate a security threat.

- **Audit Trail Creation:**

  Centralized logging is complemented by the creation of a comprehensive audit trail. Each transaction, system access, or critical operation is meticulously recorded, providing an immutable record of activities. In the financial institution, this means recording every fund transfer, account access, and system configuration change.

  Audit trails serve multiple purposes. They act as a forensic tool, aiding in post-incident investigations. Additionally, they facilitate compliance audits by providing a detailed account of actions taken within the organization. In our scenario, auditors can easily trace and verify financial transactions, ensuring the institution's adherence to financial regulations.

- **Real-Time Monitoring and Alerting:**

  Centralized logging enables real-time monitoring of activities, allowing security teams to promptly detect and respond to potential security incidents. In our financial institution, this could involve setting up alerts for suspicious account access, large fund transfers, or deviations from established transaction patterns. Anomalies trigger immediate alerts, enabling security analysts to investigate and mitigate potential threats promptly.

- **Security Information and Event Management (SIEM):**

  A Security Information and Event Management (SIEM) system is a crucial component in designing centralized logging and auditing. SIEM tools analyze and correlate data from various sources, providing actionable insights into security events. In our scenario, a SIEM solution would enable the financial institution to correlate logs from multiple branches, online platforms, and backend systems, offering a holistic view of its security posture.

- **Compliance and Reporting:**

  Centralized logging and auditing significantly simplify the compliance reporting process. In our financial institution, the system facilitates the generation of detailed compliance reports required by regulatory bodies. These reports demonstrate the institution's adherence to industry standards and provide evidence of robust security practices.

- **Incident Response and Forensics:**

  In the unfortunate event of a security incident, the centralized logging and auditing system proves invaluable for incident response and forensics. Security teams can trace the origins of an incident, identify affected systems, and assess the extent of the compromise. In our scenario, this capability enables the financial institution to quickly respond to a data breach, mitigate risks, and meet reporting obligations.

- **Scalability and Flexibility:**

  The design of centralized logging and auditing systems should be scalable to accommodate the growing needs of the organization. In our scenario, as the financial institution expands its operations, the centralized system should seamlessly scale to handle increased log volumes while maintaining performance and efficiency.

In conclusion, the design of centralized logging and auditing systems is a strategic imperative for organizations, particularly in sectors with stringent regulatory requirements. By consolidating logs, creating detailed audit trails, implementing real-time monitoring and alerting, utilizing SIEM tools, facilitating compliance reporting, and enhancing incident response capabilities, organizations can establish a robust security framework. In the business scenario of our multinational financial institution, this approach ensures the confidentiality, integrity, and availability of sensitive financial data while meeting regulatory expectations.

Crafting SIEM Solutions: Orchestrating Cybersecurity

Security Information and Event Management (SIEM) solutions serve as a cornerstone in achieving this goal. This comprehensive approach involves designing and implementing SIEM solutions that provide real-time visibility into security events, facilitate threat detection, and enhance incident response capabilities.

1. **Data Collection and Aggregation:**

   The first step in designing a SIEM solution involves identifying and collecting data from diverse sources within the organization. This includes logs from servers, network devices, firewalls, applications, and more. The goal is to aggregate this data into a centralized platform, creating a unified source of information for security analysts.

   Use Case: In a corporate environment, a SIEM solution collects logs from various endpoints, such as employee workstations and servers. It also aggregates data from network devices and firewalls, creating a centralized repository that captures the organization's digital activities.

2. **Normalization and Parsing:**

   Once the data is collected, it undergoes normalization and parsing processes to standardize formats and structures. This ensures consistency in the data, allowing for effective correlation and analysis. Normalization is critical when dealing with logs from different sources that may use diverse formats and syntax.

   Use Case: In a cloud-based infrastructure, a SIEM solution normalizes logs from different cloud service providers, standardizing event data from AWS, Azure, and Google Cloud into a common format for seamless correlation and analysis.

3. **Correlation and Analysis:**

   Correlation involves analyzing the normalized data to identify patterns, relationships, and anomalies that may indicate security incidents. Advanced correlation rules and algorithms help connect disparate events and generate actionable insights. The analysis phase assesses the severity of events and prioritizes them on the basis of the organization's risk profile.

   Use Case: In a financial institution, a SIEM solution correlates events such as multiple failed login attempts, unusual fund transfer patterns, and access to sensitive customer information. This correlation helps identify potential security threats, such as a credential compromise or a financial fraud attempt.

4. **Real-Time Monitoring:**

   A crucial feature of SIEM solutions is real-time monitoring. Security analysts gain a live view of the organization's security posture, enabling them to detect and respond to incidents as they occur. Real-time monitoring involves setting up alerts for specific events or thresholds, ensuring prompt action in response to potential threats.

   Use Case: In an e-commerce platform, a SIEM solution monitors user activity in real-time, triggering alerts for suspicious login attempts, changes in shopping cart behavior, or anomalies in payment processing. This allows immediate investigation and response to potential fraud or security breaches.

5. **Incident Response and Automation:**

   SIEM solutions play a pivotal role in incident response. Automated response mechanisms can be integrated to execute predefined actions when specific security events are detected. Automation enhances the speed of response, reduces manual intervention, and mitigates the impact of security incidents.

   Use Case: In a healthcare organization, a SIEM solution integrated with incident response automation can identify patterns indicative of a potential data breach. Automated responses may include isolating affected systems, notifying relevant personnel, and initiating a forensic investigation.

6. **Forensic Analysis and Reporting:**

   SIEM solutions facilitate forensic analysis by providing detailed historical data and audit trails. This capability is crucial for post-incident investigations and compliance reporting. Organizations can reconstruct events, identify the root cause of incidents, and generate comprehensive reports for internal review and regulatory compliance.

   Use Case: In a manufacturing environment, a SIEM solution assists in forensic analysis by reconstructing the sequence of events leading to a production system outage. This information is valuable for identifying vulnerabilities, improving security controls, and preventing future incidents.

Benefits and Considerations:

Forensic analysis and reporting provide invaluable insights for investigations, facilitating evidence gathering and legal proceedings. Highlighting both benefits and considerations enhances the understanding of related insights.

- **Enhanced Threat Detection:**

  SIEM solutions enhance an organization's ability to detect both known and unknown threats by correlating data from diverse sources. This proactive approach allows security teams to identify patterns that may go unnoticed with traditional monitoring methods.

- **Streamlined Compliance:**

  SIEM solutions aid in meeting regulatory requirements by providing comprehensive audit trails and facilitating the generation of compliance reports. This is particularly essential in industries such as finance, healthcare, and government, where adherence to regulations is critical.

- **Operational Efficiency:**

  Centralized monitoring, automated responses, and real-time alerts contribute to operational efficiency. SIEM solutions enable security teams to focus on high-priority tasks, reduce response times, and minimize the impact of security incidents.

- **Scalability and Integration:**

  SIEM solutions should be scalable to accommodate the evolving needs of organizations. Integration capabilities with other security tools, threat intelligence feeds, and third-party applications enhance the overall effectiveness of the solution.

Designing Security Information and Event Management (SIEM) solutions is paramount for organizations seeking to fortify their cybersecurity posture. By aggregating and analyzing data from diverse sources, facilitating real-time monitoring, enabling automated responses, and supporting forensic analysis, SIEM solutions empower organizations to detect, respond, and mitigate security threats effectively. In a digital landscape where cyber threats are ever-present, a well-designed SIEM solution acts as a vigilant guardian, orchestrating a robust defense against potential risks and vulnerabilities.

Designing Solutions for Detection and Response: A Real-Time Scenario

Let us explore a real-time scenario to illustrate the design of such solutions.

Scenario:

Imagine a large e-commerce platform that processes thousands of transactions daily. The platform stores sensitive customer information, including personal details and payment data. With the increasing sophistication of cyber threats, the e-commerce company recognizes the need for a comprehensive detection and response system to safeguard customer data and maintain the trust of its user base.

- **Real-Time Monitoring:**

  The design begins with the implementation of real-time monitoring solutions. Security Information and Event Management (SIEM) tools are employed to collect and analyze logs from various sources, including servers, databases, and network devices. This real-time monitoring allows the security team to have immediate visibility into the platform's activities.

- **Anomaly Detection:**

  To identify potential threats, the e-commerce platform integrates anomaly detection mechanisms into its monitoring systems. Machine learning algorithms analyze patterns of user behavior, transaction volumes, and access patterns. Any deviation from the established norms triggers alerts for further investigation.

- **Endpoint Protection:**

  Recognizing the diverse attack vectors, the organization deploys advanced endpoint protection solutions. Every device accessing the e-commerce platform undergoes continuous monitoring for signs of malicious activity. Endpoint protection not only prevents known threats but also identifies and responds to novel, previously unseen threats in real-time.

- **Threat Intelligence Integration:**

  The e-commerce company incorporates threat intelligence feeds into its detection systems. These feeds provide real-time information about the latest cyber threats and attack methodologies. Integrating threat intelligence enhances the platform's ability to recognize and respond to emerging threats promptly.

- **Incident Response Plan:**

  A well-defined incident response plan is crucial for effective handling of security incidents. The e-commerce platform establishes a comprehensive incident response team and outlines procedures for identifying, containing, eradicating, recovering, and learning from security incidents. This plan ensures a coordinated and efficient response to any detected threats.

- **Automation of Responses:**

  To expedite incident response, the organization automates certain response actions. For example, in the event of a detected phishing attempt, automated responses may include isolating affected accounts, blocking malicious IP addresses, and notifying the security team for further analysis.

- **Continuous Improvement:**

  Acknowledging the ever-evolving nature of cyber threats, the e-commerce company implements continuous improvement mechanisms. This involves regular reviews of incident response procedures, updates to detection algorithms based on new threat intelligence, and ongoing training for the incident response team to stay ahead of emerging threats.

Benefits and Outcomes:

Designing solutions for detection and response yields improved threat identification, swift incident handling, and fortified resilience. Enhanced security posture and reduced impact of cyber threats are consequential outcomes.

- **Timely Threat Detection:**

  The implemented solutions enable the e-commerce platform to detect threats as they occur, reducing the time between an incident and its identification. This swift detection minimizes the potential impact on customer data and business operations.

- **Effective Incident Response:**

  With a well-structured incident response plan and automated response actions, the organization can efficiently contain and mitigate the effects of security incidents. This proactive approach safeguards the integrity of the e-commerce platform.

- **Adaptability to Emerging Threats:**

  By integrating threat intelligence and continuously improving detection mechanisms, the organization remains adaptable to emerging cyber threats. The ability to respond to novel attack methods ensures a proactive defense against evolving risks.

Designing solutions for detection and response is imperative for organizations navigating the complex cybersecurity landscape. Through real-time monitoring, anomaly detection, endpoint protection, threat intelligence integration, a robust incident response plan, and continuous improvement, organizations can fortify their defenses and provide a secure environment for users and sensitive data. In the scenario of the e-commerce platform, these measures not only enhance security but also contribute to maintaining customer trust and sustaining business continuity.

Orchestrating Cybersecurity Excellence: Designing a SOAR Solution

Security Orchestration, Automation, and Response (SOAR) solutions have emerged as a strategic approach to streamline security operations, automate repetitive tasks, and enhance incident response capabilities. Let us explore the design of a SOAR solution through a business scenario.

Business Scenario:

Imagine a global financial institution managing vast amounts of sensitive customer data, including financial transactions and personal information. The institution recognizes the critical need for a comprehensive cybersecurity strategy that not only detects threats but also responds to incidents promptly to safeguard customer assets and uphold regulatory compliance.

- **Integration of Security Tools:**

  The first step in designing a SOAR solution involves integrating diverse security tools and technologies used within the organization. This includes Security Information and Event Management (SIEM) systems, endpoint protection, firewalls, threat intelligence feeds, and incident response platforms. The goal is to create a unified and interconnected security infrastructure.

  Use Case: In the financial institution, the SOAR solution integrates with the existing SIEM system, endpoint protection tools, and threat intelligence feeds. This ensures that all security tools work collaboratively, sharing information seamlessly for enhanced threat detection and response.

- **Incident Orchestration:**

  SOAR solutions facilitate incident orchestration by defining workflows and playbooks for various types of security incidents. Workflows outline the step-by-step processes for incident response, and playbooks automate these processes where possible. Incident orchestration ensures a coordinated and consistent response to security incidents.

  Use Case: In the financial institution, a playbook is created for responding to a potential data breach. The playbook outlines the tasks to isolate affected systems, notify the incident response team, and engage with legal and compliance teams. Automation triggers these tasks based on the severity of the incident.

- **Automated Threat Response:**

  Automation is a core component of SOAR solutions. Automated response actions are predefined for common security incidents, allowing the system to respond to threats without manual intervention. This not only accelerates response times but also reduces the risk of human error.

  Use Case: If the SOAR solution detects a malware outbreak on several endpoints, automated response actions can be triggered to isolate the affected devices from the network, update antivirus signatures, and initiate a scan to remove the malware.

- **Threat Intelligence Integration:**

  SOAR solutions leverage threat intelligence feeds to stay informed about the latest cyber threats and attack techniques. Integrating threat intelligence enhances the ability to detect and respond to emerging threats promptly.

  Use Case: The financial institution integrates threat intelligence feeds into the SOAR solution to receive real-time updates on new malware strains or phishing campaigns. This ensures that the incident response playbooks are updated to address the latest threat landscape.

- **User Authentication and Access Management:**

  SOAR solutions can automate user authentication and access management tasks. For instance, in the event of a compromised user account, the system can automatically reset passwords, revoke access privileges, and notify the affected user.

  Use Case: If the SOAR solution detects suspicious activity indicating a compromised user account, it can automatically trigger actions to reset the user's password, log them out of active sessions, and notify the security team for further investigation.

- **Reporting and Analytics:**

  Reporting and analytics capabilities within SOAR solutions provide insights into the effectiveness of incident response efforts. Organizations can analyze response times, identify recurring incidents, and fine-tune playbooks based on historical data.

  Use Case: The financial institution utilizes the reporting features of the SOAR solution to track incident response metrics, measure the effectiveness of automated actions, and identify areas for improvement in the security operations workflow.

Benefits and Outcomes:

Forensic analysis and reporting offer crucial insights into investigations, aiding in evidence collection and legal proceedings. Benefits include efficient incident response, reduction in manual workload, enhanced threat detection, and adaptability to the changing threat landscape. These outcomes underscore the importance of incorporating forensic analysis and reporting into cybersecurity strategies to bolster defense mechanisms effectively.

- **Efficient Incident Response:**

  The automated workflows and playbooks streamline incident response processes, reducing response times and ensuring a consistent approach to different types of security incidents.

- **Reduction in Manual Workload:**

  Automation of repetitive tasks, such as user authentication and access management, reduces the manual workload on security teams, allowing them to focus on more complex and strategic aspects of cybersecurity.

- **Enhanced Threat Detection:**

  Integration with diverse security tools and threat intelligence feeds enhances the SOAR solution's ability to detect and respond to a wide range of threats, including emerging and sophisticated cyber threats.

- **Adaptability to Changing Threat Landscape:**

  Regular updates from threat intelligence feeds and continuous improvement based on analytics ensure that the SOAR solution remains adaptable to the evolving threat landscape.

Designing a SOAR solution empowers organizations, such as our global financial institution, to orchestrate and automate their cybersecurity operations effectively. By integrating security tools, orchestrating incident response, automating threat response, integrating threat intelligence, managing user authentication, and providing robust reporting capabilities, a well-designed SOAR solution becomes a cornerstone in fortifying an organization's defense against cyber threats. In a world where cyber threats continue to evolve, a proactive and automated response is key to maintaining the integrity, security, and trust of critical systems and sensitive data

Safeguarding Cyber Frontiers: Designing Effective Security Workflows

In the realm of cybersecurity, the design of robust security workflows is paramount for organizations aiming to fortify their digital defenses. These workflows, comprising structured processes and procedures, ensure a systematic and efficient approach to threat detection, incident response, and overall cybersecurity management. Let us delve into the design of security workflows through a real-time scenario.

Scenario:

Consider a multinational technology corporation that develops and maintains critical software applications used by enterprises globally. The corporation handles vast amounts of sensitive data, including proprietary code, customer information, and intellectual property. Recognizing the ever-present cyber threats, the organization seeks to design comprehensive security workflows to safeguard its digital assets and maintain the trust of its clients.

- **Threat Intelligence Integration:**

  The first step in designing security workflows involves the integration of threat intelligence feeds. These feeds provide real-time information about the latest cyber threats, including malware signatures, known vulnerabilities, and emerging attack patterns. Integrating threat intelligence ensures that security workflows are informed and adaptive to the current threat landscape.

  Use Case: The technology corporation integrates threat intelligence feeds into its workflows to receive timely updates on new malware targeting software development environments. This information influences workflow decisions, such as prioritizing patching for vulnerable systems and enhancing monitoring for related indicators of compromise.

- **Continuous Monitoring:**

  Security workflows should incorporate continuous monitoring mechanisms. Automated tools analyze network traffic, system logs, and user activities in real-time to detect anomalous patterns indicative of potential security incidents. Continuous monitoring ensures a proactive stance in identifying threats as they emerge.

  Use Case: The technology corporation employs continuous monitoring in its workflows to detect unauthorized access attempts to its source code repositories. Automated alerts trigger immediate investigation and response, mitigating the risk of code theft or tampering.

- **Incident Response Procedures:**

  Clearly defined incident response procedures are a critical component of security workflows. Workflows outline the steps to be taken in the event of a security incident, including identification, containment, eradication, recovery, and lessons learned. These procedures ensure a coordinated and effective response to minimize the impact of incidents.

  Use Case: In response to a detected intrusion attempt, the technology corporation's workflows guide the incident response team through a predefined set of actions. These may include isolating affected systems, analyzing malware artifacts, and implementing measures to prevent further unauthorized access.

- **Patch Management:**

  An integral part of security workflows involves patch management processes. Workflows should detail how and when software updates and patches are applied to address known vulnerabilities promptly. Patch management is crucial for closing security gaps and reducing the risk of exploitation.

  Use Case: The technology corporation incorporates patch management into its security workflows to ensure that critical security patches are applied promptly. Workflows include procedures for testing patches in a controlled environment before deployment to production systems.

- **User Education and Awareness:**

  Security workflows should encompass initiatives for user education and awareness. Workflows may include training programs, simulated phishing exercises, and communication strategies to ensure that employees are well-informed about cybersecurity best practices and potential threats.

  Use Case: The technology corporation integrates user education into its workflows, conducting regular training sessions on topics such as phishing awareness and secure coding practices. This proactive approach enhances the organization's overall security posture.

- **Forensic Analysis and Reporting:**

  Security workflows should incorporate processes for forensic analysis and reporting. In the aftermath of a security incident, workflows guide the collection of evidence, analysis of artifacts, and generation of comprehensive reports for internal review and regulatory compliance.

Use Case: Following a data breach attempt, the technology corporation's workflows facilitate forensic analysis to understand the extent of the breach. Detailed reports are generated, documenting the incident timeline, impact assessment, and recommended improvements to security controls.

Benefits and Outcomes:

Benefits and outcomes of implementing robust security workflows are paramount in safeguarding organizations against cyber threats. Proactive threat detection, efficient incident response, reduced vulnerability exposure, and enhanced employee awareness underscore the importance of strategic cybersecurity measures.

- **Proactive Threat Detection:**

  The integration of threat intelligence and continuous monitoring in security workflows enables the early detection of potential threats, allowing organizations to respond proactively before incidents escalate.

- **Efficient Incident Response:**

  Well-defined incident response procedures ensure a swift and coordinated response to security incidents. This efficiency minimizes the impact of incidents on business operations and customer trust

- **Reduced Vulnerability Exposure:**

  Patch management processes integrated into security workflows help organizations promptly address known vulnerabilities, reducing the window of exposure to potential exploitation by malicious actors.

- **Enhanced Employee Awareness:**

  Security workflows that incorporate user education initiatives contribute to a security-aware organizational culture. Educated and aware employees become a frontline defense against social engineering and phishing attacks.

Designing effective security workflows is a strategic imperative for organizations navigating the intricate landscape of cybersecurity. By integrating threat intelligence, continuous monitoring, incident response procedures, patch management, user education, and forensic analysis into these workflows, organizations, like our multinational technology corporation, establish a comprehensive and resilient cybersecurity framework. In a digital environment where threats are dynamic and persistent, well-designed security workflows act as a shield, ensuring the protection of sensitive data, maintaining operational integrity, and fortifying the digital fortresses of modern enterprises

Fortifying Digital Ramparts: Designing Comprehensive Threat Detection Coverage

Designing robust threat detection coverage is a strategic imperative, ensuring that organizations can identify and respond to diverse cyber threats promptly. Let us delve into the intricacies of designing threat detection coverage through a real-world case study.

Case Study: Securing a Global Financial Institution

In the case study of securing a global financial institution, the imperative of enhancing threat detection capabilities within the institution's vast digital infrastructure is paramount. Let us delve into the meticulous design and implementation of comprehensive threat detection coverage.

Scenario:

A global financial institution, managing vast financial transactions and sensitive customer data, recognized the critical need to enhance its threat detection capabilities. The institution aimed to fortify its digital infrastructure against a spectrum of threats, including malware, phishing attacks, and advanced persistent threats.

Designing Threat Detection Coverage:

In the landscape of cybersecurity, establishing comprehensive threat detection coverage is essential. Let us explore the methods and considerations pivotal to designing effective defences against diverse digital threats.

1. **Risk Assessment and Asset Inventory:**

   The first step in designing threat detection coverage involved conducting a comprehensive risk assessment and creating an inventory of critical assets. Understanding the organization's risk profile and identifying high-value assets provided a foundation for designing tailored threat detection mechanisms.

   Implementation: The financial institution utilized automated tools to perform risk assessments, identifying vulnerabilities and assessing the criticality of assets. This information informed the prioritization of threat detection efforts.

2. **Endpoint Security:**

   Recognizing that endpoints are common entry points for cyber threats, the institution focused on bolstering endpoint security. Advanced endpoint protection solutions were deployed to detect and prevent malware, ransomware, and other malicious activities on employee devices.

Implementation: Endpoint security solutions were integrated into the organization's threat detection infrastructure, providing real-time monitoring, behavior analysis, and automated responses to mitigate potential threats at the device level.

3. **Network Traffic Analysis:**

   Designing comprehensive threat detection coverage involved monitoring network traffic for anomalous patterns and potential security incidents. Intrusion detection and prevention systems were implemented to analyze incoming and outgoing traffic, identifying unusual activities that could indicate a security threat.

   Implementation: The financial institution deployed network traffic analysis tools that utilized machine learning algorithms to detect deviations from normal network behavior. This approach enhanced the institution's ability to identify sophisticated threats that may attempt to traverse the network undetected.

4. **User Behavior Analytics:**

   Understanding that user behavior plays a crucial role in threat detection, the organization incorporated user behavior analytics into its strategy. This involved establishing baselines for normal user activities and leveraging analytics to detect deviations that could indicate compromised accounts or insider threats.

   Implementation: The financial institution employed user behavior analytics tools that analyzed login patterns, access privileges, and data interactions. Deviations from established norms triggered alerts for further investigation, enabling the organization to proactively address potential insider threats.

5. **Email Security and Phishing Detection:**

   Given the prevalence of phishing attacks, the institution prioritized email security. Advanced email filtering solutions and phishing detection tools were implemented to identify and quarantine malicious emails, reducing the risk of employees falling victim to phishing scams.

   Implementation: The financial institution integrated advanced email security solutions that utilized machine learning algorithms to analyze email content, sender behavior, and attachment characteristics. Suspicious emails were flagged and isolated for inspection.

6. **Threat Intelligence Integration:**

   To stay ahead of emerging threats, the organization integrated threat intelligence feeds into its threat detection coverage. Real-time information about the latest cyber threats, vulnerabilities, and attack techniques provided the context for proactive threat detection.

   Implementation: The financial institution subscribed to threat intelligence feeds from reputable sources, ensuring that its threat detection systems were regularly updated with information about new malware variants, zero-day vulnerabilities, and evolving threat landscapes.

7. **Incident Response Planning:**

   Recognizing the inevitability of security incidents, the financial institution prioritized incident response planning. Well-defined incident response procedures were established, outlining the steps to be taken in the event of a detected security incident.

   Implementation: The institution conducted regular incident response drills, involving cross-functional teams in simulated scenarios. These drills helped refine incident response plans, ensuring a coordinated and effective response in the event of a real security incident.

Outcomes and Benefits:

Effective threat detection coverage yields heightened security posture and timely identification of potential risks, ensuring proactive mitigation and safeguarding critical assets.

- **Enhanced Threat Visibility:**

  The comprehensive threat detection coverage provided the financial institution with enhanced visibility into its digital landscape, allowing for the early detection of potential security threats across various attack vectors.

- **Reduced Response Times:**

  By deploying a multifaceted approach to threat detection, the organization significantly reduced response times to security incidents. Automated responses and well-defined incident response procedures ensured a swift and coordinated reaction to emerging threats.

- **Minimized Impact of Cyber Threats:**

  The institution's proactive threat detection coverage contributed to minimizing the impact of cyber threats. Swift detection and mitigation measures prevented the escalation of incidents, protecting critical financial data and maintaining operational continuity.

- **Adaptability to Emerging Threats:**

  The integration of threat intelligence feeds ensured that the financial institution remained adaptable to emerging cyber threats. The organization could quickly adjust its threat detection strategies based on real-time information about the evolving threat landscape.

Designing comprehensive threat detection coverage is a cornerstone of effective cybersecurity, as demonstrated by the case study of the global financial institution. By conducting risk assessments, securing endpoints, analyzing network traffic, monitoring user behavior, fortifying email security, integrating threat intelligence, and prioritizing incident response planning, organizations can create a resilient defense against a wide range of cyber threats. In an era where cyber threats continue to evolve, the proactive and adaptive approach exemplified in this case study serves as a blueprint for organizations aiming to safeguard their digital assets and maintain the trust of stakeholders.

Conclusion

In conclusion, the meticulous orchestration of Security Operations Design is paramount in safeguarding digital landscapes. As technology evolves, so do the intricacies of potential threats, necessitating a dynamic and comprehensive approach. By seamlessly integrating threat intelligence, incident response, and proactive measures, organizations can fortify their defenses. A well-designed security operation not only mitigates risks but also ensures resilience in the face of emerging challenges. Embracing a holistic mindset that adapts to the ever-changing threat landscape is imperative. In the pursuit of robust security, continual refinement of Security Operations Design emerges as a linchpin for the protection of valuable assets and sensitive information. In the next chapter, we discuss the Microsoft 365 security design.

Multiple Choice Questions

1. What is the primary goal of designing solutions for security operations?
   a. Enhancing network speed
   b. Minimizing software development time
   c. Detecting, responding to, and mitigating security incidents
   d. Increasing server storage capacity

2. Which technology plays a vital role in Security Operations (SecOps) by analyzing incoming emails and attachments for suspicious content?
    a. Blockchain
    b. Augmented Reality (AR)
    c. Security Information and Event Management (SIEM)
    d. Virtual Private Network (VPN)
3. What is a key benefit of integrating threat intelligence feeds into security operations?
    a. Reducing electricity consumption
    b. Enhancing user interface design
    c. Staying informed about the latest cyber threats
    d. Improving hardware durability
4. In Security Operations, what is the purpose of incident response planning?
    a. Creating marketing campaigns
    b. Identifying potential software bugs
    c. Coordinating and responding to security incidents
    d. Analyzing financial transactions
5. Which term refers to the ability of QR codes to be read from any alignment, enhancing scanning speed?
    a. Uniform Resource Locator (URL)
    b. Position Detection Patterns
    c. Reed-Solomon Algorithm
    d. Machine Learning Algorithm

Answers

1. c
2. c
3. c
4. c
5. b

Chapter 9
Microsoft 365 Security Design

Introduction

Organizations are increasingly relying on platforms like Microsoft 365 to boost productivity. However, this heightened reliance brings forth a critical need for robust security measures. Microsoft 365, comprising Exchange Online, SharePoint Online, OneDrive for Business, and Microsoft Teams, plays a pivotal role in communication, collaboration, and data storage. Safeguarding these services is imperative for protecting sensitive information and upholding data integrity.

Structure

In this chapter, we will cover the following topics:

- Microsoft 365 Security Blueprint
- Microsoft 365 Security: Defender for Office 365
- Office 365 Security Journey: EOP to Defender
- XYZ Corporation's Microsoft 365 Security Case Study
- Designing a Microsoft Defender XDR Solution: A Real-Time Scenario
- Design Configurations and Operational Practices for Microsoft 365: A Business Scenario

Microsoft 365 Security Blueprint

As organizations increasingly rely on collaborative platforms like Microsoft 365 to enhance productivity, the need for robust security measures becomes paramount. Microsoft 365 encompasses a suite of services, including Exchange Online, SharePoint Online, OneDrive for Business, and Microsoft Teams, each playing a crucial role in communication, collaboration, and data storage.

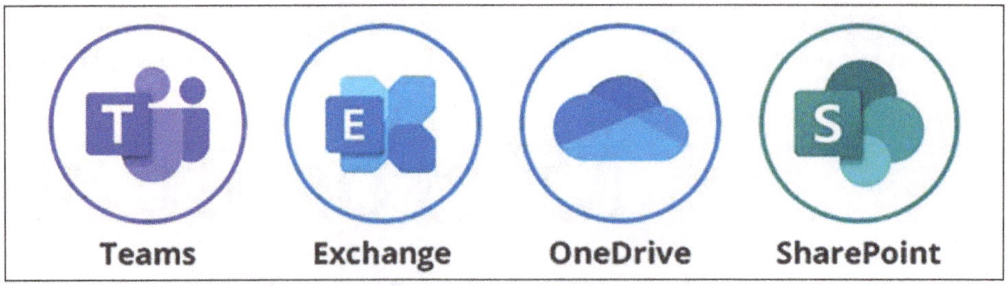

Figure 9.1: *Microsoft 365 Services (Source :* Microsoft 365 Business - Eclectics International)

Understanding and implementing security measures across these services is vital to safeguard sensitive information and maintain the integrity of organizational data.

Exchange Online

Exchange Online, the cloud-based email service within Microsoft 365, requires vigilant security practices to protect against email-based threats such as phishing and malware. Multi-Factor Authentication (MFA), email encryption, and advanced threat protection are key components in securing email communications. Regular monitoring and auditing help detect and respond to potential security incidents promptly.

SharePoint Online

SharePoint Online serves as a collaborative platform for document management and team collaboration. Security measures for SharePoint include access controls, permission management, and encryption. Organizations should define clear policies for sharing and collaboration to prevent unauthorized access. Regular audits of user permissions and activity logs contribute to a proactive security posture.

OneDrive for Business

OneDrive for Business offers secure cloud storage for individual users, necessitating granular access controls and encryption. By enforcing data loss prevention (DLP) policies, organizations can prevent the unintentional sharing of sensitive information. Backup solutions and versioning features add an extra layer of protection against data loss or accidental deletions.

Microsoft Teams

Microsoft Teams facilitates real-time collaboration through chat, videoconferencing, and file sharing. Security considerations for Teams involve controlling guest access, securing meetings, and managing file permissions. Integration with Azure Active Directory and adherence to compliance standards enhance overall security.

A comprehensive security strategy for Microsoft 365 services – Exchange Online, SharePoint Online, OneDrive for Business, and Microsoft Teams – involves a multifaceted approach encompassing user education, policy enforcement, and the utilization of advanced security features. As organizations navigate the digital landscape, prioritizing security ensures a resilient and protected collaborative environment.

Microsoft 365 Security: Defender for Office 365

Defender for Office 365 Security is a comprehensive cloud-based security solution provided by Microsoft to safeguard organizations using Microsoft 365 applications. Formerly known as Office 365 Advanced Threat Protection (ATP), Defender for Office 365 goes beyond traditional antivirus measures, offering advanced threat protection against a wide range of cyber threats.

This security platform is designed to protect against various email-based attacks, including phishing, malware, and ransomware. It employs sophisticated threat intelligence, machine learning, and behavioral analytics to detect and mitigate potential risks in real-time. Defender for Office 365 integrates seamlessly with Exchange Online Protection to enhance the security posture of email communications within the Microsoft 365 environment.

Key features of Defender for Office 365 include Safe Attachments, which examines email attachments in a virtual environment to detect malicious behavior, and Safe Links, which scans URLs in emails to identify and block malicious links. Additionally, the solution provides robust anti-phishing capabilities to identify and thwart phishing attempts targeting organizational users.

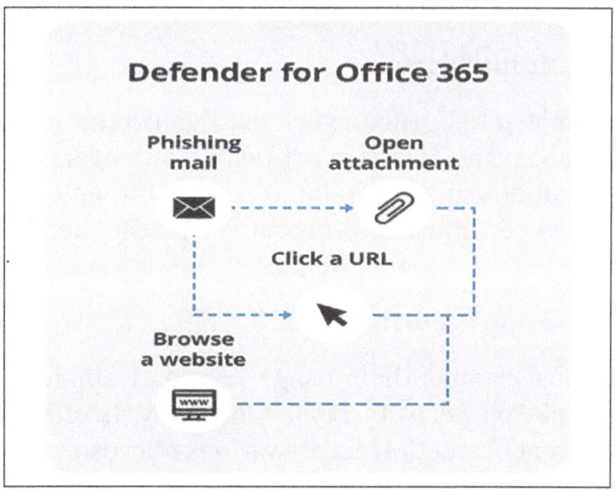

Figure 9.2: *Defender for Office 365 (Source:* SC-100: Design solutions that align with security best practices and priorities - Training | Microsoft Learn)

By offering advanced threat detection and response capabilities, Defender for Office 365 Security plays a crucial role in fortifying the overall cybersecurity infrastructure for Microsoft 365 users, ensuring a safer and more secure digital communication and collaboration experience.

Office 365 Security Journey: EOP to Defender

The Office 365 security ladder represents a progression of security features and capabilities designed to fortify the defenses of organizations relying on Microsoft 365 services. This journey typically starts with Exchange Online Protection (EOP) and ascends to the advanced threat protection offered by Microsoft Defender for Office 365. Let's explore the key steps on this security ladder:

1. **Exchange Online Protection (EOP)**

   At the base of the security ladder, EOP serves as the first line of defense for Microsoft 365 users. It includes fundamental security features such as anti-malware and anti-spam filters, helping to protect email communications from common threats. EOP analyzes email content, attachments, and links to filter out malicious content before it reaches users' inboxes.

2. **Advanced Threat Protection (ATP)**

   Building on the foundation of EOP, Advanced Threat Protection (ATP) introduces additional layers of security. ATP includes features such as Safe Attachments, which detonates email attachments in a sandbox environment to identify and block potentially malicious content, and Safe Links, which examines URLs in emails for signs of malicious activity.

3. **Office 365 Threat Intelligence**

   Office 365 Threat Intelligence provides organizations with insights into the global threat landscape. It offers actionable intelligence and threat analytics to help organizations understand and respond to emerging security threats. Threat Intelligence enhances proactive threat detection and response capabilities.

4. **Microsoft Cloud App Security**

   As organizations expand their usage of cloud applications beyond email, Microsoft Cloud App Security comes into play. It offers advanced visibility, control, and threat protection across various Microsoft 365 services, including SharePoint Online, OneDrive for Business, and Teams. This step reinforces security beyond email, covering a broader spectrum of cloud-based activities.

5. **Microsoft Defender for Office 365**

   At the pinnacle of the security ladder is Microsoft Defender for Office 365, representing the most advanced threat protection for Microsoft 365 environments. Defender integrates threat protection capabilities across email, collaboration, and cloud storage services. It leverages AI, machine learning, and behavioral analytics to detect and remediate sophisticated threats, including phishing attacks, zero-day exploits, and other advanced malware.

By ascending the Office 365 security ladder from EOP to Microsoft Defender for Office 365, organizations can create a robust and layered defense strategy. This multi-tiered approach is essential for adapting to the evolving threat landscape and safeguarding sensitive data and communications in today's dynamic digital environment. Each step on the ladder adds depth and sophistication to the security posture, providing a comprehensive solution for modern cybersecurity challenges.

XYZ Corporation's Microsoft 365 Security Case Study

In today's business landscape, ensuring a strong security posture for collaboration and productivity workloads is crucial for protecting sensitive information, maintaining regulatory compliance, and mitigating the evolving threat landscape. Let's evaluate the security posture in the context of a fictional business scenario:

Business Scenario: XYZ Corporation

XYZ Corporation is a multinational enterprise that heavily relies on Microsoft 365 collaboration and productivity tools to facilitate communication, document sharing, and project management. The company's workforce is dispersed globally, accessing services such as Exchange Online, SharePoint Online, OneDrive for Business, and Microsoft Teams for seamless collaboration.

- **Exchange Online**
  - **Current State:** XYZ Corporation uses Exchange Online for email communication. Basic security measures, such as Exchange Online Protection (EOP), are in place to filter out spam and malware.
  - **Enhancements:** Implement Advanced Threat Protection (ATP) to enhance email security, utilizing features like Safe Attachments and Safe Links for advanced threat detection and prevention.
- **SharePoint Online and OneDrive for Business**
  - **Current State:** The organization extensively uses SharePoint Online for document collaboration and OneDrive for individual file storage.

- **Enhancements:** Strengthen access controls and permissions, implement data loss prevention (DLP) policies to prevent unauthorized data sharing, and regularly audit and monitor user activities to ensure compliance.

- **Microsoft Teams**
  - **Current State:** Microsoft Teams is a central hub for virtual collaboration, including chat, videoconferencing, and file sharing.
  - **Enhancements:** Enable and configure guest access controls, implement secure meeting policies, and utilize information barriers to control communication between different teams or departments.
- **Microsoft Defender for Office 365**
  - **Current State:** The organization relies on Exchange Online Protection and other native security features.
  - **Enhancements:** Upgrade to Microsoft Defender for Office 365 for advanced threat protection across email, collaboration, and cloud storage services. Leverage AI and machine learning to detect and respond to sophisticated threats.
- **User Training and Awareness**
  - **Current State:** Employees are trained on basic security practices but may benefit from ongoing awareness programs.
  - **Enhancements**: Implement regular cybersecurity training sessions to educate users about the latest threats, social engineering tactics, and the importance of adhering to security policies.
- **Compliance and Auditing**
  - **Current State:** The organization has compliance policies in place but needs to enhance auditing capabilities.
  - **Enhancements:** Implement Microsoft 365 compliance center features to streamline compliance management, conduct regular compliance audits, and generate reports to meet regulatory requirements.

By evaluating and enhancing the security posture for collaboration and productivity workloads in this scenario, XYZ Corporation can create a more resilient and secure digital environment. Regularly reviewing and adapting security measures will ensure that the organization stays ahead of potential threats and safeguards its critical data and communication channels effectively.

Designing a Microsoft Defender XDR Solution: A Real-Time Scenario

Let's explore the design of a Microsoft Defender XDR solution in a real-time scenario for a fictional company, GlobalTech Innovations.

Scenario: GlobalTech Innovations

GlobalTech Innovations is a leading technology company specializing in innovative software solutions. With a global workforce and a vast digital infrastructure, the company recognizes the need for an advanced XDR solution to protect against evolving cyber threats.

Key Requirements:

- **Comprehensive Endpoint Protection**

  GlobalTech's diverse workforce operates on various devices and platforms. The XDR solution must integrate seamlessly with Microsoft Defender for Endpoint to provide advanced endpoint protection. This includes real-time threat detection, response, and continuous monitoring across all endpoints, regardless of their location.

- **Email Security**

  Email remains a critical vector for cyber threats. The XDR solution should integrate with Microsoft Defender for Office 365 to fortify email security. This includes anti-phishing measures, attachment and link scanning, and real-time threat intelligence to identify and neutralize email-borne threats.

- **Cloud Security**

  As GlobalTech utilizes cloud services extensively, the XDR solution must extend its protective capabilities to cloud environments. Integration with Microsoft Defender for Cloud, encompassing Azure Security Center, is essential. This ensures continuous monitoring, threat detection, and response across cloud workloads and services.

- **Threat Intelligence Integration**

  To stay ahead of emerging threats, the XDR solution must leverage threat intelligence feeds. Integration with Microsoft Threat Intelligence ensures that GlobalTech has access to up-to-date information on the latest cybersecurity threats and trends.

- **Automated Incident Response**

  GlobalTech requires an XDR solution that automates incident response processes. Microsoft Defender XDR's automated investigation and remediation capabilities will play a critical role in rapidly containing and neutralizing threats and minimizing their impact on the organization.

- **Centralized Security Management**

  To streamline security operations, the XDR solution should offer a centralized management console. Microsoft Defender Security Center provides a unified interface for monitoring and managing security incidents across endpoints, email, and cloud services.

Design Considerations:

- **Implementation of Microsoft Defender for Endpoint**

  Deploy Microsoft Defender for Endpoint across all endpoints, ensuring comprehensive protection. Configure detection and response policies tailored to GlobalTech's specific needs, considering factors such as user behavior analytics, endpoint vulnerability management, and exploit protection.

- **Integration with Microsoft Defender for Office 365**

  Seamlessly integrate Microsoft Defender for Office 365 to enhance email security. Enable anti-phishing policies, use Safe Attachments and Safe Links to protect against malicious email attachments and links, and configure real-time threat intelligence for proactive threat detection.

- **Extending Protection to Cloud Environments**

  Leverage Microsoft Defender for Cloud to extend security coverage to Azure workloads. Implement policies for continuous monitoring, threat detection, and response in the cloud. Ensure that security configurations align with best practices for cloud security.

- **Threat Intelligence Integration**

  Integrate Microsoft Threat Intelligence to enrich the XDR solution with real-time insights. Leverage threat indicators and contextual information to enhance the accuracy of threat detection and automate response actions based on the latest threat intelligence.

- **Automation of Incident Response**

  Configure automated investigation and remediation workflows in Microsoft Defender XDR. Define playbooks for common security incidents, allowing the XDR solution to autonomously respond to and mitigate threats. This accelerates response times and reduces manual intervention.

- **Centralized Management with Microsoft Defender Security Center**

  Utilize Microsoft Defender Security Center as the central hub for security management. This unified console provides a holistic view of security incidents, allowing security teams at GlobalTech to monitor, investigate, and respond to threats across different attack surfaces.

Designing a Microsoft Defender XDR solution for GlobalTech Innovations involves a comprehensive approach that integrates advanced endpoint protection, email security, cloud security, threat intelligence, and automated incident response. By leveraging the capabilities of Microsoft Defender for Endpoint, Office 365, Cloud,

Threat Intelligence, and the Security Center, GlobalTech can establish a proactive defense strategy against a wide range of cyber threats, ensuring the security and resilience of its digital infrastructure.

Design Configurations and Operational Practices for Microsoft 365: A Business Scenario

Designing effective configurations and operational practices is essential to ensure a secure and efficient use of Microsoft 365 services. Let's explore this concept in the context of a fictional business scenario: TechSolutions Inc.

Scenario: TechSolutions Inc.

TechSolutions Inc. is a rapidly growing technology consulting firm with a diverse workforce spread across multiple locations. The company has embraced Microsoft 365 to facilitate seamless communication, collaboration, and data management. To optimize their Microsoft 365 environment, TechSolutions needs to design configurations and operational practices that align with their business goals and ensure a secure, productive, and compliant digital workplace.

Key Configurations and Operational Practices:

- **Identity and Access Management**
  - **Scenario Implementation**: TechSolutions opts for Azure Active Directory (AAD) as the identity provider to manage user identities and access to Microsoft 365 services.
  - **Operational Practice**: Implement Single Sign-On (SSO) to enhance user experience, simplify access management, and enforce strong password policies. Enable Multi-Factor Authentication (MFA) to add an extra layer of security.
- **Data Governance and Compliance**
  - **Scenario Implementation:** TechSolutions utilizes Microsoft 365 Compliance Center to enforce data governance policies and meet regulatory compliance requirements.
  - **Operational Practice:** Implement Data Loss Prevention (DLP) policies to prevent unauthorized sharing of sensitive information. Regularly conduct compliance audits and leverage eDiscovery capabilities to respond to legal and regulatory requests promptly.

- **Collaboration and Communication**
    - **Scenario Implementation:** TechSolutions heavily relies on Microsoft Teams for collaboration and communication.
    - **Operational Practice:** Establish governance policies for Teams, defining naming conventions, access controls, and lifecycle management. Encourage the use of SharePoint Online and OneDrive for Business for document collaboration, ensuring version control and data security.
- **Security and Threat Protection**
    - **Scenario Implementation**: TechSolutions deploys Microsoft Defender for Office 365 to protect against email-based threats and Microsoft Defender for Endpoint for endpoint security.
    - **Operational Practice:** Regularly update security configurations, conduct threat simulations, and monitor security dashboards. Implement security awareness training for employees to recognize and report potential security threats.
- **Mobile Device Management (MDM)**
    - **Scenario Implementation:** Recognizing the need for mobile productivity, TechSolutions implements Microsoft Intune for mobile device management.
    - **Operational Practice:** Enforce device compliance policies, configure application protection policies, and enable conditional access to ensure secure access from mobile devices. Regularly review and update device management configurations based on evolving security requirements.
- **Monitoring and Reporting**
    - **Scenario Implementation:** TechSolutions uses Microsoft 365 Security Center for centralized monitoring and reporting.
    - **Operational Practice:** Establish a routine for reviewing security reports, investigating anomalies, and addressing incidents promptly. Implement proactive monitoring for service health and performance to minimize downtime and disruptions.

In the TechSolutions Inc. scenario, designing configurations and operational practices for Microsoft 365 involves a holistic approach. By implementing identity and access management best practices, enforcing data governance, securing collaboration tools, protecting against threats, managing mobile devices, and establishing robust monitoring, TechSolutions ensures a resilient and secure Microsoft 365 environment. This approach not only enhances security but also contributes to a more efficient and compliant digital workplace, aligning with the company's goals for growth and innovation. Regularly reviewing and updating these configurations and practices will enable TechSolutions to adapt to evolving business needs and security challenges.

Conclusion

In conclusion, the effective implementation of Microsoft 365 security measures, as outlined in the comprehensive blueprint, is essential for organizations to navigate the evolving digital landscape securely. Prioritizing security across Exchange Online, SharePoint Online, OneDrive for Business, and Microsoft Teams ensures the protection of sensitive information and data integrity. The integration of Defender for Office 365 Security further fortifies the overall cybersecurity infrastructure, providing advanced threat protection against a spectrum of cyber threats. The Office 365 security ladder offers a structured progression, culminating in Microsoft Defender for Office 365, creating a multi-tiered defense strategy crucial for adapting to the dynamic threat landscape. Through careful design, configuration, and operational practices, organizations can establish a resilient and secure Microsoft 365 environment, fostering productivity and collaboration while safeguarding critical data from evolving cyber threats. In the next chapter, we will be discussing about design aspects of application security.

Multiple Choice Questions

1. What is a key component for securing identities in Microsoft 365?
    a. Microsoft Teams
    b. SharePoint Online
    c. Azure Active Directory (AAD)
    d. OneDrive for Business
2. Which Microsoft 365 tool is designed for advanced threat protection against email-based threats, including phishing and malware?
    a. Microsoft Defender for Endpoint
    b. Microsoft Intune
    c. Microsoft Defender for Office 365
    d. Microsoft 365 Compliance Center
3. What is recommended for enhancing user authentication security in Microsoft 365?
    a. Disabling Multi-Factor Authentication (MFA)
    b. Using simple and easily guessable passwords

   c. Enabling Single Sign-On (SSO)
   d. Ignoring password policies

4. Which practice is essential for securing collaboration and communication in Microsoft 365, especially in the context of Microsoft Teams?
   a. Avoiding the use of SharePoint Online
   b. Implementing naming conventions and access controls for Teams
   c. Disabling Multi-Factor Authentication (MFA)
   d. Ignoring document version control
5. What is a recommended tool for monitoring and reporting security incidents in Microsoft 365?
   a. Microsoft Defender for Endpoint
   b. Microsoft 365 Security Center
   c. Microsoft Intune
   d. Microsoft 365 Compliance Center

Answers

1. c
2. c
3. c
4. b
5. b

Chapter 10
Application Security Design

Introduction

Application security is a critical aspect of modern software development, aimed at safeguarding applications from unauthorized access, data breaches, and other cyber threats. As technology evolves, applications become more complex, interconnected, and susceptible to various vulnerabilities. The primary goal of application security is to identify, fix, and prevent these vulnerabilities throughout the development lifecycle. One of the key principles of application security is the implementation of robust coding practices. Secure coding helps developers create software that is resilient to common threats such as injection attacks, cross-site scripting, and security misconfigurations. Additionally, authentication and authorization mechanisms play a pivotal role in ensuring that only authorized users can access sensitive data and functionalities within an application. Regular security assessments, including penetration testing and code reviews, are essential components of application security. These practices help identify and address potential weaknesses before they can be exploited by malicious actors. Furthermore, the integration of security into the DevOps pipeline ensures that security measures are seamlessly woven into the software development process. Application security is an indispensable discipline that strives to fortify software against an ever-evolving landscape of cyber threats. By adopting proactive measures, adhering to secure coding practices, and conducting thorough assessments, organizations can build and maintain resilient applications that protect sensitive information and maintain the trust of users.

Structure

In this chapter, we will cover the following topics:

- Securing Applications in the DevOps Era: A Case Study
- Implementation of Secure Coding Practices

- Design and Implementing Standards to Secure Application Development: A Comprehensive Approach
- Evaluating the Security Posture of Existing Application Portfolios: A Strategic Imperative
- Methodology for Security Posture Evaluation
- Microsoft Threat Modeling Tool (MTMT): An Overview
- Designing a Security Lifecycle Strategy for Applications: A Proactive Approach for Business Resilience
- Designing a Solution for Secure Access to Applications: Navigating the Digital Frontier

Securing Applications in the DevOps Era: A Case Study

In the fast-paced world of software development, the integration of security into the entire application lifecycle has become paramount. As organizations embrace DevOps practices to accelerate development and deployment, ensuring the security of applications is a complex challenge that demands a holistic and continuous approach. In this case study, we explore the journey of a fictional company, TechSecure, in implementing Application and DevOps security measures to safeguard their critical software assets.

Background

TechSecure, a leading software development firm, was facing the dual challenge of rapidly delivering innovative applications to meet market demands while safeguarding their systems from evolving cyber threats. Traditional security approaches, often implemented as a separate phase after development, were proving inadequate in the dynamic landscape of modern software deployment.

Challenges

The challenges faced by TechSecure included vulnerabilities in their application code, misconfigurations, and the need to align security with the high-velocity DevOps pipeline. Security measures were often seen as impediments to speed, leading to a trade-off between agility and resilience.

Implementation of Secure Coding Practices

TechSecure initiated the transformation by emphasizing secure coding practices from the outset of development. Developers received training on identifying and mitigating common vulnerabilities such as SQL injection, cross-site scripting, and insecure direct object references. Automated code analysis tools were integrated into the CI/CD pipeline, providing real-time feedback to developers and preventing insecure code from progressing to the next stage.

Authentication and Authorization Mechanisms

To fortify access controls, TechSecure revamped its authentication and authorization mechanisms. Multi-factor authentication was implemented for critical systems, and a robust role-based access control (RBAC) system was introduced to ensure that users had the least privilege necessary to perform their tasks. This not only bolstered security but also enhanced overall system governance.

Continuous Security Assessments

Recognizing that security is an ever-evolving landscape, TechSecure adopted continuous security assessments as a fundamental practice. Regular penetration testing, performed by both internal and external experts, helped identify and remediate vulnerabilities in both application code and infrastructure. Automated vulnerability scanning tools were integrated into the DevOps pipeline, enabling rapid detection and remediation of issues in pre-production environments.

DevOps Security Integration

TechSecure embraced the concept of "DevSecOps" by integrating security into the entire DevOps pipeline. Security measures were treated as code, with security configurations stored alongside application code in version control. Automated security testing, including static application security testing (SAST) and dynamic application security testing (DAST), became integral parts of the continuous integration and continuous deployment (CI/CD) process.

Case Study Results

The implementation of comprehensive application and DevOps security measures yielded significant benefits for TechSecure. The frequency of security incidents decreased, and the company experienced a notable reduction in the time and resources required to address vulnerabilities. By integrating security into the DevOps pipeline, the development team maintained agility without compromising on security. Furthermore, TechSecure witnessed an improvement in customer trust and satisfaction as the security posture of their applications became a differentiator in the competitive market. Compliance with industry regulations also became more seamless, as security controls were consistently applied throughout the development lifecycle.

The case study of TechSecure demonstrates that the integration of application and DevOps security is not only feasible but also essential in today's software development landscape. By adopting secure coding practices, enhancing authentication and authorization mechanisms, and embracing continuous security assessments, organizations can fortify their applications against evolving cyber threats without sacrificing speed and agility. As the DevOps journey continues to evolve, the emphasis on security as an integral part of the process will be crucial for organizations seeking to build resilient, secure, and innovative software solutions. TechSecure's success serves as a testament to the effectiveness of a holistic approach to application and DevOps security in meeting the demands of the modern digital era.

Design and Implementing Standards to Secure Application Development: A Comprehensive Approach

In the ever-evolving landscape of technology, the security of application development has become a paramount concern for businesses. As organizations increasingly rely on software to drive innovation and productivity, ensuring the confidentiality, integrity, and availability of their applications is imperative. This section explores the design and implementation of standards to secure application development, emphasizing the importance of a comprehensive approach to mitigate risks and fortify digital assets.

Business Scenario

Consider a hypothetical scenario faced by a financial services company, FinSecure Corp. The company, like many in its industry, manages sensitive financial data and operates in a highly regulated environment. Facing the constant threat of cyber attacks and data breaches, FinSecure Corp. recognizes the critical need to establish robust security standards for its application development processes. The business scenario involves FinSecure Corp. developing and maintaining a suite of financial applications, including online banking, mobile payment solutions, and customer relationship management tools. These applications process and store vast amounts of sensitive customer information, making them attractive targets for cybercriminals.

To safeguard their reputation, customer trust, and regulatory compliance, FinSecure Corp. is compelled to design and implement stringent security standards throughout the application development lifecycle.

Designing Security Standards

The first step in securing application development is the design of comprehensive security standards that encompass the entire software development lifecycle. These standards should be tailored to the specific needs and risks of the organization. For FinSecure Corp., the security standards would include guidelines for secure coding practices, authentication mechanisms, data encryption, and secure configuration management.

- **Secure Coding Practices:** The security standards would mandate the use of secure coding practices to mitigate common vulnerabilities such as injection attacks, cross-site scripting, and security misconfigurations. Developers would undergo training to understand and implement coding techniques that minimize the risk of introducing security flaws.
- **Authentication Mechanisms:** Given the sensitivity of financial data, robust authentication mechanisms are essential. The security standards would specify the use of multi-factor authentication for user access to applications, protecting against unauthorized access and identity theft.
- **Data Encryption:** To protect customer information during transit and storage, the security standards would mandate the use of encryption protocols. This ensures that even if data is intercepted, it remains unreadable and secure.
- **Secure Configuration Management**: Configuration errors can expose applications to vulnerabilities. The security standards would include guidelines for secure configuration management, ensuring that servers, databases, and other components are configured with the principle of least privilege and hardened against potential threats.

Implementation of Security Standards

Once the security standards are designed, their effective implementation is crucial. This involves integrating security measures into the day-to-day practices of the development team and the broader organization.

- **Integration into Development Processes**

  The security standards should seamlessly integrate into the development processes. Automated tools for static code analysis, dynamic application security testing, and vulnerability scanning should be integrated into the continuous integration and continuous deployment (CI/CD) pipeline. This ensures that security checks are performed at every stage of development, preventing insecure code from progressing further.

- **Developer Training and Awareness**

  Developers play a pivotal role in the success of security standards. Regular training sessions and awareness programs should be conducted to keep developers informed about the latest security threats, best practices, and the importance of adhering to the established standards.

- **Regular Security Audits and Assessments**

  To validate the effectiveness of the security standards, regular security audits and assessments should be conducted. External penetration testing, code reviews, and compliance checks can identify vulnerabilities and areas for improvement.

Benefits and Future Considerations

By designing and implementing robust security standards, FinSecure Corp. can enjoy several benefits, including reduced risk of data breaches, enhanced customer trust, and compliance with regulatory requirements. The ongoing monitoring and adaptation of these standards to address emerging threats and technologies are crucial for staying ahead of potential risks. In conclusion, the design and implementation of standards to secure application development are essential components of a proactive and resilient cybersecurity strategy. Through a comprehensive approach that integrates security into the entire development lifecycle, organizations like FinSecure Corp. can navigate the complex threat landscape and build applications that not only meet business objectives but also prioritize the protection of sensitive data and customer trust.

Evaluating the Security Posture of Existing Application Portfolios: A Strategic Imperative

Evaluating the security of existing applications is not merely a compliance exercise but a strategic imperative to identify vulnerabilities, mitigate risks, and ensure the continued protection of sensitive data. This section delves into the significance of assessing the security posture of application portfolios, providing insights through a business case study.

Business Case Study

Consider a multinational corporation, GlobalTech Enterprises, operating in the highly competitive technology sector. With a diverse range of applications supporting internal operations, customer interactions, and product offerings, GlobalTech faces the challenge of maintaining a secure digital environment amidst an ever-evolving threat landscape. The business case involves GlobalTech's realization that its application portfolios have grown organically over the years, incorporating diverse technologies and functionalities. As the company expands its digital footprint, executives acknowledge the need to systematically evaluate the security posture of existing applications to proactively address vulnerabilities and strengthen the overall cyber resilience of the organization.

Significance of Evaluating Security Posture

Evaluating security posture is crucial for organizations to gauge the effectiveness of their cybersecurity measures. It identifies vulnerabilities, strengthens defenses, and ensures resilience against evolving threats. Regular assessments enable proactive adjustments, fostering a robust security stance that safeguards sensitive data and bolsters overall resilience in the face of cybersecurity challenges.

- **Risk Mitigation**

  Regular evaluation of the security posture enables organizations to identify and mitigate potential risks associated with their application portfolios. This includes vulnerabilities that could be exploited by cybercriminals to gain unauthorized access, manipulate data, or disrupt critical business processes.

- **Compliance and Regulatory Adherence**

  Many industries are subject to stringent regulatory requirements governing the protection of sensitive information. Assessing the security posture ensures that applications comply with relevant regulations, avoiding potential legal consequences and safeguarding the organization's reputation.

- **Protecting Sensitive Data**

  Applications often handle sensitive data, ranging from customer information to intellectual property. Assessing security posture is crucial in preventing unauthorized access to and unauthorized disclosure of this data, safeguarding the organization's assets and maintaining customer trust.

- **Adapting to Emerging Threats**

  The threat landscape is dynamic, with new vulnerabilities and attack vectors emerging regularly. Evaluating the security posture allows organizations to stay ahead of potential threats, adapt security measures, and implement countermeasures to address evolving cybersecurity challenges.

Methodology for Security Posture Evaluation

GlobalTech Enterprises initiated a comprehensive methodology to evaluate the security posture of its existing application portfolios:

- **Inventory and Categorization**

  A detailed inventory of all applications was created, categorizing them based on their criticality, functionality, and data they handle. This step laid the foundation for prioritizing assessments based on the importance and potential impact of each application.

- **Vulnerability Scanning and Penetration Testing**

  Automated vulnerability scanning tools were deployed to identify known vulnerabilities in application code, infrastructure, and configurations. Penetration testing, conducted by ethical hackers, simulated real-world attack scenarios to uncover potential weaknesses.

- **Code Reviews and Secure Coding Practices**

  In-depth code reviews were performed to assess the security of application code. Emphasis was placed on evaluating adherence to secure coding practices, identifying and remediating potential vulnerabilities in the source code.

- **Access Controls and Authentication Mechanisms**

  The evaluation included a thorough examination of access controls and authentication mechanisms within applications. This ensured that only authorized users had access to sensitive functionalities and data, reducing the risk of unauthorized access.

- **Incident Response and Monitoring**

  The organization's incident response capabilities and monitoring systems were evaluated to assess its readiness to detect and respond to security incidents promptly. This proactive approach aimed to minimize the impact of potential security breaches.

Outcomes and Future Roadmap

As a result of the security posture evaluation, GlobalTech Enterprises gained valuable insights into potential vulnerabilities and weaknesses within its application portfolios. Immediate remediation efforts were prioritized based on the criticality of the identified issues. Looking forward, GlobalTech is committed to integrating security into the entire application lifecycle, adopting secure coding practices, and implementing continuous monitoring mechanisms. Regular security assessments will be embedded into the organization's cybersecurity strategy, ensuring that the security posture remains robust amid the ever-changing threat landscape. Evaluating the security posture of existing application portfolios is not just a reactive measure; it is a strategic imperative for organizations seeking to thrive in the digital age. Through a proactive and comprehensive approach, businesses can identify and address vulnerabilities, fortifying their applications and ensuring the continued trust of customers and stakeholders. The case of GlobalTech Enterprises illustrates the importance of such assessments in navigating the complex and dynamic cybersecurity landscape.

Evaluating Application Threats with Threat Modeling: A Proactive Security Approach

Threat modeling has emerged as a crucial methodology, allowing businesses to proactively assess and address security risks in their application ecosystems. This section explores the significance of evaluating application threats through threat modeling, offering insights through a case study to illustrate its practical implementation.

Case Study

Consider a scenario involving a financial technology (FinTech) company, SecureFin, which provides online banking services. As SecureFin continually expands its digital presence, the company recognizes the importance of safeguarding its applications against evolving cyber threats. In response to this, SecureFin decides to leverage threat modeling to systematically evaluate and enhance the security of its online banking application.

Significance of Threat Modeling

Threat modeling is pivotal in cybersecurity, offering a proactive approach to identify and mitigate potential risks. By systematically analyzing system components and vulnerabilities, it enhances security measures, informs strategic defenses, and bolsters resilience. Threat modeling empowers organizations to pre-emptively address threats, fortify their systems, and adapt to emerging risks effectively.

- **Identifying Potential Vulnerabilities**

  Threat modeling enables organizations to systematically identify and analyze potential vulnerabilities within their applications. By understanding how attackers might exploit weaknesses, businesses can take proactive steps to address these issues before they can be leveraged for malicious purposes.

- **Proactive Risk Management**

  Threat modeling is a proactive approach to risk management. Rather than reacting to security incidents after they occur, organizations can anticipate and mitigate risks during the development and design phases, minimizing the impact of potential threats.

- **Resource Optimization**

  By focusing on the most critical threats and vulnerabilities, organizations can optimize their resources and efforts. Threat modeling allows for prioritization, ensuring that security measures are directed toward the areas with the highest risk and potential impact.

- **Integration with Development Lifecycle**

  Threat modeling can be seamlessly integrated into the software development lifecycle. By incorporating it into the early stages of application design and development, organizations can instill a security mindset throughout the entire process, reducing the likelihood of introducing vulnerabilities.

Implementation of Threat Modeling at SecureFin

SecureFin embarked on a comprehensive threat modeling process for its online banking application, encompassing the following key steps:

1. **Define the System**

   The first step involved a detailed understanding of the online banking system. This included identifying the components, data flows, and interactions within the application. SecureFin created a comprehensive diagram to visualize the architecture and functionality of the system.

2. **Identify Assets and Data Flows**

   SecureFin identified the critical assets in its online banking application, such as user accounts, transaction data, and authentication mechanisms. Data flows, representing the movement of information between components, were carefully mapped to understand how sensitive data traversed the system.

3. **Threat Identification**

   With a clear understanding of the system and its components, SecureFin systematically identified potential threats and vulnerabilities. This involved considering various attack vectors, such as unauthorized access, injection attacks, and data manipulation. Common threat modeling frameworks, like

STRIDE (Spoofing, Tampering, Repudiation, Information Disclosure, Denial of Service, Elevation of Privilege), were applied to categorize threats.

4. **Risk Assessment**

   Each identified threat was assessed in terms of its likelihood and potential impact. Risks were prioritized based on their severity, allowing SecureFin to focus on addressing the most critical threats first. This risk assessment provided valuable insights for resource allocation and mitigation strategies.

5. **Mitigation Strategies**

   SecureFin developed and implemented mitigation strategies for the identified threats. This involved a combination of secure coding practices, access controls, encryption, and monitoring mechanisms. By integrating these measures into the application design and development process, SecureFin aimed to create a more resilient and secure online banking platform.

Outcomes and Future Considerations

The threat modeling initiative at SecureFin resulted in a strengthened security posture for its online banking application. The organization not only identified and addressed existing vulnerabilities but also established a framework for ongoing threat monitoring and mitigation. Looking ahead, SecureFin is committed to integrating threat modeling into its continuous improvement processes. As the online banking application evolves, regular threat modeling sessions will be conducted to adapt to emerging threats and changes in the application landscape. This proactive approach ensures that SecureFin remains resilient in the face of evolving cybersecurity challenges.

Evaluating application threats through threat modeling is a proactive and strategic approach to cybersecurity. By systematically identifying and addressing potential vulnerabilities, organizations can fortify their applications against evolving threats. The case study of SecureFin demonstrates how threat modeling can be integrated into the development lifecycle, providing a roadmap for other organizations seeking to enhance the security of their application portfolios. In a digital landscape where cyber threats are dynamic and pervasive, threat modeling stands as a crucial practice in building resilient and secure applications.

Overview of Microsoft Threat Modeling Tool

Cybersecurity has become a top priority for businesses aiming to protect their critical assets and maintain customer trust. Threat modeling, a proactive approach to identifying and mitigating potential security threats, plays a pivotal role in this endeavor. Microsoft's Threat Modeling Tool (MTMT) is a robust solution designed to help organizations systematically assess and address security risks in their applications. Let us explore the key features of the Microsoft Threat Modeling Tool and its practical application in a real-time business scenario.

Microsoft Threat Modeling Tool (MTMT): An Overview

Microsoft Threat Modeling Tool is a free, standalone application that enables developers, architects, and security professionals to create and analyze threat models for software systems. The tool provides a structured methodology for identifying and mitigating potential security issues during the design and development phases of an application.

Key Features of Microsoft Threat Modeling Tool:

- **System Diagrams**: MTMT allows users to create system diagrams, providing a visual representation of the components and interactions within an application. This includes identifying data flows, trust boundaries, and external entities.
- **STRIDE Framework**: The tool leverages the STRIDE framework, which categorizes threats into six main types: Spoofing, Tampering, Repudiation, Information Disclosure, Denial of Service, and Elevation of Privilege. This systematic approach helps users identify potential threats comprehensively.
- **Threat Identification**: MTMT assists users in systematically identifying potential threats based on the components and data flows defined in the system diagram. It prompts users to consider various attack vectors and security weaknesses, fostering a thorough threat assessment.
- **Risk Assessment**: Users can assess the risks associated with identified threats by evaluating their likelihood and potential impact. This risk assessment aids in prioritizing mitigation efforts and allocating resources effectively.
- **Mitigation Strategies:** MTMT provides guidance on mitigation strategies for identified threats. It assists users in developing countermeasures and implementing security controls to address vulnerabilities and enhance the overall security posture of the application.

Real-time Business Scenario

Let us consider a real-time business scenario where a financial institution, FinSecure Bank, is in the process of developing a new online banking application. In this scenario, the implementation of Microsoft Threat Modeling Tool proves instrumental in identifying and addressing potential security threats.

Step 1: System Diagram CreationFin

Secure Bank initiates the threat modeling process by creating a system diagram using MTMT. The diagram includes components such as user authentication, transaction processing, database storage, and external interfaces. Data flows are clearly outlined to depict the movement of sensitive information within the application.

Step 2: STRIDE Framework Application

Using the STRIDE framework, FinSecure Bank systematically evaluates potential threats to its online banking application.

a. **Spoofing:** MTMT prompts the identification of potential spoofing threats, such as unauthorized access attempts or identity theft.

b. **Tampering:** Threats related to data tampering, such as unauthorized modification of transaction details, are considered.

c. **Repudiation:** FinSecure Bank assesses threats related to repudiation, ensuring that transaction records cannot be easily repudiated by users.

d. **Information Disclosure:** Potential threats to information disclosure, including unauthorized access to customer data, are carefully examined.

e. **Denial of Service**: Threats leading to denial of service, such as server overload or distributed denial-of-service (DDoS) attacks, are considered.

f. **Elevation of Privilege**: FinSecure Bank evaluates threats associated with the elevation of privilege, aiming to prevent unauthorized escalation of user privileges.

Step 3: Threat Identification and Risk Assessment

MTMT guides FinSecure Bank in identifying specific threats, such as SQL injection vulnerabilities, inadequate encryption mechanisms, and insufficient access controls. Each identified threat is then assessed for its likelihood and potential impact on the online banking application.

Step 4: Mitigation Strategies Implementation

Based on the identified threats and associated risks, FinSecure Bank employs mitigation strategies recommended by MTMT. This may involve implementing secure coding practices, enhancing encryption protocols, and strengthening access controls. The tool assists in developing a roadmap for integrating these security measures into the development process.

Outcomes and Future Considerations

Through the application of Microsoft Threat Modeling Tool, FinSecure Bank successfully identifies and mitigates potential security threats in its online banking application. The risk assessment enables the bank to prioritize mitigation efforts, allocating resources efficiently and ensuring a robust security posture for the application. Looking ahead, FinSecure Bank incorporates threat modeling into its regular development practices, conducting periodic assessments as the application evolves. This proactive approach allows the bank to adapt to emerging threats and changes in the cybersecurity landscape, maintaining a resilient defense against potential security risks.

Microsoft Threat Modeling Tool emerges as a valuable asset for organizations like FinSecure Bank, providing a systematic and visual approach to evaluating and addressing potential security threats in real-time business scenarios. By leveraging this tool, businesses can enhance their cybersecurity posture, safeguard critical assets, and instill a proactive security mindset throughout the application development lifecycle. As cyber threats continue to evolve, tools like MTMT empower organizations to stay ahead and build robust, secure applications that meet the highest standards of data protection and integrity.

Evaluate Application Threats with Threat Modeling

Threat modeling, a proactive and systematic approach to identifying and mitigating potential security threats, has become a crucial practice for businesses aiming to fortify their applications. Here, we explore the significance of evaluating application threats through threat modeling, illustrating its practical implementation in a business scenario.

Business Scenario

Imagine a global e-commerce giant, TechMart, that operates an extensive online platform connecting millions of buyers and sellers. The company recognizes the critical need to ensure the security of its e-commerce application, which handles sensitive customer information, financial transactions, and a vast array of products and services. In this scenario, TechMart decides to employ threat modeling as a strategic initiative to systematically assess and address potential security threats to its e-commerce application.

Significance of Threat Modeling:

- **Proactive Risk Identification**

  Threat modeling is a proactive approach that allows organizations to identify potential security risks early in the development lifecycle. By systematically analyzing the application's architecture and design, businesses can uncover vulnerabilities and weaknesses before they can be exploited by malicious actors.

- **Resource Optimization**

  Through the prioritization of identified threats, organizations can optimize resource allocation. By focusing efforts on addressing the most critical and impactful threats, businesses can effectively strengthen their security posture without spreading resources too thin.

- **Alignment with Business Objectives**

  Threat modeling ensures that security measures align with business objectives. By understanding the potential threats that could impact the application and, consequently, the business, organizations can make informed decisions to protect both their assets and their customers.

- **Integration into Development Lifecycle**

  Threat modeling can be seamlessly integrated into the software development lifecycle. By conducting threat assessments during the design and development phases, businesses can instill a security mindset among developers and architects, reducing the likelihood of introducing vulnerabilities

Implementation of Threat Modeling at TechMart

TechMart initiates the threat modeling process to evaluate potential threats to its e-commerce application systematically.

1. Define the System

The first step involves defining the e-commerce system. This includes creating a detailed system diagram that outlines the various components, data flows, and interactions within the application. The diagram provides a comprehensive view of how information moves through the system.

2. Identify Assets and Data Flows

TechMart identifies critical assets within its e-commerce application, such as customer profiles, payment information, and inventory databases. Data flows are mapped to understand how these assets are processed and shared between different components of the application.

3. STRIDE Framework Application

Leveraging the STRIDE framework, TechMart evaluates potential threats.

a. **Spoofing**

   Ensuring that user authentication processes are robust to prevent unauthorized access attempts.

b. **Tampering**

Identifying and mitigating threats related to unauthorized modifications to product listings, prices, or transaction details.

c. **Repudiation**

Preventing situations where users can repudiate their actions, such as denying a purchase or transaction.

d. **Information Disclosure**

Addressing threats related to unauthorized access to customer data, ensuring privacy and confidentiality.

e. **Denial of Service**

Evaluating and mitigating risks associated with potential denial-of-service attacks that could disrupt the availability of the platform.

f. **Elevation of Privilege**

Ensuring that there are no vulnerabilities that could lead to unauthorized elevation of user privileges within the application.

4. Threat Identification and Risk Assessment

TechMart systematically identifies specific threats based on the components, assets, and data flows defined in the system. Each threat is assessed for its likelihood and potential impact, enabling TechMart to prioritize mitigation efforts based on risk severity.

5. Mitigation Strategies Implementation

TechMart develops and implements mitigation strategies based on the identified threats. This may involve introducing secure coding practices, enhancing encryption mechanisms, and reinforcing access controls. The goal is to systematically address vulnerabilities and enhance the overall security posture of the e-commerce application.

Outcomes and Future Considerations

Through the application of threat modeling, TechMart successfully identifies and mitigates potential security threats to its e-commerce application. The risk assessment enables the company to prioritize mitigation efforts effectively, allocating resources where they are needed most. Looking forward, TechMart incorporates threat modeling into its regular development practices. Periodic assessments are conducted as the e-commerce application evolves, ensuring that emerging threats are identified and addressed promptly. This proactive approach helps TechMart maintain a resilient defense against potential security risks in the dynamic landscape of cybersecurity.

Evaluating application threats through threat modeling is a proactive and strategic approach to cybersecurity. The case of TechMart illustrates how this methodology can be applied in real business scenarios to systematically identify, assess, and mitigate potential security risks. In an era where digital platforms are central to business operations, threat modeling emerges as a critical practice for organizations aiming to build and maintain secure applications that inspire trust and confidence among users.

Designing a Security Lifecycle Strategy for Applications: A Proactive Approach for Business Resilience

A robust security lifecycle strategy is essential to ensure that applications are designed, developed, and maintained with the highest standards of protection against evolving cyber threats. Let us explore the significance of designing a security lifecycle strategy for applications, demonstrating its practical implementation through a business scenario.

Business Scenario

Consider a multinational financial institution, SecureBank, that relies heavily on a suite of applications to deliver a wide range of financial services to its customers. In this scenario, SecureBank is acutely aware of the constant and sophisticated cyber threats targeting the financial sector. Recognizing the critical need to fortify its applications against potential security vulnerabilities, SecureBank decides to formulate a comprehensive security lifecycle strategy.

Significance of a Security Lifecycle Strategy:

Proactive Risk Management: A security lifecycle strategy ensures proactive risk management by integrating security measures into every phase of the application development process. This proactive approach identifies and mitigates potential vulnerabilities before they can be exploited by malicious actors.

Regulatory Compliance: Many industries, especially finance, are subject to strict regulatory requirements regarding the protection of sensitive information. A well-defined security lifecycle strategy helps organizations adhere to these regulations, avoiding legal consequences and maintaining the trust of customers and stakeholders.

Cost-Efficient Security Measures

By incorporating security measures throughout the lifecycle, organizations can optimize resource allocation. This avoids the costly repercussions of addressing security issues post-production and reduces the risk of financial losses associated with data breaches.

Enhanced Resilience: A security-focused approach from the inception of application development enhances the overall resilience of the business. It ensures that applications can withstand cyber threats, ensuring continuous service delivery and protecting sensitive data.

Designing the Security Lifecycle Strategy for SecureBank

SecureBank initiates the process of designing a security lifecycle strategy tailored to its unique business needs:

1. **Requirements Gathering**

   The strategy begins with an in-depth analysis of the business requirements and the security considerations associated with each application. This phase involves collaboration between security experts, developers, and business stakeholders to establish clear security requirements.

2. **Threat Modeling**

   SecureBank employs threat modeling to systematically identify potential security threats and vulnerabilities in the early stages of application design. This involves creating a comprehensive overview of the application architecture, identifying assets, and assessing potential risks using frameworks such as STRIDE.

3. **Secure Coding Practices**

   The security lifecycle strategy emphasizes the adoption of secure coding practices throughout the development phase. Developers receive training on writing secure code, avoiding common vulnerabilities like SQL injection, cross-site scripting, and buffer overflows.

4. **Continuous Integration and Continuous Deployment (CI/CD) Security**

   Security measures are integrated into the CI/CD pipeline, ensuring that security checks, such as automated vulnerability scanning and code analysis, are performed at every stage of development. This reduces the risk of introducing security flaws during rapid development cycles.

5. **Access Controls and Encryption**

   The strategy mandates robust access controls and encryption mechanisms to protect sensitive data. Role-based access controls are implemented to ensure that users have the minimum necessary privileges, and encryption is applied to data both in transit and at rest.

6. **Regular Security Assessments**

   SecureBank incorporates regular security assessments into its strategy. This includes penetration testing, code reviews, and vulnerability assessments to identify and remediate emerging threats and vulnerabilities.

7. **Incident Response and Monitoring**

   The security lifecycle strategy includes the establishment of an effective incident response plan and continuous monitoring mechanisms. This ensures that security incidents are detected promptly, and the organization can respond swiftly to mitigate potential impacts.

Outcomes and Future Considerations

As a result of implementing the security lifecycle strategy, SecureBank experiences a strengthened security posture across its application portfolio. Potential vulnerabilities are identified and addressed early in the development process, reducing the risk of security incidents. Customer trust is bolstered as the institution demonstrates a commitment to protecting sensitive financial information. Looking forward, SecureBank remains committed to adapting its security lifecycle strategy to address emerging threats and technological advancements. The strategy becomes an integral part of the organizational culture, fostering a proactive and security-conscious mindset across development teams.

Designing a security lifecycle strategy for applications is not just a technical requirement but a strategic imperative for organizations operating in a digital landscape. The case of SecureBank demonstrates how a proactive and comprehensive security approach, integrated from the initial design phases through ongoing maintenance, can enhance business resilience and protect against the evolving threat landscape. As businesses increasingly rely on applications, a well-designed security lifecycle strategy becomes a cornerstone in building and maintaining secure, resilient, and trustworthy digital ecosystems.

Safeguarding Digital Ecosystems in Real-time Scenarios

Securing access for workload identities is a critical aspect of ensuring the integrity and confidentiality of sensitive data. As organizations transition to cloud-based environments and distributed systems, the need to protect the identities of workloads that interact with various services becomes paramount. This example explores the importance of securing access for workload identities and illustrates its practical application through a real-time business scenario.

Real-time Business Scenario

Consider a multinational e-commerce platform, GlobalMarket, which relies on a complex network of cloud services and microservices to handle a massive influx of online transactions. In this scenario, GlobalMarket is grappling with the challenge of securing access for workload identities to prevent unauthorized access, data breaches, and potential disruptions in service.

Significance of Securing Access for Workload Identities:

- **Protecting Digital Assets**

  Workload identities, representing the various services and applications within a digital ecosystem, are prime targets for cyber threats. Securing access ensures that only authorized entities can interact with sensitive data, protecting digital assets from unauthorized access or tampering.

- **Maintaining Data Integrity**

  Unauthorized access to workload identities can lead to data integrity issues. Securing access helps in preventing malicious actors from tampering with or manipulating the data processed by workloads, preserving its accuracy and reliability.

- **Ensuring Confidentiality**

  Workload identities often handle sensitive information such as customer data, payment details, and proprietary algorithms. Securing access is crucial for maintaining the confidentiality of this information, safeguarding the trust of customers and stakeholders.

- **Mitigating Operational Risks**

  Unauthorized access to workload identities can introduce operational risks, leading to service disruptions and downtime. A robust access security strategy helps mitigate these risks, ensuring the continuous and reliable operation of digital services.

- **Implementing Access Security at GlobalMarket**

  GlobalMarket adopts a comprehensive approach to secure access for workload identities, addressing key aspects of identity management, authentication, and authorization.

- **Identity Management**

  The first step involves establishing a robust identity management system. GlobalMarket implements centralized identity and access management (IAM) to ensure that each workload identity is uniquely identified, authenticated, and authorized based on predefined roles and permissions.

- **Authentication Mechanisms**

  To enhance access security, GlobalMarket implements strong authentication mechanisms for workload identities. Multi-factor authentication (MFA) is enforced, requiring multiple forms of verification before granting access. This includes factors such as passwords, biometrics, or temporary security tokens.

- **Role-Based Access Control (RBAC)**

  GlobalMarket adopts RBAC to streamline access permissions for workload identities. Roles are defined based on the principle of least privilege, ensuring that each workload has access only to the resources and data necessary for its specific function. This minimizes the risk associated with excessive permissions.

- **Secure Communication Channels**

  Securing communication channels is critical in distributed systems. GlobalMarket employs secure protocols such as Transport Layer Security (TLS) for encrypting data in transit, ensuring that communication between workloads is protected from eavesdropping and tampering.

- **Continuous Monitoring and Logging**

  A real-time monitoring and logging system is implemented to track access activities and detect any anomalies. GlobalMarket utilizes security information and event management (SIEM) tools to analyze access logs, providing insights into potential security threats or unusual behavior associated with workload identities.

Outcomes and Future Considerations

Through the implementation of a robust access security strategy, GlobalMarket witnesses tangible outcomes in its digital ecosystem. Instances of unauthorized access are significantly reduced, and the organization experiences enhanced data integrity, confidentiality, and operational resilience. Looking forward, GlobalMarket is committed to staying ahead of emerging threats and technology advancements. The access security strategy is continuously refined to adapt to evolving cyber threats, industry regulations, and changes in the digital landscape. Regular security audits and assessments are conducted to identify and address new challenges associated with securing access for workload identities.

Securing access for workload identities is a crucial component of safeguarding digital ecosystems in an era where cloud services and distributed architectures are prevalent. The real-time scenario of GlobalMarket highlights the practical importance of implementing a comprehensive access security strategy to protect against unauthorized access and potential data breaches. As organizations navigate the complexities of modern digital environments, prioritizing the security of workload identities is instrumental in building and maintaining resilient, secure, and trustworthy systems.

Designing a Robust Solution for API Management and Security: Empowering Business Innovation

Application Programming Interfaces (APIs) have become the linchpin for seamless connectivity and innovation. However, the widespread adoption of APIs brings forth the need for a comprehensive solution that not only efficiently manages the API lifecycle but also prioritizes robust security measures. This section delves into the critical aspects of designing a solution for API management and security, showcasing its practical application through a relevant business scenario.

Business Scenario

Imagine a cutting-edge financial technology firm, FinTech Innovations, which has revolutionized the industry by providing a suite of financial applications and services. The firm's success is underpinned by a sophisticated network of APIs that facilitate secure interactions between various applications, partners, and external services. However, recognizing the escalating cyber threats and the need for seamless API management, FinTech Innovations is seeking a solution that ensures optimal performance, scalability, and, most importantly, stringent security

Key Considerations in Designing the Solution: API Lifecycle Management

The solution prioritizes an end-to-end API lifecycle management approach. This encompasses API design, development, testing, deployment, versioning, and retirement. By incorporating a systematic and standardized lifecycle, FinTech Innovations can streamline processes, enhance collaboration among development teams, and ensure the longevity of its APIs.

- **Developer Experience (DX)**

  The design places a strong emphasis on providing an exceptional Developer Experience. User-friendly API documentation, interactive sandboxes for testing, and developer support resources are integral components. A positive DX not only accelerates the adoption of APIs but also fosters a collaborative ecosystem, attracting developers to contribute to the success of FinTech Innovations.

- **Scalability and Performance**

  Recognizing the potential growth in API usage, the solution is architected to be highly scalable. It incorporates load balancing, caching mechanisms, and efficient resource utilization to handle increased traffic without compromising performance. This ensures that FinTech Innovations can seamlessly scale its operations as its user base expands.

- **Security Measures**

  Security is embedded at every layer of the solution. It includes robust authentication mechanisms, authorization controls, and encryption protocols to protect data in transit and at rest. Additionally, the solution implements threat detection, monitoring, and response mechanisms to promptly address any suspicious activities, ensuring the confidentiality and integrity of financial data.

- **API Gateway**

  A central component of the solution is an API gateway that acts as the entry point for external requests. The API gateway handles request routing, rate limiting, and enforces security policies. This centralized control point enhances visibility into API traffic, simplifies management, and provides a unified interface for security measures.

- **Monitoring and Analytics**

  Real-time monitoring and analytics capabilities are integrated into the solution. This includes logging, performance metrics, and usage analytics. These insights empower FinTech Innovations to proactively identify issues, optimize API performance, and make informed decisions regarding API enhancements and updates.

Outcomes and Future Considerations

The implementation of the API management and security solution yields tangible benefits for FinTech Innovations. API development becomes more efficient, with accelerated time-to-market for new financial services. The enhanced security measures instill confidence among users, partners, and regulators, reinforcing FinTech Innovations' reputation as a secure and trustworthy financial technology provider. Looking ahead, the solution evolves in tandem with technological advancements and emerging threats. Continuous monitoring, regular security audits, and periodic updates to accommodate new API standards and best practices ensure that FinTech Innovations remains at the forefront of API innovation while maintaining the highest standards of security.

Designing a robust solution for API management and security is a strategic imperative for organizations navigating the digital landscape. In the context of FinTech Innovations, the seamless integration of API lifecycle management and stringent security measures not only propels innovation but also establishes a foundation for sustained growth and user trust. As businesses increasingly rely on APIs to drive their digital initiatives, a well-crafted solution becomes pivotal in unlocking the full potential of APIs while safeguarding against evolving cybersecurity challenges.

Designing a Solution for Secure Access to Applications: Navigating the Digital Frontier

As organizations leverage an array of applications to drive operations and services, ensuring a robust solution for access management becomes paramount. This section explores the intricacies of designing a solution for secure access to applications, shedding light on its practical implementation through a real-time business scenario.

Real-time Business Scenario

Imagine a global healthcare consortium, HealthConnect Solutions, entrusted with managing and disseminating critical patient data among various healthcare providers, professionals, and researchers. As the custodian of sensitive health information, HealthConnect Solutions faces the challenge of enabling authorized access to applications while safeguarding patient confidentiality and complying with stringent regulatory requirements.

Key Considerations in Designing the Solution: Identity and Access Management (IAM)

The solution adopts a comprehensive Identity and Access Management system to establish and manage user identities. Through IAM, HealthConnect Solutions ensures that each user is uniquely identified, authenticated, and authorized based on their roles and responsibilities. This approach enhances security by employing the principle of least privilege, granting users access only to the resources necessary for their tasks.

- **Single Sign-On (SSO)**

  To simplify user experience without compromising security, the solution incorporates Single Sign-On functionality. This allows users to access multiple applications with a single set of credentials, thus streamlining the login process. SSO enhances productivity and reduces the likelihood of password-related security vulnerabilities.

- **Multi-Factor Authentication (MFA)**

  Recognizing the vulnerabilities associated with relying solely on passwords, the solution integrates Multi-Factor Authentication. Users are required to provide additional authentication factors, such as biometrics or one-time passcodes, adding an extra layer of security. MFA mitigates the risks associated with compromised passwords and enhances the overall access security posture.

- **Role-Based Access Control (RBAC)**

  RBAC is a pivotal component of the solution, ensuring that access privileges align with users' roles and responsibilities. By defining roles and associating them with specific permissions, HealthConnect Solutions can precisely control access to applications and sensitive data. This not only enhances security but also facilitates compliance with regulatory frameworks.

- **Secure Remote Access**

  Considering the evolving nature of work environments, the solution prioritizes secure remote access. Virtual Private Network (VPN) and secure tunneling mechanisms are employed to enable authorized users to access applications securely from remote locations. This approach caters to the flexibility demanded by modern work practices without compromising security.

- **Encryption Protocols**

  Robust encryption protocols, such as Transport Layer Security (TLS), are implemented to secure data in transit. This ensures that sensitive information exchanged between users and applications remains confidential and immune to eavesdropping or unauthorized interception.

Outcomes and Future Considerations

The implementation of the secure access solution yields tangible outcomes for HealthConnect Solutions. Authorized users can seamlessly access applications, fostering collaboration among healthcare providers and researchers. The adoption of stringent access controls and encryption measures instills confidence in patients, ensuring the confidentiality and integrity of their health information. Looking ahead, HealthConnect Solutions remains committed to the ongoing enhancement of its secure access solution. Regular security·assessments, updates to address emerging threats, and the incorporation of new technologies ensure that the solution evolves in tandem with the dynamic landscape of cybersecurity. The organization's proactive approach positions it to adapt to changing regulatory requirements and emerging security challenges.

Designing a solution for secure access to applications is a strategic imperative for organizations entrusted with sensitive information. The real-time scenario of HealthConnect Solutions exemplifies the critical importance of balancing accessibility with stringent security measures in the healthcare domain. As businesses across industries increasingly rely on digital applications, a well-crafted secure access solution becomes instrumental in ensuring not only operational efficiency but also the trust and confidence of users and stakeholders.

Conclusion

A robust application security design is imperative in safeguarding digital assets and user data from evolving cyber threats. By implementing comprehensive measures such as secure coding practices, encryption protocols, and regular security audits, organizations can fortify their applications against potential vulnerabilities. Continuous vigilance, proactive threat assessments, and user education contribute to a resilient security posture. In an era marked by increasing digital interconnectivity, prioritizing application security is not only a necessity but a commitment to ensuring the trust and integrity of systems. Through these concerted efforts, we pave the way for a safer digital landscape and user experience. The next chapter discusses data protection strategy development.

Multiple Choice Questions

1. What is the primary purpose of secure coding practices in application security design?
    a. Enhancing user interface design
    b. Improving application performance
    c. Preventing and mitigating security vulnerabilities
    d. Optimizing database management
2. What does encryption in application security design primarily address?
    a. Improving network speed
    b. Protecting sensitive data by converting it into unreadable format
    c. Enhancing user authentication
    d. Streamlining code development
3. Why is regular security auditing essential in application security design?
    a. To increase application speed
    b. To identify and address potential security weaknesses

   c. To enhance user experience

   d. To improve graphical user interface (GUI)

4. What role does user education play in application security?

   a. Speeding up application processes

   b. Reducing development costs

   c. Enhancing user awareness and responsible online behavior

   d. Improving database efficiency

5. In the context of application security design, what is the significance of a firewall?

   a. Optimizing code execution

   b. Preventing unauthorized access to a network

   c. Improving user interface design

   d. Enhancing data storage capacity

Answers

1. c
2. b
3. b
4. c
5. b

CHAPTER 11
Data Protection Strategy Development

Introduction

Data Protection Strategy Development involves crafting comprehensive plans to safeguard sensitive information within an organization. This strategic process includes assessing data vulnerabilities, implementing encryption protocols, establishing access controls, and ensuring compliance with relevant regulations. The strategy aims to mitigate potential risks such as data breaches, unauthorized access, and privacy violations. By adopting robust security measures, organizations can build resilience against evolving cyber threats, bolstering trust among stakeholders. Continuous evaluation and adaptation are integral, ensuring that the data protection strategy remains effective in safeguarding valuable assets in an ever-changing technological landscape.

Structure

In this chapter, we will cover the following topics:

- Securing Digital Information in a Growing Landscape
- Securing Data: A Dual Focus on Protecting Data at Rest and in Transit
- Designing a Data Discovery and Classification Solution with Microsoft Purview
- Navigating Data Governance: The Importance of Data Maps in a Retail Scenario
- Designing a Comprehensive Data Protection Solution

Securing Digital Information in a Growing Landscape

Data security is a critical aspect of information technology that focuses on protecting digital information from unauthorized access, disclosure, alteration, or destruction. As our reliance on digital data continues to grow, ensuring the confidentiality, integrity, and availability of sensitive information has become paramount for individuals, businesses, and governments alike.

Confidentiality is one of the fundamental principles of data security, emphasizing the need to prevent unauthorized access to sensitive information. This involves implementing access controls, encryption, and other mechanisms to ensure that only authorized individuals or systems can access and view specific data. For example, encrypting files and communications helps safeguard data during transmission and storage, making it unreadable to unauthorized parties.

Integrity, the second pillar of data security, revolves around maintaining the accuracy and reliability of information. This means protecting data from unauthorized modifications, deletions, or alterations. Implementing data integrity measures involves using checksums, digital signatures, and access controls to ensure that data remains unaltered and trustworthy.

Availability is the third crucial element, ensuring that authorized users have timely and reliable access to data when needed. This involves implementing measures to prevent or mitigate disruptions, such as hardware failures, cyber attacks, or natural disasters. Redundancy, backups, and disaster recovery plans are essential components of maintaining data availability.

The field of data security encompasses various strategies and technologies, including firewalls, antivirus software, intrusion detection systems, and security protocols. As cyber threats evolve, data security practices must adapt to address new challenges. This includes staying informed about emerging threats, regularly updating security measures, and educating users about best practices for safeguarding sensitive information.

Data security is a multidimensional discipline that aims to protect digital information from unauthorized access, maintain its accuracy and reliability, and ensure timely access for authorized users. As technology advances, the importance of data security continues to grow, making it a critical consideration for anyone handling digital information.

Protecting data at rest is a crucial component of overall data security, focusing on safeguarding information when it is stored or archived. This encompasses data stored in databases, file systems, or on physical devices such as hard drives and servers. The goal is to prevent unauthorized access to the stored data and maintain its confidentiality and integrity.

Securing Data: A Dual Focus on Protecting Data at Rest and in Transit

One primary method to protect data at rest is encryption. By encrypting data, it is transformed into an unreadable format without the corresponding decryption key, rendering it useless to unauthorized individuals even if they gain access to the storage medium. This adds an extra layer of security, especially in the event of physical theft or unauthorized access to storage devices.

Additionally, access controls and authentication mechanisms play a crucial role in protecting data at rest. By implementing strong access policies and ensuring that only authorized individuals have the necessary credentials to access stored data, organizations can mitigate the risk of unauthorized breaches

Overall, safeguarding data at rest is essential for maintaining the privacy and security of sensitive information, and encryption along with access controls are key tools in achieving this protection.

Protecting data in transit is a critical aspect of data security, ensuring that information remains confidential and secure while it is being transmitted from one location to another, typically over a network. This is particularly important in the era of digital communication, where sensitive data is frequently exchanged between systems, devices, and users.

Encryption is a fundamental technique used to safeguard data in transit. Through the use of encryption protocols such as Transport Layer Security (TLS) or Secure Sockets Layer (SSL), data is transformed into a secure, unreadable format during transmission. This cryptographic process ensures that even if intercepted by unauthorized entities, the data remains protected and inaccessible without the appropriate decryption key.

Secure communication channels, such as Virtual Private Networks (VPNs), also play a crucial role in protecting data during transit. VPNs create encrypted tunnels that facilitate secure data transfer over potentially insecure networks, adding an extra layer of protection against eavesdropping and interception.

Authentication mechanisms further enhance data security in transit by verifying the identities of the communicating parties. This prevents unauthorized entities from injecting or tampering with data during transmission. Digital signatures and certificates are commonly used to establish the authenticity and integrity of the data being exchanged.

In addition to encryption and authentication, organizations employ firewalls and intrusion detection/prevention systems to monitor and filter incoming and outgoing network traffic. These security measures help identify and block potential threats, ensuring the integrity and confidentiality of the data during transit.

Overall, protecting data in transit is vital for maintaining the privacy and security of sensitive information. By employing a combination of encryption, secure communication channels, authentication, and network security measures, organizations can establish robust defenses against unauthorized access and interception, thereby safeguarding data as it travels across networks.

Designing a Data Discovery and Classification Solution with Microsoft Purview

Embarking on the journey of data governance and security requires a robust solution, and Microsoft Purview emerges as a key player in this landscape. The need to discover, classify, and manage data is paramount. Microsoft Purview offers a comprehensive platform designed to empower organizations in understanding and controlling their data landscape. From automated data discovery to custom classification policies, Purview enables businesses to enhance compliance, strengthen security, and gain valuable insights. This introduction sets the stage for delving into the intricacies of designing an effective data discovery and classification solution with Microsoft Purview.

Business Scenario

In a multinational financial institution, managing and securing sensitive financial data is of utmost importance. The organization deals with a vast amount of data, ranging from customer transactions to financial reports, and compliance with data protection regulations is a top priority. The need for efficient data discovery and classification is critical to ensure compliance, protect sensitive information, and streamline data governance processes.

Solution Design:

1. Microsoft Purview Integration:
    a. Implement Microsoft Purview, a comprehensive data governance solution, to centralize data discovery and classification capabilities.
    b. Leverage Purview's connectors to seamlessly integrate with various data sources within the organization, such as databases, cloud storage, and on-premises repositories.
2. **Automated Data Discovery:**
    a. Utilize Purview's automated scanning capabilities to discover and catalog data across the organization's diverse data landscape.
    b. Schedule regular scans to ensure real-time visibility into newly created or modified data.

3. **Classification Policies:**

    a. Define classification policies based on regulatory requirements, data sensitivity, and business rules.

    b. Leverage Purview's pre-built classifiers for personally identifiable information (PII), financial data, and other sensitive categories.

4. **Custom Classifiers:**

    a. Develop custom classifiers tailored to the organization's unique data types and structures.

    b. Incorporate machine learning models to enhance accuracy in identifying sensitive information.

5. **Metadata Enrichment:**

    a. Leverage Purview's metadata enrichment capabilities to add contextual information to discovered data, such as data owners, business units, and compliance tags.

6. **Integration with Azure Information Protection:**

    a. Integrate Purview with Azure Information Protection for seamless enforcement of data classification and labeling policies.

    b. Ensure consistent classification across the data lifecycle, from creation to archival.

7. **Role-Based Access Control (RBAC):**

    a. Implement RBAC in Purview to control access to sensitive data classifications.

    b. Define roles for data stewards, compliance officers, and administrators to manage and monitor the data governance framework.

8. **Auditing and Monitoring:**

    a. Activate Purview's auditing features to track changes, access, and usage of classified data.

    b. Establish alerts for potential policy violations or unusual data access patterns.

Benefits

- Enhanced compliance with data protection regulations.
- Improved data visibility and understanding across the organization.

- Streamlined data governance processes, reducing the risk of data breaches.
- Empowered data stewards with tools for efficient data management and classification.

Implementing this solution ensures that the financial institution can confidently manage and secure its data, adhere to regulatory requirements, and make informed decisions based on a well-governed data landscape.

Navigating Data Governance: The Importance of Data Maps in a Retail Scenario

A data map is a visual representation of an organization's data landscape, illustrating the flow, relationships, and characteristics of data within its systems. It serves as a valuable tool for understanding and managing data assets, enhancing data governance, and ensuring compliance with regulatory requirements. Let us explore a real-time scenario to illustrate the importance of a data map.

Real-Time Scenario

Consider a multinational retail corporation that operates both physical stores and an extensive e-commerce platform. The company manages vast amounts of customer data, including purchase history, personal information, and preferences. To ensure effective data governance and compliance with data protection regulations such as GDPR or CCPA, the organization decides to create a comprehensive data map.

1. **Data Discovery:** The initial step involves deploying data discovery tools to scan and catalog data across various systems, including the customer relationship management (CRM) system, e-commerce database, inventory management, and point-of-sale terminals.
2. **Mapping Data Flows:** With the data discovery results, the organization creates a data map illustrating how customer data flows through different touchpoints. This includes the journey from online interactions, such as website visits and mobile app usage, to in-store purchases.
3. **Identifying Sensitive Data**: The data map allows the organization to identify sensitive customer information, such as credit card details or personally identifiable information (PII). This information is crucial for implementing appropriate security measures and ensuring compliance with privacy regulations.

4. **Data Ownership and Stewardship:** The data map specifies data ownership at each stage of the process. It identifies data stewards responsible for ensuring the accuracy, quality, and security of the data. This clear delineation of responsibilities enhances accountability and data management practices.
5. **Risk Mitigation:** Through the data map, the organization identifies potential risks, such as data silos or points of vulnerability. This enables proactive measures to mitigate risks, implement access controls, and ensure data integrity.
6. **Regulatory Compliance:** The data map assists in demonstrating compliance with data protection regulations by providing a visual representation of how customer data is handled, stored, and processed. This is especially crucial for responding to regulatory audits and inquiries.
7. **Data Lifecycle Management:** Understanding the data lifecycle is essential. The data map helps in visualizing data from creation to archival, enabling the organization to implement effective data lifecycle management strategies.

Benefits

- **Enhanced Data Governance:** The organization gains a holistic view of its data, facilitating effective governance.
- **Regulatory Compliance:** The data map ensures adherence to data protection regulations, avoiding potential legal consequences.
- **Risk Management:** Identifying vulnerabilities allows the organization to proactively address security risks.
- **Improved Decision-Making:** Data maps empower decision-makers with a clear understanding of data relationships and dependencies.

In summary, a data map serves as a strategic asset for organizations, providing a comprehensive and visual understanding of their data landscape. In our retail scenario, it enables the company to navigate the complexities of managing customer data, ensuring compliance, and making informed decisions about data governance.

Designing a Comprehensive Data Protection Solution

A Data Protection Solution serves as the bedrock of an organization's strategy to safeguard sensitive information in today's digitally-driven landscape. This comprehensive approach involves a multifaceted framework that addresses the intricate challenges of data security, ensuring confidentiality, integrity, and availability of critical assets.

At its core, a robust Data Protection Solution encompasses encryption methodologies to shield data during transmission and storage. This cryptographic safeguard acts as a formidable barrier, rendering unauthorized access futile even in the event of a breach. Access controls further refine this defense, delineating permissions and restricting data accessibility to authorized personnel, thus minimizing the risk of internal threats.

Proactive threat detection and response mechanisms constitute another pivotal facet. Leveraging advanced analytics, machine learning, and behavioral analysis, these solutions identify anomalous patterns indicative of potential cyber threats. Timely detection allows for swift response, mitigating risks, and minimizing the impact of security incidents.

Data masking and anonymization techniques contribute to privacy compliance by obscuring sensitive information in non-production environments. This ensures that, even in scenarios where data is shared for testing or analytics, the confidentiality of personally identifiable information remains intact.

As organizations grapple with an ever-evolving threat landscape, a Data Protection Solution must also incorporate adaptive security measures. Continuous monitoring, regular security audits, and updates keep the defense mechanisms agile, capable of thwarting emerging threats and vulnerabilities.

Compliance with global data protection regulations, such as GDPR and CCPA, is integral to the design of these solutions. By aligning with regulatory requirements, organizations not only fortify their security posture but also mitigate legal risks associated with data breaches.

In an era where data is an invaluable asset, a well-crafted Data Protection Solution is indispensable. Beyond fortifying against external threats, it instills confidence among stakeholders, clients, and partners, fostering trust in the organization's commitment to data integrity and privacy. As technology advances, the evolution of Data Protection Solutions remains critical to staying one step ahead in the ongoing battle for digital security.

Business Scenario

Imagine a healthcare organization, HealthGuard, that handles a vast amount of sensitive patient information, including medical records, personal details, and insurance data. With the increasing frequency of cyber threats and the stringent regulations in the healthcare industry, HealthGuard recognizes the critical need for a robust data protection solution. The organization is committed to ensuring the confidentiality, integrity, and availability of patient data while complying with regulations such as the Health Insurance Portability and Accountability Act (HIPAA).

Solution Design:

1. **Data Classification:**

   Implement a data classification system to categorize data based on sensitivity and importance. Classify data into categories such as public, internal use, confidential, and restricted, with a focus on patient health records and personally identifiable information (PII).

2. **Encryption:**

   Utilize strong encryption algorithms to protect data both at rest and in transit. Implement encryption mechanisms for databases, file systems, and communication channels to ensure that even if unauthorized access occurs, the data remains unreadable.

3. **Access Controls:**

   Implement robust access controls to restrict data access to authorized personnel. Assign roles and permissions based on job responsibilities, ensuring that only authorized users have access to specific categories of data. Regularly audit and update access privileges.

4. **Endpoint Protection:**

   Deploy advanced endpoint protection solutions on devices that access patient data. This includes antivirus software, endpoint detection and response (EDR) tools, and mobile device management (MDM) solutions to safeguard against malware and unauthorized access.

5. **Data Loss Prevention (DLP):**

   Implement DLP tools to monitor and control the movement of sensitive data within and outside the organization. Define policies to prevent unauthorized transfers of patient data and ensure compliance with data protection regulations.

6. **Secure Communication:**

   Utilize secure communication protocols, such as Transport Layer Security (TLS), for all internal and external data transmissions. Encrypt emails containing patient information and implement secure messaging platforms to protect the confidentiality of communication.

7. **Regular Audits and Monitoring:**

   Establish a continuous monitoring system to track data access, modifications, and potential security incidents. Conduct regular security audits to identify vulnerabilities and ensure compliance with industry regulations.

8. **Data Backups and Recovery:**

   Implement a robust data backup and recovery strategy to ensure data availability in the event of accidental deletion, hardware failure, or a cyber attack. Regularly test backup restoration processes to verify their effectiveness.

9. **Incident Response Plan:**

   Develop a comprehensive incident response plan outlining the steps to be taken in the event of a data breach or security incident. Define roles and responsibilities, establish communication protocols, and conduct regular drills to ensure preparedness.

10. **Employee Training and Awareness:**

    Conduct regular training sessions for employees on data protection best practices, security policies, and the importance of safeguarding patient information. Foster a culture of cybersecurity awareness to mitigate risks associated with human error.

11. **Compliance Management:**

    Implement a compliance management system to track and adhere to healthcare industry regulations, particularly HIPAA. Ensure that the data protection solution aligns with regulatory requirements and undergoes regular compliance assessments.

Benefits

- **Patient Trust:** A robust data protection solution instills confidence in patients, demonstrating a commitment to safeguarding their sensitive information.
- **Regulatory Compliance:** HealthGuard can confidently comply with healthcare regulations, avoiding legal consequences and reputational damage.
- **Reduced Risk:** The organization minimizes the risk of data breaches, ensuring the confidentiality and integrity of patient data.
- **Operational Continuity:** With effective data backups and recovery processes, HealthGuard ensures uninterrupted operations even in the face of data loss incidents.

A comprehensive data protection solution is paramount for organizations handling sensitive information, especially in industries with stringent regulations. In the healthcare sector, such a solution is essential for maintaining patient trust, complying with regulations, and safeguarding the integrity of medical records. HealthGuard, through the implementation of this robust data protection framework, ensures the security and privacy of its patients' health information.

Designing a Data Protection Solution: A Case Study

Designing a robust Data Protection Solution is the linchpin in fortifying digital ecosystems against cyber threats and ensuring compliance with stringent privacy regulations. This intricate process involves meticulous planning, encompassing encryption protocols, access controls, and proactive threat detection mechanisms. Balancing the twin objectives of data accessibility and security, the solution must adapt to dynamic technological landscapes. As organizations navigate the complexities of modern data management, crafting a resilient Data Protection Solution becomes pivotal in fostering trust, maintaining integrity, and safeguarding the confidentiality of invaluable digital assets.

Business Scenario

ABC Financials, a global financial institution, processes vast amounts of sensitive customer information daily. The organization, keenly aware of the increasing threats to data security and compliance requirements, faces the challenge of designing a robust data protection solution. The objective is to safeguard customer data, maintain regulatory compliance, and build trust in an industry where data security is paramount.

Challenges:

- **Data Sensitivity:** ABC Financials handles a range of sensitive data, including financial transactions, personal information, and credit card details. Protecting this data is crucial to maintain customer trust and comply with financial industry regulations.
- **Global Operations:** With a global presence, ABC Financials operates in various jurisdictions with different data protection and privacy laws. The solution needs to be scalable and adaptable to diverse regulatory environments.
- **Emerging Threat Landscape:** The financial industry is a prime target for cyber attacks. ABC Financials needs a solution that evolves with the dynamic threat landscape, protecting against both known and emerging cybersecurity risks.

Solution Design:

1. **Data Encryption:**

   Implement end-to-end encryption to protect customer data at rest, in transit, and during processing. Utilize strong encryption algorithms for databases, file systems, and communication channels to ensure that even if unauthorized access occurs, the data remains unreadable.

2. **Tokenization:**

   Integrate tokenization techniques to replace sensitive information with tokens, reducing the risk associated with storing and transmitting sensitive data. Tokenization enhances security while maintaining the functionality required for financial transactions.

3. **Access Controls:**

   Implement a robust access control system to restrict data access to authorized personnel. Utilize role-based access controls (RBAC) to ensure that employees only have access to the data necessary for their roles, reducing the risk of internal breaches.

4. **Multi-Factor Authentication (MFA):**

   Enforce multi-factor authentication for all user access, especially for systems that handle sensitive customer data. MFA adds an extra layer of security, mitigating the risk of unauthorized access even if credentials are compromised.

5. **Data Loss Prevention (DLP):**

   Deploy DLP solutions to monitor and control the movement of sensitive data within the organization. Define policies to prevent unauthorized transfers of financial and personal information, ensuring compliance with data protection regulations.

6. **Threat Intelligence Integration:**

   Integrate threat intelligence feeds to stay updated on the latest cybersecurity threats. Implement advanced threat detection mechanisms to identify and respond to emerging threats promptly.

7. **Secure APIs and Integrations:**

   Ensure that APIs and integrations follow secure coding practices. Implement secure data exchange protocols to safeguard customer data during interactions with third-party services and partners.

8. **Regular Security Audits**

   Conduct regular security audits and penetration testing to identify vulnerabilities in the system. Regular audits ensure that the security measures remain effective and aligned with industry best practices.

9. **Employee Training:**

   Conduct ongoing cybersecurity awareness training for employees to educate them about data protection best practices. Foster a security-conscious culture to minimize the risk of human error leading to security incidents.

10. **Incident Response Plan:**

    Develop and regularly test an incident response plan to ensure a swift and coordinated response to potential security incidents. Clearly define roles and responsibilities for incident resolution and communication.

Benefits:

- **Enhanced Customer Trust:** ABC Financials establishes itself as a trustworthy institution by prioritizing the security of customer data.
- **Global Compliance:** The solution ensures compliance with diverse global data protection and privacy regulations.
- **Adaptability to Emerging Threats:** Integrating threat intelligence and regular security audits enables ABC Financials to adapt to evolving cybersecurity threats.
- **Operational Resilience:** With robust data protection measures, ABC Financials ensures the resilience of its operations, even in the face of potential security incidents.

In this case study, ABC Financials successfully designs and implements a comprehensive data protection solution, addressing the unique challenges of the financial industry. By combining encryption, access controls, threat intelligence, and employee training, the organization not only protects sensitive customer data but also establishes itself as a leader in data security and regulatory compliance within the global financial sector.

Designing Security for Azure Storage: Real-time Examples

Designing Security for Azure Storage is a critical endeavor in establishing a robust and resilient defense against cyber threats within the Microsoft Azure cloud environment. Azure Storage serves as a cornerstone for storing vast amounts of data, ranging from blobs and files to tables and queues, making it imperative to implement comprehensive security measures.

One fundamental aspect of securing Azure Storage involves access control. Utilizing Azure Active Directory (Azure AD) integration, role-based access control (RBAC), and shared access signatures (SAS), organizations can define and enforce granular access policies, ensuring that only authorized personnel can interact with the stored data. Encryption plays a pivotal role, and Azure Storage provides options for both data in transit and at rest. Transport Layer Security (TLS) safeguards data during transmission, while Azure Storage Service Encryption (SSE) encrypts data at rest, providing an additional layer of protection against unauthorized access.

Furthermore, Azure Storage benefits from Azure Defender, an intelligent threat protection solution that leverages advanced analytics and machine learning to detect and respond to potential security incidents. Azure Defender for Storage offers real-time monitoring, anomaly detection, and automated responses, fortifying the storage infrastructure against emerging cyber threats.

Audit logs and monitoring capabilities within Azure Storage contribute to a proactive security posture, allowing organizations to track user activities, analyze trends, and promptly identify any suspicious behavior. By integrating Azure Policy, organizations can enforce compliance standards, ensuring that storage configurations align with security best practices.

Designing security for Azure Storage is a multifaceted process encompassing access controls, encryption, threat detection, monitoring, and compliance enforcement. Embracing these security measures not only protects the confidentiality and integrity of data stored in Azure but also strengthens the overall resilience of cloud-based storage solutions in the face of an ever-evolving threat landscape.

1. **Authentication and Authorization:**

   Example: Implement Azure Active Directory (Azure AD) authentication for Azure Storage. This ensures that only authorized users and applications can access storage resources. Utilize role-based access control (RBAC) to grant specific permissions to users or groups, for instance, assign the "Storage Account Contributor" role to individuals who need to manage storage accounts.

2. **Encryption:**

   Example: Enable Azure Storage Service Encryption (SSE) to automatically encrypt data at rest. SSE uses Azure-managed keys or customer-managed keys stored in Azure Key Vault. This ensures that even if unauthorized access occurs, the data remains encrypted. Additionally, use Azure Storage client-side encryption to encrypt data before it is sent to Azure Storage.

3. **Network Security:**

   Example: Configure virtual network service endpoints for Azure Storage. By doing this, you restrict access to Azure Storage to resources within your virtual network, minimizing exposure to the public internet. This adds an extra layer of security, especially for sensitive data.

4. **Azure Private Link:**

   Example: Implement Azure Private Link to access Azure Storage securely over a private network connection. This allows organizations to access Azure Storage using private IP addresses, reducing exposure to the public internet. This is particularly useful for scenarios where direct internet access should be limited.

5. **Shared Access Signatures (SAS):**

   Example: Use Shared Access Signatures to grant time-limited and scoped permissions to clients. For instance, generate an SAS token that provides read-only access to a specific blob for a limited time. This ensures that clients have temporary and specific access without sharing storage account credentials.

6. **Azure Monitor and Azure Security Center:**

   Example: Leverage Azure Monitor and Azure Security Center for continuous monitoring of storage activity and security threats. Set up alerts for suspicious activities, such as multiple failed login attempts. The Security Center can provide recommendations and threat intelligence to enhance the overall security posture.

7. **Firewall and Virtual Networks:**

   Example: Configure Azure Storage firewalls and virtual networks to allow or deny traffic based on IP addresses. This ensures that only specified IP ranges, such as those within the organization's virtual network, can access Azure Storage accounts. It acts as an additional layer of defense against unauthorized access.

8. **Threat Detection and Logging:**

   Example: Enable Azure Storage Analytics logging and Azure Monitor Diagnostic Settings. Analyze logs for unusual patterns or potential security incidents, for example, detect spikes in data access during non-business hours, which could indicate a security threat.

9. **Regulatory Compliance:**

   Example: Implement Azure Policy and Azure Blueprints to enforce regulatory compliance requirements. For example, define policies to ensure that all Azure Storage accounts adhere to specific security configurations mandated by industry regulations, such as GDPR or HIPAA.

10. **Geo-redundancy for Disaster Recovery:**

    Example: Configure Azure Storage geo-redundancy to replicate data across multiple regions. This not only ensures high availability but also serves as a disaster recovery mechanism. In the event of a regional outage, data remains accessible from the replicated copy in another region.

Benefits:

- **Enhanced Data Security:** By combining these security measures, organizations can significantly enhance the security of data stored in Azure Storage, protecting it from unauthorized access and potential threats.

- **Compliance Assurance:** The implemented security features help organizations meet regulatory requirements and industry standards, ensuring that data is handled in a compliant and secure manner.
- **Operational Resilience:** The design ensures the availability and resilience of data, both in terms of disaster recovery and continuous monitoring for potential security incidents.

Designing security for Azure Storage involves a multi-faceted approach that addresses authentication, encryption, network security, monitoring, and compliance. Real-time examples illustrate how organizations can implement these security features to protect their data effectively in Microsoft Azure Storage.

Designing a Comprehensive Security Solution: Microsoft Defender for SQL and Microsoft Defender for Storage

Microsoft Defender for SQL and Microsoft Defender for Storage represent cutting-edge solutions within the comprehensive Microsoft Defender suite, designed to fortify data security across SQL databases and storage environments. Microsoft Defender for SQL stands as a sentinel against evolving cyber threats, providing advanced threat protection, vulnerability assessment, and intelligent security insights for SQL Server databases. Leveraging machine learning, behavioral analytics, and threat intelligence, it proactively identifies and mitigates potential risks, ensuring the integrity and confidentiality of critical data.

Complementing this, Microsoft Defender for Storage extends its protective umbrella over cloud storage solutions, addressing the challenges posed by modern data repositories. With real-time threat detection, automated responses, and integrated security management, it safeguards against unauthorized access, data breaches, and ransomware attacks. As organizations increasingly migrate to cloud-based storage solutions, this robust defense mechanism becomes indispensable in preserving the sanctity of stored information.

Both defenders synergize to provide a holistic security architecture, allowing seamless integration with Microsoft 365 Defender for unified threat protection. By combining these solutions, businesses can confidently navigate the digital landscape, proactively mitigating risks, and ensuring the resilience of their data infrastructure in the face of ever-evolving cybersecurity challenges.

Business Scenario

Imagine a global e-commerce enterprise, TechMart, that relies heavily on its digital infrastructure for processing transactions, managing customer data, and ensuring the availability of its online platform. Recognizing the critical importance of securing sensitive information, including customer details and transaction records, TechMart decided to design a robust security solution leveraging Microsoft Defender for SQL and Microsoft Defender for Storage.

Challenges:

- **Data Sensitivity:** TechMart handles a vast amount of sensitive data, including customer payment information, personal details, and purchase history. Protecting this data is paramount to maintain customer trust and comply with data protection regulations.
- **Complex Infrastructure:** With a complex digital infrastructure that includes a SQL Server database for transaction processing and Azure Storage for data storage and retrieval, TechMart needs a unified security solution that covers both databases and storage.
- **Cybersecurity Threats:** The e-commerce sector is a prime target for cyber attacks, including SQL injection, ransomware, and unauthorized access to storage resources. TechMart must defend against evolving cybersecurity threats to ensure the integrity and availability of its systems.

Solution Design:

1. **Microsoft Defender for SQL:**

   Example: Implement Microsoft Defender for SQL to protect the SQL Server database. Utilize its advanced threat protection capabilities, including vulnerability assessments, SQL injection detection, and anomaly detection. Regularly conduct vulnerability assessments to identify and remediate potential weaknesses in the database.

2. **Threat Intelligence Integration:**

   Example: Integrate threat intelligence feeds into Microsoft Defender for SQL. Stay informed about the latest cybersecurity threats and leverage this intelligence to enhance the database's defense mechanisms. For instance, update security rules based on real-time threat intelligence to block known malicious activities.

3. **Encryption for Data at Rest and in Transit:**

   Example: Enable Transparent Data Encryption (TDE) for SQL Server to encrypt data at rest. Utilize 'always encrypted' to encrypt sensitive data in transit between the application and the database. This ensures that even if there is unauthorized access, the data remains encrypted and unreadable.

4. **Role-Based Access Controls (RBAC):**

   Example: Implement RBAC in Microsoft Defender for SQL to control access to the database. Define roles based on job responsibilities and grant minimal necessary permissions. For instance, limit access to payment information only to authorized finance personnel.

5. **Microsoft Defender for Storage:**

   Example: Utilize Microsoft Defender for Storage to secure data stored in Azure Storage. Leverage its threat detection capabilities to identify and respond to potential security incidents. Configure alerts for suspicious activities, such as unauthorized access or changes to critical files.

6. **Advanced Threat Protection:**

   Example: Enable advanced threat protection features in Microsoft Defender for Storage to detect and mitigate ransomware attacks. For example, set up behavior analytics to identify abnormal file access patterns that may indicate a ransomware infection. Automatically quarantine affected files to prevent further spread.

7. **Access Controls for Storage:**

   Example: Implement fine-grained access controls for Azure Storage. Utilize Shared Access Signatures (SAS) to grant time-limited and scoped permissions to clients. This ensures that only authorized applications and users have access to specific storage resources for the required duration.

8. **Continuous Monitoring:**

   Example: Leverage Azure Monitor and Microsoft Defender for continuous monitoring of both SQL Server and Azure Storage. Set up dashboards to provide real-time visibility into security events, performance metrics, and potential vulnerabilities across the infrastructure.

9. **Incident Response Plan:**

   Example: Develop and regularly test an incident response plan that encompasses both SQL Server and Azure Storage. Clearly define roles, responsibilities, and communication protocols for responding to security incidents. Conduct simulated exercises to ensure a swift and coordinated response.

10. **Regulatory Compliance Management:**

    Example: Utilize Microsoft Defender's compliance management features to ensure that both the SQL Server database and Azure Storage adhere to relevant data protection regulations. Regularly assess and enforce compliance with industry standards such as PCI DSS or GDPR.

Benefits:

- **Holistic Security Coverage:** The integrated approach using Microsoft Defender for SQL and Microsoft Defender for Storage provides comprehensive security coverage for both databases and storage resources, ensuring end-to-end protection.
- **Real-time Threat Response:** Leveraging threat intelligence and continuous monitoring allows TechMart to respond promptly to emerging cybersecurity threats, minimizing the impact of potential security incidents.
- **Regulatory Compliance Assurance:** By incorporating compliance management features, TechMart ensures that its security solution aligns with industry regulations, safeguarding customer data and avoiding legal consequences.
- **Operational Resilience:** With role-based access controls, encryption, and incident response planning, TechMart enhances the resilience of its digital infrastructure, ensuring uninterrupted operations even in the face of security challenges.

The designed security solution for TechMart, combining Microsoft Defender for SQL and Microsoft Defender for Storage, addresses the unique challenges of securing both databases and storage in a complex e-commerce environment. This approach ensures the protection of sensitive data, regulatory compliance, and operational resilience against evolving cybersecurity threats.

Conclusion

The development of a robust Data Protection Strategy is paramount in safeguarding sensitive information. This strategic framework not only ensures compliance with regulatory standards but also mitigates the risks associated with data breaches. By fostering a culture of data privacy and security, organizations can build trust with stakeholders and protect their reputation. The continuous evolution of technology underscores the necessity for an adaptive strategy that addresses emerging threats. With a well-crafted Data Protection Strategy, organizations can navigate the complex landscape of data management, foster innovation, and uphold the integrity of the information they handle. In the next chapter, we will discuss Security Specifications for Cloud Services.

Multiple Choice Questions

1. What is the primary purpose of developing a Data Protection Strategy?

    a. Enhancing employee productivity.

    b. Ensuring compliance and safeguarding sensitive information.

   c. Reducing electricity consumption.
   d. Improving office aesthetics.
2. Why is a continuous evolution of Data Protection Strategy necessary?
   a. To increase operational costs.
   b. To comply with outdated regulations.
   c. To address emerging threats and technology changes.
   d. To limit innovation within the organization.
3. What role does a Data Protection Strategy play in building trust with stakeholders?
   a. It has no impact on trust.
   b. It increases operational efficiency.
   c. It fosters a culture of data privacy and security.
   d. It solely focuses on profit generation.
4. How does a well-crafted Data Protection Strategy contribute to organizational reputation?
   a. By ignoring data protection measures.
   b. By exposing sensitive information.
   c. By mitigating risks associated with data breaches.
   d. By avoiding compliance with regulations.
5. What is the significance of an adaptive Data Protection Strategy?
   a. To limit innovation.
   b. To maintain a static approach to data protection.
   c. To address changing threats and technologies.
   d. To discourage employee engagement.

Answers

1. b
2. c
3. c
4. c
5. c

CHAPTER 12
Security Specifications for Cloud Services

Introduction

Infrastructure security encompasses the protective measures implemented to defend vital systems, networks, and assets from cyber threats, physical attacks, and unauthorized access. As our reliance on interconnected technologies grows, the vulnerability of critical infrastructure to malicious actors intensifies. This field demands a holistic approach, integrating robust cybersecurity protocols, resilient physical defenses, and proactive risk management strategies. Addressing infrastructure security challenges requires collaboration across sectors, innovative technologies, and a constant commitment to adaptability in the face of evolving threats. Only through such comprehensive measures can we fortify our foundational systems against potential disruptions, ensuring the continuity of essential services and the overall well-being of society.

Infrastructure as a Service (IaaS), Platform as a Service (PaaS), and Software as a Service (SaaS) are all cloud computing models offering varying levels of IT resources, platforms, and software, respectively, on a subscription basis.

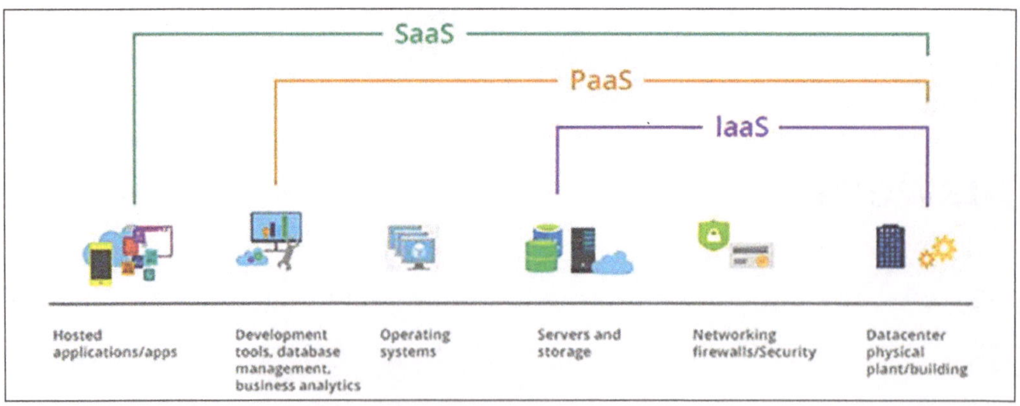

Figure 12.1: *Ias vs Paas vs Saas* (*Source*: Cloud Migration | Adatis)

Security considerations are paramount for Software as a Service (SaaS), Platform as a Service (PaaS), and Infrastructure as a Service (IaaS). These cloud service models offer businesses scalable and flexible solutions, but they also introduce unique security challenges.

Structure

In this chapter, we will cover the following topics:

- Introduction to security for SaaS, PaaS, and IaaS
- Specify Security Baselines for SaaS, PaaS, and IaaS Services
- Specify Security Requirements for Web Workloads
- Specify Security Requirements for Containers and Container Orchestration

Introduction to Security for SaaS, PaaS, and IaaS

Let us explore the security requirements for cloud service models.

SaaS

Software as a Service (SaaS) is a cloud computing model that delivers software applications over the internet, eliminating the need for users to install, maintain, and update software locally. In this model, the responsibility for maintenance and workability is shared between the cloud provider and the client, with the provider typically handling the majority of maintenance tasks.

A real-time example is Google Workspace, which provides collaborative tools like Gmail, Google Docs, and Google Drive. Security for SaaS involves protecting user data, ensuring secure authentication, and guarding against unauthorized access. Encryption protocols, multi-factor authentication, and regular security audits are essential components to safeguard sensitive information in SaaS applications.

Cloud Provider Responsibilities:

The cloud provider is responsible for approximately 90% of the maintenance and workability of the software. This includes tasks such as:

- **Infrastructure Management:** The provider manages the underlying infrastructure, ensuring high availability, scalability, and reliability of the software applications.

- **Security Measures:** Implementing robust security measures to protect user data, ensuring secure authentication, and guarding against unauthorized access.
- **Updates and Upgrades:** Regularly updating and upgrading the software to incorporate new features, fix bugs, and enhance performance.
- **Performance Optimization:** Monitoring and optimizing the performance of the software to ensure optimal user experience.
- **Backup and Disaster Recovery:** Implementing backup and disaster recovery solutions to protect against data loss and ensure business continuity.

Client Responsibilities:

While the cloud provider handles the majority of maintenance tasks, clients are responsible for the operations and configuration of the software. Client responsibilities may include:

- **User Configuration:** Configuring user accounts, permissions, and settings according to the organization's requirements.
- **Customization:** Tailoring the software to meet specific business needs through customization options provided by the SaaS platform.
- **Data Management:** Managing and organizing data within the software, including data input, storage, and retrieval.
- **Training and Support:** Providing training and support to end-users to ensure effective utilization of the software.
- **Compliance:** Ensuring compliance with industry regulations and standards applicable to the use of the software and handling of sensitive data.

PaaS

Platform as a Service (PaaS) offers a platform allowing developers to build, deploy, and manage applications without dealing with the underlying infrastructure. Microsoft Azure's Azure app service exemplifies PaaS, providing a platform for web and mobile app development. Security in PaaS is paramount, focusing on securing the development process, ensuring secure APIs, and protecting the runtime environment. Access controls, code analysis tools, and secure API design contribute to a robust PaaS security framework.

Security Principles Across Cloud Service Models:

In the broader context of cloud computing, security principles like encryption, access controls, and secure API design are fundamental across Software as a Service (SaaS), Platform as a Service (PaaS), and Infrastructure as a Service (IaaS). However, the application of these principles varies according to the specific cloud service model.

Examples of Security Measures:

- **SaaS Security:** SaaS providers implement encryption protocols, multi-factor authentication, and regular security audits to safeguard user data. Access controls are enforced to manage user permissions within the software applications.
- **PaaS Security:** In PaaS environments, access controls are crucial to secure the development and deployment processes. Code analysis tools help identify and mitigate vulnerabilities in applications. Secure API design ensures the integrity and confidentiality of data exchanged between applications and services.
- **IaaS Security:** Infrastructure security in IaaS involves securing virtual machines, networks, and storage resources. Encryption is applied to data at rest and in transit. Network access controls and firewalls protect against unauthorized access to cloud resources.

IaaS

Infrastructure as a Service (Iaas) provides virtualized computing resources over the internet, allowing users to manage and control virtualized infrastructure. Amazon Web Services (AWS) is a prominent IaaS provider. Security in IaaS involves securing virtual machines, networks, and data storage. For instance, implementing network firewalls, encryption for data at rest and in transit, and continuous monitoring are crucial for IaaS security. Users must also manage access controls and regularly update and patch virtualized infrastructure components. As organizations increasingly rely on cloud services, understanding and implementing robust security measures for SaaS, PaaS, and IaaS is imperative. By embracing encryption, access controls, and a proactive security posture, businesses can harness the full potential of these cloud models while safeguarding their data and applications in real-world scenarios.

Security Baselines for SaaS, PaaS, and IaaS Services

Businesses are increasingly leveraging SaaS, PaaS, and IaaS to enhance flexibility, scalability, and efficiency. However, with this transition to cloud-based services comes the critical responsibility of defining and implementing robust security baselines to safeguard sensitive data and maintain the integrity of business operations.

SaaS

Consider a scenario where a multinational corporation adopts a cloud-based Customer Relationship Management (CRM) SaaS solution to streamline its sales and customer management processes. In this context, establishing security baselines for SaaS involves several key considerations:

- **Authentication and Access Controls**

  Implementing multi-factor authentication ensures that only authorized users can access the CRM platform. Defining role-based access controls ensures that employees have the appropriate permissions based on their roles within the organization. For instance, sales representatives might have access to customer data, while marketing professionals may only need access to campaign analytics.

- **Data Encryption**

  The security baseline for SaaS should mandate the use of encryption mechanisms for data both in transit and at rest. This ensures that sensitive customer information, such as contact details and purchase history, remains confidential. The organization may employ Transport Layer Security (TLS) for data in transit and encryption algorithms for data stored within the SaaS application.

- **Regular Audits and Monitoring**

  Establishing a baseline for regular security audits and continuous monitoring is crucial. Automated tools can scan the SaaS application for vulnerabilities, while log analysis helps detect and respond to potential security incidents promptly. Regular audits provide insights into the overall security posture, helping the organization stay proactive in addressing emerging threats.

PaaS

In the same business scenario, the organization decides to develop custom applications for its CRM processes using a PaaS solution. Defining security baselines for PaaS involves addressing the specific challenges associated with application development and deployment.

- **Secure Development Practices**

  The security baseline should enforce the adoption of secure coding practices throughout the software development lifecycle. This includes regular code reviews, static and dynamic analysis tools, and training for developers on secure coding techniques. By embedding security into the development process, the organization reduces the risk of vulnerabilities in the custom applications.

- **API Security**

  As the PaaS solution involves the use of APIs to connect different components, establishing baselines for API security is essential. This includes implementing secure authentication mechanisms, encrypting data transmitted via APIs, and validating user input to prevent injection attacks. These measures enhance the overall security of the integrated applications.

- **Container Security**

  If the PaaS solution incorporates containerization technologies like Docker, specifying security baselines for container orchestration and management becomes crucial. This involves configuring secure container images, managing access controls within the container environment, and monitoring containerized applications for vulnerabilities.

IaaS

Now, let us imagine the organization decides to host critical backend services, databases, and networking infrastructure on an IaaS platform. Defining security baselines for IaaS involves safeguarding the foundational components of the IT infrastructure.

- **Network Security**

  The security baseline should include measures to secure the virtual networks within the IaaS environment. This involves setting up firewalls, implementing network segmentation, and monitoring network traffic for anomalous behavior. Network security ensures that communication between different components remains secure and isolated.

- **Identity and Access Management**

  Defining clear baselines for identity and access management is essential. This involves the creation of least privilege policies, regular review and revocation of access credentials, and the use of identity federation for seamless and secure authentication across services. Proper identity management reduces the risk of unauthorized access to critical infrastructure components.

- **Data Encryption and Backup**

  Establishing baselines for data encryption at rest and in transit is equally important in an IaaS scenario. Additionally, implementing regular data backup and recovery processes ensures business continuity in the event of data loss or a security incident. The organization should define the frequency of backups and conduct periodic recovery drills to validate the effectiveness of these measures.

- **Unified Security Governance**

  In this business scenario, a unified security governance framework should be established, ensuring consistency across SaaS, PaaS, and IaaS security baselines. This includes defining policies, conducting regular security training for employees, and establishing incident response plans that encompass the entire cloud infrastructure.

- **Compliance Management**

  The security baseline should address industry-specific compliance requirements and regulations. This ensures that the organization remains compliant with data protection laws, industry standards, and regulatory frameworks applicable to its operations.

- **Collaboration with Cloud Service Providers**

  Given the shared responsibility model in cloud computing, collaborating with SaaS, PaaS, and IaaS providers is crucial. The security baseline should include guidelines for engaging with providers, conducting due diligence on their security practices, and ensuring contractual agreements align with the organization's security requirements.

- **Incident Response and Communication**

  Establishing a baseline for incident response is crucial to ensure effective detection, containment, and recovery from security incidents within an organization. It is essential to establish clear communication protocols to notify relevant stakeholders, including customers, partners, and regulatory bodies, in the event of a data breach or security incident. When it comes to cloud computing, specifying security baselines tailored to Software as a Service (SaaS), Platform as a Service (PaaS), and Infrastructure as a Service (IaaS) is imperative. Organizations need to customize security measures according to the distinct characteristics and risks of each service model, aligning them with business objectives.

  For instance, in SaaS environments, emphasis should be placed on robust authentication mechanisms and data encryption to safeguard user information. In PaaS, securing the development environment and APIs becomes critical, while in IaaS, securing virtualized infrastructure components is paramount.

  This strategic approach not only protects sensitive data but also strengthens the overall resilience and security of the digital ecosystem, fostering sustainable business growth.

Specify Security Requirements for Web Workloads

As the importance of web-based applications grows, so does the need for robust security requirements to protect against evolving cyber threats. Let us delve into a real-time business scenario to explore the critical aspects of specifying security requirements for web workloads.

Business Scenario

Imagine a rapidly expanding e-commerce platform that caters to a diverse customer base, offering a wide range of products and services. The platform operates primarily through its web-based application, allowing users to browse products, make purchases, and manage their accounts. With the increasing volume of online transactions and customer data, ensuring the security of the web workloads becomes paramount.

Key Security Requirements for Web Workloads

Key security requirements for web workloads encompass robust encryption protocols, secure authentication mechanisms, regular vulnerability assessments, and stringent access controls. Implementing HTTPS, multi-factor authentication, and continuous monitoring are essential. These measures fortify web applications, protecting against data breaches and ensuring a resilient defense against evolving cyber threats.

- **Data Encryption and Privacy**

  Data encryption is a fundamental tool in safeguarding privacy and securing sensitive information. In an era dominated by digital transactions and communication, encryption plays a pivotal role in protecting data from unauthorized access. It involves converting plain text into a coded format using complex algorithms, rendering the information unreadable without the corresponding decryption key. Privacy concerns have escalated with the growing prevalence of cyber threats and data breaches. Encryption acts as a powerful defense mechanism, ensuring that even if data is intercepted, it remains unintelligible to unauthorized entities. This is particularly crucial in sectors like finance, healthcare, and communications, where the confidentiality of personal and sensitive information is paramount.

  End-to-end encryption is widely adopted in messaging applications, ensuring that only the intended recipient can decipher the messages. However, debates around encryption often arise, as some argue it hinders law enforcement efforts by impeding access to potentially crucial information. Despite these debates, the significance of data encryption in preserving privacy cannot be overstated. As technology continues to advance, the responsible use of encryption will remain integral to maintaining the trust of individuals and organizations in the digital age.

  - **Security Requirement:** All data transmitted between users and the e-commerce platform, including personal information, payment details, and login credentials, must be encrypted using industry-standard protocols such as HTTPS. Additionally, customer data at rest within the database should be encrypted to safeguard against unauthorized access in case of a breach.

- **Rationale:** Encryption ensures the confidentiality and integrity of sensitive data during transmission and storage. This requirement aligns with best practices for protecting customer privacy and complying with data protection regulations.

- **Authentication and Authorization**
  - **Security Requirement:** Implement a robust authentication mechanism, requiring users to create strong, unique passwords and supporting multi-factor authentication (MFA) for added security. Role-based access control (RBAC) should be enforced, granting users the minimum necessary permissions based on their roles within the platform.
  - **Rationale:** Strong authentication prevents unauthorized access to user accounts, while RBAC ensures that each user has access only to the functionalities essential for their role. MFA adds an extra layer of security by requiring users to provide multiple forms of identification.

- **Vulnerability Management**

  Vulnerability management is a pivotal aspect of cybersecurity, especially in cloud environments where shared responsibility models are prevalent. It involves identifying, assessing, and mitigating security vulnerabilities within systems or networks. Given the dynamic nature of the digital landscape, organizations encounter a growing array of threats, underscoring the need for proactive vulnerability management.

  Effective collaboration with Cloud Service Providers (CSPs) is essential in cloud environments. Organizations should prioritize understanding service level agreements (SLAs) and leverage CSP-provided security features to enhance vulnerability management. Integrating CSP-specific security recommendations into vulnerability management processes is crucial for maximizing protection.

  The vulnerability management process typically commences with vulnerability assessment, utilizing automated tools and manual techniques to scan for vulnerabilities across software, hardware, and network infrastructure. Identified vulnerabilities are then prioritized based on severity and potential impact on the organization's security posture. This prioritization ensures efficient resource allocation, enabling organizations to address critical vulnerabilities promptly and effectively.

  Once vulnerabilities are identified and ranked, organizations develop and implement mitigation strategies. This may involve applying patches, reconfiguring systems, or deploying additional security measures. Regular updates and ongoing monitoring are essential to adapt to emerging threats and maintain a robust security posture. Effective vulnerability management not only safeguards against potential cyber threats but also ensures compliance with regulatory requirements. It is a proactive approach to cybersecurity that minimizes the risk of exploitation and helps organizations maintain a resilient and secure digital environment.

- **Security Requirement:** Regularly conduct vulnerability assessments and penetration testing on the web application to identify and remediate potential security weaknesses. Ensure that security patches and updates are promptly applied to both the underlying infrastructure and third-party components.
- **Rationale:** Proactive vulnerability management reduces the risk of exploitation by malicious actors. Timely application of security patches is crucial to addressing known vulnerabilities and maintaining a secure web environment.

- **Logging and Monitoring**

  Logging and monitoring are essential components of effective IT and cybersecurity practices. Logging involves the systematic recording of events, activities, and errors within a system, creating a detailed chronicle that can be analyzed for troubleshooting, auditing, and security purposes. Monitoring, on the other hand, is the continuous observation of system performance, user activities, and network behavior in real-time. By implementing robust logging mechanisms, organizations can track changes, detect anomalies, and investigate incidents. This not only aids in troubleshooting technical issues but also plays a crucial role in compliance adherence and forensic analysis during security incidents. Monitoring complements logging by providing immediate insights into system health and performance. Continuous monitoring allows for the timely identification of unusual patterns or suspicious activities, enabling proactive responses to potential threats.

  Together, logging and monitoring enhance the overall resilience of IT infrastructures. They empower organizations to maintain operational efficiency, identify and mitigate security risks promptly, and meet regulatory requirements. In an ever-evolving digital landscape, effective logging and monitoring strategies are integral to maintaining the integrity, confidentiality, and availability of systems and data.

  - **Security Requirement:** Implement comprehensive logging for web workloads, capturing user activities, authentication attempts, and system events. Set up real-time monitoring to detect and respond to anomalous activities, and establish alerting mechanisms for potential security incidents.
  - **Rationale:** Logging and monitoring enhance the platform's ability to detect and respond to security incidents promptly. By analyzing

logs, the organization gains insights into user behavior and potential threats, enabling a proactive security posture.

- **DDoS Protection**
  - **Security Requirement:** Deploy a Distributed Denial of Service (DDoS) protection solution to mitigate the risk of service disruptions caused by malicious traffic. Implement rate limiting, traffic filtering, and scalability measures to ensure the platform can withstand sudden surges in web traffic.
  - **Rationale:** DDoS attacks pose a significant threat to web workloads, aiming to overwhelm servers and disrupt services. DDoS protection measures help maintain the availability and performance of the e-commerce platform during periods of high traffic.

In cloud environments, logging and monitoring play pivotal roles in maintaining the security and operational integrity of IT infrastructures. Logging entails systematically recording events, activities, and errors within cloud systems, creating a comprehensive chronicle for troubleshooting, auditing, and security analysis. Meanwhile, monitoring involves the continuous observation of system performance, user activities, and network behavior in real-time, offering immediate insights into cloud health and potential security threats.

Robust logging mechanisms enable organizations to track changes, detect anomalies, and investigate security incidents effectively within cloud environments. This aids in troubleshooting technical issues, ensuring compliance adherence, and facilitating forensic analysis during security breaches. Complementing logging, real-time monitoring provides immediate visibility into cloud performance, allowing for timely identification of unusual patterns or suspicious activities, thus enabling proactive threat responses.

In the cloud context, effective logging and monitoring strategies are vital for maintaining the integrity, confidentiality, and availability of cloud systems and data. For instance, for web workloads hosted in the cloud, implementing comprehensive logging to capture user activities, authentication attempts, and system events is essential. Additionally, setting up real-time monitoring to detect and respond to anomalous activities, along with establishing alerting mechanisms for potential security incidents, enhances the platform's ability to maintain security and operational resilience.

Moreover, deploying a Distributed Denial of Service (DDoS) protection solution is crucial to mitigate the risk of service disruptions caused by malicious traffic in cloud-based e-commerce platforms. By implementing rate limiting, traffic filtering, and scalability measures, organizations can ensure that the platform withstands sudden surges in web traffic, thereby safeguarding availability and performance during potential DDoS attacks.

In summary, within the cloud context, effective logging, monitoring, and DDoS protection measures are indispensable for maintaining the security, resilience, and performance of cloud-based IT infrastructures, ensuring seamless operations and mitigating potential security risks.

- **Incident Response and Communication**

  Incident response and communication are integral components of effective cybersecurity strategies. In the rapidly evolving landscape of digital threats, organizations must have robust mechanisms in place to detect, respond to, and recover from security incidents. Incident response involves the systematic approach to managing and mitigating the impact of cybersecurity events, such as data breaches or malware infections.

  Communication plays a pivotal role throughout the incident response process. Timely and transparent communication is crucial for maintaining trust with stakeholders, including customers, employees, and regulatory bodies. Clear and accurate information helps in managing the public perception and minimizing reputational damage. Moreover, internal communication is vital to coordinate the efforts of various teams involved in incident response, ensuring a swift and effective resolution.

  Establishing a well-defined incident response plan that includes communication protocols is essential. This plan should outline roles and responsibilities, escalation procedures, and communication channels. Regular drills and simulations can help organizations test and refine their incident response and communication strategies, ensuring readiness when a real incident occurs. In the ever-changing threat landscape, a proactive and communicative approach is key to minimizing the impact of security incidents and safeguarding the overall resilience of an organization.

  - **Security Requirement:** Develop and regularly update an incident response plan outlining procedures for identifying, containing, and recovering from security incidents. Establish clear communication channels to notify internal stakeholders, customers, and relevant authorities in the event of a data breach or significant security incident.
  - **Rationale:** An effective incident response plan minimizes the impact of security incidents and facilitates a swift and coordinated response. Transparent communication builds trust with customers and demonstrates a commitment to addressing security concerns.

- **Compliance with Regulatory Standards:**

  Compliance with regulatory standards is a paramount consideration for organizations across various industries. These standards are established by government bodies and industry authorities to ensure that businesses operate ethically, transparently, and in accordance with legal requirements.

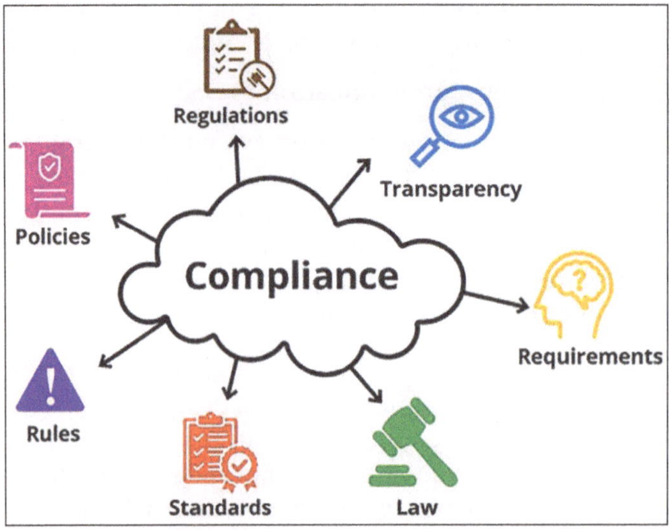

Figure 12.2: *Compliance Requirements*

Adhering to regulatory standards is not only a legal obligation but also a crucial aspect of maintaining trust and credibility with stakeholders. In the financial sector, for instance, compliance with regulations such as Anti-Money Laundering (AML) and Know Your Customer (KYC) is essential to prevent illicit activities and safeguard the integrity of the financial system. Similarly, in healthcare, organizations must comply with strict data protection laws like the Health Insurance Portability and Accountability Act (HIPAA) to protect patient information.

Non-compliance can result in severe consequences, including legal penalties, financial losses, and damage to reputation. Therefore, companies invest significant resources in implementing robust compliance programs, conducting regular audits, and staying informed about evolving regulatory landscapes. Embracing compliance not only mitigates risks but also fosters a culture of responsibility within an organization. It demonstrates a commitment to ethical practices, social responsibility, and the overall well-being of the business ecosystem. Ultimately, a proactive approach to compliance ensures that organizations not only meet regulatory standards but also contribute to a sustainable and trustworthy business environment.

  - **Security Requirement:** Ensure that the e-commerce platform complies with relevant regulatory standards and data protection laws. This includes implementing measures to protect customer data in accordance with regulations such as the General Data Protection Regulation (GDPR) or the Payment Card Industry Data Security Standard (PCI DSS).

- **Rationale:** Compliance with regulatory standards not only mitigates legal risks but also reflects the platform's dedication to protecting customer rights and privacy. Adherence to industry-specific standards fosters trust among users and partners.

Specifying security requirements for web workloads in the context of a dynamic e-commerce platform is integral to the success and sustainability of the business. By addressing data privacy, authentication, vulnerability management, monitoring, DDoS protection, incident response, and compliance, the organization establishes a comprehensive security framework. This proactive approach not only safeguards the integrity and availability of the web workloads but also instills confidence in customers, supporting the platform's growth and reputation in the competitive digital marketplace. As cyber threats continue to evolve, ongoing evaluation and adaptation of security requirements will be crucial to ensuring the resilience of web-based applications in the face of emerging challenges.

Specify Security Requirements for Containers and Container Orchestration

Let us explore the security requirements for containers and container orchestration in a real-time scenario, focusing on a dynamic e-commerce platform that relies heavily on microservices architecture.

Business Scenario

Imagine an e-commerce giant that has transitioned from a traditional monolithic architecture to a microservices-based architecture using containers and container orchestration. The platform handles a vast array of services, including user authentication, product catalog management, order processing, and payment transactions. In this scenario, ensuring the security of containers and the orchestration environment is paramount to safeguard sensitive customer information, maintain business continuity, and uphold the platform's reputation.

Security Requirements for Containers

Security requirements for containers are vital considerations in modern IT environments where containerization, using tools like Docker and Kubernetes, has become ubiquitous. Containers package applications and their dependencies into isolated units, but ensuring their security is crucial to prevent potential vulnerabilities.

Firstly, container images must be built from trusted sources, and the images themselves should be regularly scanned for vulnerabilities. Implementing a secure supply chain for container images helps prevent the deployment of compromised or outdated software.

Access control is another critical aspect. Container orchestration platforms need to enforce strong access controls, limiting permissions based on the principle of least privilege. This prevents unauthorized access and reduces the risk of malicious activities within the containerized environment.

Network security is equally important. Containers should communicate securely, and communication between containers should be restricted to necessary connections. Implementing network policies and using secure communication channels, such as TLS, enhances overall container security.

Regular updates and patch management are essential to address vulnerabilities promptly. Continuous monitoring and logging provide visibility into container activities, helping detect and respond to security incidents effectively.

A comprehensive security approach for containers involves secure image management, access controls, network security, regular updates, and continuous monitoring. As containerization continues to shape the IT landscape, addressing these security requirements is crucial for maintaining the integrity and resilience of containerized applications.

- **Image Security**

  Image security is a critical aspect of safeguarding visual assets in today's digital age. As the volume of digital images continues to surge, ensuring the protection of these visuals has become imperative for individuals and organizations alike. Image security involves implementing measures to prevent unauthorized access, manipulation, or distribution of images. One key concern in image security is the prevention of unauthorized usage or distribution, especially in the era of social media and online sharing. Watermarking, encryption, and digital rights management (DRM) are common techniques employed to secure images and control their dissemination. Watermarking, for instance, involves embedding subtle and often imperceptible marks within an image to deter unauthorized use and attribute ownership.

  In addition to protecting against unauthorized use, image security addresses the rising threat of image manipulation or "deepfakes," where sophisticated technologies alter images to deceive or manipulate viewers. Developing advanced algorithms to detect manipulations, along with educating users on the risks associated with manipulated visuals, is crucial in mitigating these challenges.

  Preserving the integrity of images is vital in various sectors, including journalism, entertainment, and forensics. As images play a pivotal role in shaping narratives and conveying information, maintaining their security ensures the authenticity and credibility of visual content in the digital landscape. Implementing comprehensive image security measures is essential to uphold trust and reliability in an era dominated by visual communication.

- **Requirement:** All container images must be sourced from trusted repositories, and a strict image scanning process should be in place to identify and remediate vulnerabilities before deployment.
- **Rationale:** Trustworthy sources and regular image scanning help mitigate the risk of deploying containers with known vulnerabilities, ensuring that only secure and approved images are used in the production environment.

- **Runtime Security**

Runtime security is a critical component of a comprehensive cybersecurity strategy, focusing on the protection of software and systems during their execution. Unlike traditional security measures that primarily address vulnerabilities in the development phase, runtime security is designed to detect and respond to threats in real-time while applications are actively running.

This approach is crucial in today's dynamic and interconnected digital landscape, where cyber threats constantly evolve. Runtime security solutions employ various techniques, such as intrusion detection systems, behavior analytics, and anomaly detection, to monitor and analyze system activities for signs of malicious behavior. They can identify and thwart threats like malware, unauthorized access attempts, and suspicious network activities during the runtime phase.

By actively monitoring and responding to potential security incidents, runtime security helps prevent and mitigate the impact of attacks, protecting sensitive data and ensuring the integrity of systems. This is especially important as cyber threats become more sophisticated, leveraging advanced techniques to exploit vulnerabilities.

Incorporating runtime security into an organization's cybersecurity framework enhances its ability to adapt to emerging threats, providing a dynamic layer of defense that complements static security measures. As technology continues to advance, runtime security remains a fundamental element in safeguarding digital assets and maintaining the resilience of modern IT infrastructures.

- **Requirement:** Employ runtime protection mechanisms, such as container firewalls and runtime vulnerability scanners, to monitor and control the behavior of containers in real-time.
- **Rationale:** Runtime security measures add an additional layer of defense, preventing malicious activities within containers and detecting unauthorized changes or anomalies during runtime.

- **Access Controls**
    - **Requirement:** Implement strong access controls for containers, restricting permissions based on the principle of least privilege. Ensure that only authorized personnel can access, modify, or interact with containers.
    - **Rationale:** Limiting access to containers helps prevent unauthorized actions and reduces the attack surface. Strict access controls are essential for maintaining the integrity and confidentiality of containerized applications.
- **Network Security**

  Network security is a paramount concern in the realm of cybersecurity, dedicated to safeguarding the integrity, confidentiality, and availability of data transmitted over computer networks. As businesses and individuals increasingly rely on interconnected systems, the importance of robust network security measures cannot be overstated.

  Key components of network security include firewalls, intrusion detection and prevention systems, virtual private networks (VPNs), and antivirus software. Firewalls act as barriers, monitoring and controlling incoming and outgoing network traffic based on predetermined security rules. Intrusion detection and prevention systems identify and respond to potential threats, ensuring a proactive defense against malicious activities. Securing communication channels through VPNs is crucial, particularly for remote access and protection of sensitive data during transmission. Additionally, antivirus software plays a pivotal role in detecting and removing malicious software, including viruses, worms, and Trojans, before they compromise network integrity.

  Regular updates, patches, and security audits are essential practices to address emerging vulnerabilities and strengthen the overall resilience of a network. With the growing sophistication of cyber threats, network security measures must evolve to counteract new attack vectors and techniques. In essence, network security is a multifaceted discipline that encompasses a range of technologies and processes, aiming to create a secure and trustworthy digital environment. As organizations and individuals continue to navigate an interconnected world, prioritizing network security is imperative to mitigate risks and ensure the confidentiality and reliability of digital communications.

    - **Requirement:** Employ network segmentation for containers to isolate communication between services. Implement network policies to control inbound and outbound traffic, and use encryption for data in transit between containers.
    - **Rationale:** Network security measures prevent lateral movement of threats within the containerized environment, enhancing the overall resilience of the microservices architecture.

- **Logging and Auditing**

  Logging and auditing are integral components of robust cybersecurity strategies, providing organizations with essential tools to monitor, analyze, and review activities within their IT environments.

  Logging involves the systematic recording of events, activities, and transactions across a network or system. This comprehensive record, known as logs, captures information such as user logins, system changes, and network traffic. Logging is crucial for troubleshooting, forensic analysis, and identifying security incidents. Additionally, logs play a key role in compliance, aiding organizations in meeting regulatory requirements by maintaining an audit trail of relevant activities.

  Auditing, on the other hand, refers to the systematic examination and analysis of these logs to ensure compliance, detect anomalies, and investigate security incidents. Auditing provides insights into user behavior, potential security threats, and adherence to security policies. Regular audits can uncover vulnerabilities, unauthorized access, or suspicious activities, enabling organizations to proactively address security concerns.

  Together, logging and auditing contribute to the overall cybersecurity posture by offering transparency, accountability, and the ability to trace and investigate security incidents. These practices are especially critical in sectors with stringent regulatory requirements, such as finance and healthcare, where maintaining a secure and auditable environment is imperative. In essence, logging and auditing form a crucial feedback loop in cybersecurity, helping organizations understand, respond to, and learn from the ever-evolving landscape of cyber threats.

  - **Requirement:** Enable comprehensive logging for container activities, capturing events such as container creation, modifications, and runtime events. Regularly audit logs to detect and investigate security incidents.
  - **Rationale:** Logging and auditing provide visibility into container behavior, aiding in the identification of security incidents and supporting forensic analysis in the event of a breach.

Security Requirements for Container Orchestration

Security requirements for container orchestration are crucial for ensuring the robustness of containerized environments in today's dynamic IT landscape. Container orchestration systems, such as Kubernetes, enable the efficient deployment, scaling, and management of containerized applications, but they also introduce unique security challenges that must be addressed proactively.

Firstly, access control and authentication mechanisms are paramount. Properly configured identity and access management help restrict permissions, preventing unauthorized access to critical resources. Additionally, encryption of data in transit and at rest is essential to safeguard sensitive information exchanged between containers and stored within the orchestration environment.

Network security plays a significant role in container orchestration security. Implementing network policies, firewalls, and segmentation ensures that communication between containers is secure, minimizing the attack surface. Regularly updating container images and the underlying orchestration platform is vital to patch vulnerabilities and maintain a secure environment.

Furthermore, runtime monitoring and logging are indispensable for detecting and responding to potential security incidents promptly. Security audits, vulnerability assessments, and compliance checks should be conducted regularly to identify and address any security gaps.

Lastly, organizations should foster a security-first culture, promoting awareness among development and operations teams. Educating stakeholders on best practices, secure coding principles, and the importance of adhering to security policies helps create a resilient container orchestration environment, ultimately mitigating risks and ensuring the integrity of containerized applications.

- **Authentication and Authorization**

  Authentication and authorization are fundamental concepts in the realm of cybersecurity, playing crucial roles in ensuring the security and integrity of digital systems.

  Authentication is the process of verifying the identity of a user, device, or system attempting to access a network or application. Common authentication methods include passwords, biometrics, and multi-factor authentication (MFA). Strong authentication mechanisms are essential to prevent unauthorized access and protect sensitive information from being compromised.

  Authorization, on the other hand, comes into play after authentication. Once a user's identity is confirmed, authorization determines the level of access or permissions granted to that user within the system. Authorization is about defining and enforcing policies that dictate what actions a user is allowed to perform, what data they can access, and what operations they can execute. This helps ensure that users only have the necessary privileges required for their roles and responsibilities.

  Together, authentication and authorization form a robust security framework. Properly implemented, they safeguard against unauthorized access, data breaches, and other security threats. Organizations often use these measures in conjunction with other security practices to create a layered defense strategy, enhancing the overall cybersecurity posture and protecting valuable digital assets from compromise or misuse.

- **Requirement:** Implement strong authentication mechanisms for accessing the container orchestration platform. Employ role-based access control (RBAC) to define and enforce access policies for users and services interacting with the orchestration environment.
- **Rationale:** Authentication and RBAC ensure that only authorized entities can manage and interact with the orchestration platform, preventing unauthorized access and potential malicious activities.

- **Secure Configuration**
  - **Requirement:** Configure the container orchestration platform securely, following best practices and industry standards. This includes securing API endpoints, using strong encryption for communication, and disabling unnecessary features or components.
  - **Rationale:** Secure configuration reduces the attack surface of the orchestration platform and helps protect against common vulnerabilities, ensuring the overall stability and security of the containerized infrastructure.

- **Image Signature Verification**

  Image signature verification is a process that involves confirming the authenticity and integrity of digital images through the analysis of unique signatures or fingerprints associated with each image. These signatures are cryptographic hash values generated based on the content of the image, making them distinct and resistant to alterations.

  In image signature verification, a digital signature is created using algorithms like MD5, SHA-256, or other hash functions. This signature is a fixed-length string of characters that serves as a unique identifier for the image's content. When an image is to be verified, the system recalculates the signature and compares it to the original. If the signatures match, it indicates that the image has not been tampered with or altered.

  This technology is particularly crucial in fields such as forensics, digital rights management, and content authentication. It helps ensure the integrity of visual information, preventing unauthorized modifications or manipulations. Image signature verification is extensively used in legal contexts, ensuring the credibility of digital evidence in legal proceedings. As the digital landscape evolves, image signature verification continues to play a pivotal role in maintaining trust and authenticity in various applications, providing a reliable method for confirming the legitimacy of digital images in an increasingly digitized and interconnected world.

- **Requirement:** Enable image signature verification to ensure the authenticity and integrity of container images before deployment. Only allow the execution of signed and trusted images within the orchestration environment.
- **Rationale:** Verifying image signatures prevents the deployment of tampered or malicious images, enhancing the overall trustworthiness of the containerized applications.

- **Network Isolation and Segmentation**

  Network isolation and segmentation are fundamental strategies in cybersecurity aimed at enhancing the overall resilience of IT infrastructures. These practices involve dividing a network into distinct segments or isolating certain components to control and restrict access, limiting the potential impact of security incidents. Isolation prevents lateral movement within a network, making it more challenging for cyber threats to propagate. In the event of a security breach, segmenting the network ensures that the compromised area is contained, preventing the unauthorized access of critical systems or sensitive data.

  Segmentation is often based on factors such as department, function, or user roles. By creating separate zones, organizations can implement customized security measures according to the specific requirements and risk profiles of each segment. This not only limits the attack surface but also allows for more granular control over network traffic, enabling better monitoring and threat detection.

  Network isolation and segmentation are especially crucial in large enterprises where diverse systems coexist. It adds an additional layer of defense, making it harder for cybercriminals to navigate through a network undetected. Additionally, these practices align with the principle of least privilege, ensuring that users and systems only have access to the resources necessary for their functions.

  In summary, network isolation and segmentation contribute significantly to a robust cybersecurity posture by minimizing the impact of security incidents, restricting lateral movement, and providing organizations with better control over their network infrastructure.

  - **Requirement:** Implement network isolation and segmentation within the container orchestration platform to prevent unauthorized communication between different services or clusters. Utilize network policies to control traffic flow between components

- **Rationale:** Network isolation enhances the security of individual services and prevents the lateral movement of threats, limiting the impact of a potential compromise within the orchestration environment.

- **Secrets Management**

  Secrets management is a critical aspect of cybersecurity and data protection, involving the secure storage, access, and distribution of sensitive information such as passwords, API keys, and encryption keys. In the digital age, where data breaches are prevalent, effective secrets management is essential to safeguarding confidential information and maintaining the integrity of systems.

  Organizations employ secrets management solutions to securely store and manage access to sensitive data, preventing unauthorized users or malicious actors from gaining unauthorized access. These solutions often incorporate encryption, access controls, and auditing mechanisms to ensure that only authorized personnel can retrieve and use sensitive information.

  In a cloud-centric and DevOps-oriented landscape, secrets management becomes even more crucial. Automated deployment pipelines and continuous integration processes require secure handling of credentials and keys to ensure the smooth and secure operation of applications. Secrets management tools help mitigate the risk of accidental exposure or compromise of sensitive data during these dynamic and automated workflows.

  Adopting robust secrets management practices enhances overall cybersecurity posture, mitigates the risk of data breaches, and ensures compliance with regulatory standards. As organizations increasingly rely on interconnected systems and digital platforms, effective secrets management becomes integral to protecting valuable assets and maintaining trust in the secure handling of sensitive information.

  - **Requirement:** Implement a secure and centralized secrets management system for handling sensitive information, such as API keys, passwords, and cryptographic keys. Ensure that secrets are stored securely and are only accessible to authorized services and users.
  - **Rationale:** Effective secrets management mitigates the risk of unauthorized access to sensitive information, reducing the likelihood of data breaches and maintaining the confidentiality of critical credentials.

- **Monitoring and Incident Response**

  - **Requirement:** Deploy robust monitoring tools to track the performance and security of the container orchestration platform. Establish an incident response plan that includes procedures for detecting, responding to, and recovering from security incidents.

  - **Rationale:** Monitoring and incident response capabilities are essential for identifying and mitigating security threats promptly, minimizing the impact on the containerized infrastructure and ensuring business continuity.

- **Regular Audits and Compliance Checks**

  Regular audits and compliance checks are indispensable practices for organizations seeking to ensure adherence to regulatory standards, industry norms, and internal policies. These systematic reviews serve as proactive measures to identify, rectify, and prevent potential issues related to legal compliance, operational efficiency, and risk management.

  Through periodic audits, companies assess their internal processes, financial records, and data security protocols. This helps in verifying the accuracy of information, detecting fraudulent activities, and ensuring that resources are utilized efficiently. In addition, compliance checks evaluate whether the organization aligns with external regulations, such as data protection laws, environmental standards, or industry-specific guidelines.

  These audits provide a comprehensive overview of a company's health, highlighting areas of improvement and potential vulnerabilities. They also play a crucial role in fostering a culture of transparency and accountability within the organization. By regularly reviewing and updating compliance measures, companies not only mitigate legal risks but also build trust among stakeholders, including customers, partners, and regulatory authorities.

  In industries like finance and healthcare, where regulatory requirements are stringent, regular audits are even more essential. They demonstrate a commitment to ethical practices and contribute to the establishment of a robust governance framework. Ultimately, the combination of regular audits and compliance checks forms a cornerstone for sustainable business operations and long-term success

  - **Requirement:** Conduct regular security audits and compliance checks for the container orchestration platform. This includes reviewing configurations, assessing adherence to security policies, and ensuring compliance with industry regulations and standards.
  - **Rationale:** Regular audits and compliance checks help identify and address security gaps, ensuring that the container orchestration platform remains aligned with security best practices and regulatory requirements.

Specifying comprehensive security requirements for both containers and container orchestration is critical to safeguarding sensitive data, maintaining business continuity, and fostering customer trust. By addressing image security, runtime protection, access controls, network security, and logging for containers, and authentication, secure configuration, image signature verification, network isolation, secrets management, monitoring, and compliance for container orchestration, organizations can establish a robust security posture. This proactive approach not only mitigates the risk of security incidents but also ensures the resilience of the containerized infrastructure in the face of evolving cyber threats. As container technologies continue to evolve, ongoing evaluation and adaptation of security requirements will be essential to stay ahead of emerging challenges and protect the integrity of containerized applications.

Conclusion

As our reliance on interconnected technologies burgeons in the digital era, the imperative to secure critical infrastructure stands as a linchpin for societal well-being. Infrastructure security, spanning cyber and physical realms, necessitates a holistic strategy, blending robust cybersecurity protocols, resilient physical defenses, and proactive risk management. Collaboration across sectors, technological innovation, and adaptability to evolving threats are pivotal. Safeguarding foundational systems through comprehensive measures not only ensures continuity of essential services but also fortifies against potential disruptions. In this dynamic landscape, the synergy of these elements serves as a bulwark, ensuring the integrity of our interconnected infrastructure in the face of an ever-evolving threat landscape. In the next chapter, we will discuss hybrid and multi-cloud security frameworks.

CHAPTER 13
Hybrid and Multi-Cloud Security Framework

Introduction

This chapter provides a comprehensive exploration of hybrid and multicloud management, delving into the nuances of security control, posture, and vulnerability management. It addresses the benefits, challenges, and strategic imperatives associated with designing integrated posture management, workload protection, and cloud application security. Real-world scenarios and case studies illuminate the business imperative of evaluating security posture, implementing real-time measures, and leveraging Microsoft Defender for Cloud for optimal defense strategies.

Structure

In this chapter, we will cover the following topics:

- Introduction to Hybrid Cloud Management
- Multicloud Management: Navigating Complexity for Agility
- Evaluating Security with Microsoft Cloud Benchmark: A Business Priority
- Security Control: Posture and Vulnerability Management – A Case Study
- Integrated Posture Management and Workload Protection: Strategic Priority
- Comprehensive Posture Management: Integrated Protection
- Securing Cloud Applications: A Real-time Scenario
- Improving Your Security Posture: A Business Scenario
- Protecting Cloud Workloads: A Real-time Scenario
- Defender for Cloud Planning and Operations: A Real-time Scenario

- Posture Evaluation with Microsoft Defender for Cloud Secure Score: A Business Scenario
- Designing Cloud Workload Protection with Microsoft Defender for Cloud: A Business Scenario

Introduction to Hybrid Cloud Management

Businesses are constantly seeking efficient and flexible solutions to manage their data and applications. The emergence of hybrid cloud management has become a game-changer, offering a powerful combination of on-premises infrastructure and cloud services. This integration allows organizations to capitalize on the strengths of both environments, thus creating a dynamic and scalable IT infrastructure that meets the demands of the modern digital era.

Understanding Hybrid Cloud

Hybrid cloud entails the strategic utilization of both public and private cloud services, alongside on-premises infrastructure, to establish a cohesive and integrated computing environment.

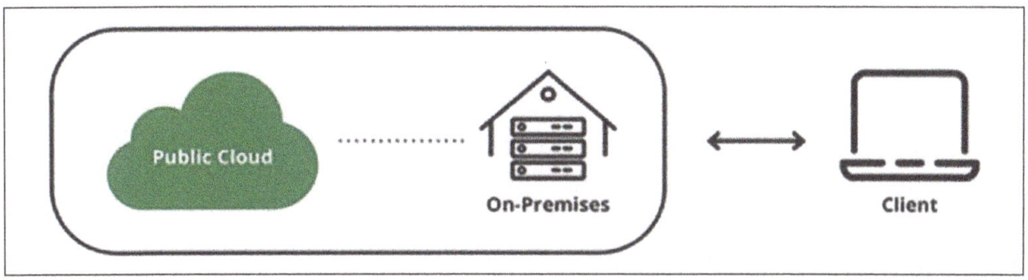

***Figure 13.1**: Hybrid Cloud (Source :* How does hybrid cloud architecture work? | Cloudflare)

This approach empowers organizations to capitalize on the scalability and cost-effectiveness of public clouds while benefiting from the control and security afforded by private clouds and on-premises data centers.

In a practical scenario, envision a global e-commerce enterprise facing fluctuating demands throughout the year, particularly during peak seasons like Black Friday or holiday sales. To accommodate the surge in web traffic and transactions during these periods, the company necessitates rapid scaling of its resources. A hybrid cloud solution proves invaluable in this context, enabling the company to harness public cloud resources for additional computing power during peak times, all while safeguarding sensitive customer data and critical applications within a private cloud or on-premises infrastructure.

While this depiction offers a foundational comprehension of hybrid cloud, it is essential to delve deeper into the technical intricacies encompassing the technologies, tools, and strategies integral to implementing and managing a hybrid cloud environment effectively.

Benefits of Hybrid Cloud Management

Hybrid cloud management offers to businesses a dynamic solution, seamlessly integrating private and public cloud services. This approach optimizes flexibility, scalability, and cost-efficiency, enhancing performance, data security, and overall operational agility.

- **Scalability**

  Scalability in hybrid cloud management extends beyond merely adjusting resources during peak seasons. It encompasses a range of considerations aimed at optimizing resources, leveraging auto-scaling capabilities, and implementing effective workload management strategies. This holistic approach ensures optimal performance not only during periods of heightened activity but also during slower times, preventing overcommitment of resources.

- **Cost Efficiency**

  Hybrid cloud solutions provide cost-effective options by allowing organizations to use public cloud resources for non-sensitive workloads or temporary projects, reducing the need for massive upfront investments in hardware.

- **Flexibility and Agility**

  Businesses operating in dynamic environments benefit from the agility offered by hybrid cloud management. The flexibility to move workloads between environments allows for quick adaptation to changing business requirements.

- **Data Security and Compliance**

  For industries dealing with sensitive data, compliance with regulations is paramount. Hybrid cloud solutions enable organizations to keep critical data on-premises or in a private cloud, ensuring compliance with industry-specific regulations and data protection laws.

Challenges and Considerations

While hybrid cloud management offers significant advantages, it also presents challenges that organizations must navigate. Seamless integration, consistent performance, and effective data management across diverse environments require careful planning and robust management solutions. Security concerns, such as data breaches and compliance issues, necessitate robust measures to safeguard sensitive information.

Real-time Implementation

Consider a multinational financial institution that operates in a heavily regulated environment. The organization utilizes a hybrid cloud approach to streamline its operations. Customer-facing applications are hosted on a public cloud for scalability, while sensitive financial data and compliance-critical applications remain on-premises or in a private cloud. This setup allows the company to meet regulatory requirements, ensure data security, and deliver a seamless user experience to its clients.

In the era of digital transformation, hybrid cloud management has emerged as a strategic imperative for businesses seeking a balance between innovation, efficiency, and security. By combining the strengths of public and private clouds with on-premises infrastructure, organizations can build a dynamic and responsive IT ecosystem that meets the diverse needs of the modern business landscape. As technology continues to advance, the role of hybrid cloud management will only become more critical in shaping the future of IT infrastructure.

Multicloud Management: Navigating Complexity for Agility

Multicloud management involves the orchestration and coordination of resources across different cloud environments to optimize performance, mitigate risks, and enhance overall agility. This approach provides organizations with the flexibility to choose the best-in-class services from various providers, fostering innovation and resilience in the face of dynamic business demands.

Understanding Multicloud Management

Multicloud refers to the use of services and resources from multiple cloud providers to meet specific business requirements. These providers may include industry giants like Amazon Web Services (AWS), Microsoft Azure, and Google Cloud Platform (GCP). Multicloud management, therefore, is the practice of efficiently handling and coordinating workloads, applications, and data across these diverse cloud environments. Consider a scenario in which a global enterprise, operating across various regions, uses AWS for its robust artificial intelligence services, Azure for seamless integration with Microsoft applications, and GCP for its advanced machine learning capabilities. Multicloud management allows this organization to leverage the unique strengths of each provider, creating a cohesive and optimized IT infrastructure tailored to its specific needs.

Benefits of Multicloud Management

Multicloud management empowers organizations with diverse cloud environments, fostering resilience, redundancy, and resource optimization. This approach enhances agility, minimizes vendor lock-in, and ensures optimal performance across multiple platforms.

- **Flexibility and Choice**

  Multicloud strategies empower organizations to select the most suitable services and features from different cloud providers based on performance, cost, and specific capabilities. This flexibility ensures that businesses are not locked into a single vendor and can adapt to evolving technology trends.

- **Risk Mitigation**

  Distributing workloads across multiple cloud providers reduces the risk of service disruptions or outages. If one provider experiences issues, the organization can seamlessly redirect its operations to another, minimizing the impact on business continuity.

- **Optimized Performance**

  Multicloud management allows businesses to strategically place workloads in regions where a particular cloud provider excels, optimizing performance and reducing latency. This is particularly crucial for applications with high-performance requirements or those catering to a global user base.

- **Cost Optimization**

  By strategically allocating workloads to the most cost-effective cloud services, organizations can optimize their cloud spending. Multicloud strategies enable businesses to take advantage of competitive pricing and leverage discounts offered by different providers.

Challenges and Considerations of Multicloud Management

While multicloud management offers compelling advantages, it comes with its set of challenges. Coordinating security measures across diverse environments, ensuring data interoperability, and managing complexities in network connectivity require thoughtful planning and robust management solutions. Additionally, organizations must invest in tools that provide visibility and control over their multicloud architecture to effectively monitor performance and enforce governance policies.

Real-time Implementation

Consider a digital media company that relies on AWS for its content delivery services due to its global reach, Azure for its integration with Microsoft 365 applications, and Oracle Cloud for its database requirements. The company employs multicloud management solutions to seamlessly orchestrate these services, ensuring optimal performance, high availability, and cost-effective operations. If there is a sudden surge in demand for its streaming services, the multicloud setup allows the company to dynamically scale resources across different providers to meet the increased load.

Multicloud management is becoming a strategic imperative for organizations aiming to harness the full potential of cloud computing while mitigating risks associated with vendor lock-in and service disruptions. The ability to seamlessly integrate and manage resources across diverse cloud environments provides businesses with the agility needed to thrive in today's dynamic and competitive landscape. As the adoption of multicloud strategies continues to grow, effective management solutions will play a pivotal role in unlocking the true benefits of this innovative approach to cloud computing.

Evaluating Security with Microsoft Cloud Benchmark: A Business Priority

As organizations increasingly migrate to cloud environments, ensuring a robust security posture becomes paramount. Microsoft Cloud Security Benchmark (MCSB) emerges as a crucial tool, empowering businesses to evaluate and enhance their security measures within Microsoft cloud services. Let us delve into how a hypothetical business scenario can benefit from this benchmark to fortify its security defenses.

Understanding Microsoft Cloud Security Benchmark

Microsoft Cloud Security Benchmark is a set of best practices and recommendations curated by cybersecurity experts to help organizations strengthen their security posture on Microsoft cloud platforms, such as Microsoft 365 and Azure. This benchmark provides a comprehensive framework for evaluating configurations, detecting vulnerabilities, and implementing security controls aligned with industry standards and regulations.

Business Scenario: Global Financial Services Firm

Consider a global financial services firm that manages sensitive customer data and conducts numerous transactions daily. With a significant portion of its operations relying on Microsoft cloud services, the company recognizes the critical importance of maintaining a high level of security. In this scenario, the firm decides to leverage the Microsoft Cloud Security Benchmark to assess and enhance its security posture.

Key Steps in Evaluating Security Posture:

1. **Assessment and Benchmarking**

   The firm initiates the process by conducting a thorough assessment of its existing security configurations within Microsoft cloud services. Leveraging the Microsoft Cloud Security Benchmark, the IT security team benchmarks current configurations against the recommended best practices outlined in the benchmark.

2. **Identification of Vulnerabilities**

   Using the benchmark as a guide, the security team identifies potential vulnerabilities and gaps in the existing security measures. This includes areas such as identity and access management, data protection, network security, and threat detection.

3. **Remediation Planning**

   Based on the assessment findings, the firm devises a comprehensive remediation plan. This plan prioritizes addressing critical vulnerabilities and aligning configurations with the recommended best practices outlined in the Microsoft Cloud Security Benchmark.

4. **Implementation of Security Controls**

   The IT security team systematically implements the recommended security controls outlined in the benchmark. This involves configuring identity and access management policies, strengthening data encryption practices, and optimizing network security settings.

5. **Continuous Monitoring and Improvement**

   Security is an ongoing process. The firm establishes a continuous monitoring system to track changes in the cloud environment, detect new vulnerabilities, and ensure that security configurations remain aligned with the evolving Microsoft Cloud Security Benchmark.

Benefits of Using Microsoft Cloud Security Benchmark: Comprehensive Guidance

The benchmark provides a comprehensive set of guidelines and best practices, offering a clear roadmap for securing Microsoft cloud environments.

- **Alignment with Industry Standards**

  By aligning security configurations with the benchmark, the financial services firm ensures compliance with industry standards and regulatory requirements, enhancing trust with customers and regulatory bodies.

- **Reduced Risk of Breaches**

  The proactive approach to identifying and addressing vulnerabilities reduces the risk of security breaches, protecting sensitive financial data and maintaining the integrity of transactions.

- **Optimized Resource Utilization**

  Implementing the recommended security controls helps optimize resource utilization within the cloud environment, ensuring that resources are configured efficiently without sacrificing security.

Leveraging tools such as the Microsoft Cloud Security Benchmark provides organizations, like our global financial services firm, with a systematic and effective way to fortify their defenses, protect sensitive data, and uphold the trust of clients and stakeholders in an increasingly interconnected and data-driven business landscape.

Security Control: Posture and Vulnerability Management – A Case Study

This case study delves into the implementation of security control measures, specifically focusing on posture and vulnerability management, within a multinational technology corporation.

Business Scenario: Multinational Technology Corporation

Our case study revolves around a multinational technology corporation that operates in diverse geographical locations, offering a range of cloud-based services and products. With a vast digital footprint and an extensive user base, the company recognizes the paramount importance of maintaining a robust security posture and promptly addressing vulnerabilities to safeguard its sensitive intellectual property and user data.

Challenges Faced

Navigating the business landscape as a Multinational Technology Corporation presents multifaceted challenges. Managing scale and complexity is an ongoing struggle, compounded by a dynamic threat landscape that demands constant adaptation. Regulatory compliance adds an additional layer of complexity, requiring vigilance and strategic planning to ensure adherence to ever-evolving global regulations.

- **Scale and Complexity**

  The corporation's extensive cloud infrastructure, spanning multiple regions, introduces complexity in managing security configurations consistently across diverse environments.

- **Dynamic Threat Landscape**

  The dynamic nature of cybersecurity threats poses a constant challenge. New vulnerabilities and attack vectors emerge regularly, requiring proactive measures to stay ahead of potential risks.

- **Regulatory Compliance**

  As a global entity, the corporation must comply with various international data protection and privacy regulations. Ensuring that security measures align with these regulations adds an extra layer of complexity.

Implementation of Posture and Vulnerability Management: Comprehensive Security Assessment

The corporation begins by conducting a thorough assessment of its security posture using industry standards and frameworks. This involves evaluating configurations across its cloud infrastructure, networks, and endpoints.

- **Utilizing Posture Management Tools**

  To streamline the process, the corporation invests in advanced posture management tools that provide a centralized view of its security configurations. These tools assess adherence to security best practices and regulatory requirements.

- **Identification of Vulnerabilities**

  Concurrently, vulnerability scans are conducted across the infrastructure to identify potential weaknesses. Automated tools, combined with manual assessments, help create an inventory of vulnerabilities, ranging from misconfigurations to outdated software.

- **Prioritization and Risk Assessment**

  The security team prioritizes identified vulnerabilities based on their severity and potential impact on the organization's operations. A risk assessment is conducted to align remediation efforts with the most critical vulnerabilities first.

- **Patch Management and Remediation**

  An efficient patch management process is established to address software vulnerabilities promptly. Automated patch deployment tools are employed, ensuring that security patches are applied across the organization's systems in a timely manner.

- **Continuous Monitoring and Adaptation**

  Recognizing that cybersecurity is an ever-evolving field, the corporation establishes continuous monitoring mechanisms. This includes real-time threat intelligence feeds, regular vulnerability scans, and ongoing evaluations of its security posture to adapt to emerging threats.

Results and Benefits

The implementation of posture and vulnerability management is instrumental in fortifying an organization's security framework. This comprehensive security assessment yields numerous results and benefits, such as an enhanced security posture, critical vulnerabilities mitigation, ensuring regulatory compliance, and significantly improving incident response capabilities.

- **Enhanced Security Posture**

  By adopting a proactive approach to posture management, the corporation achieves a heightened security posture. The systematic assessment and adherence to best practices contribute to a more resilient and secure infrastructure.

- **Mitigation of Critical Vulnerabilities**

  Through the implementation of a robust vulnerability management program, the corporation successfully mitigates critical vulnerabilities, reducing the risk of exploitation by malicious actors.

- **Regulatory Compliance**

  The corporation aligns its security controls with various regulatory requirements, ensuring compliance with international data protection laws. This, in turn, enhances trust among users and facilitates smooth business operations.

- **Improved Incident Response**

  The continuous monitoring and adaptation strategy enables the corporation to detect and respond to security incidents more effectively. Rapid response to emerging threats minimizes the impact of potential breaches.

In a cybersecurity landscape characterized by complexity and constant threats, the implementation of effective posture and vulnerability management is crucial for organizations, especially those with extensive digital footprints. This case study highlights the importance of a proactive and systematic approach, leveraging advanced tools and continuous monitoring, to fortify the security posture of a multinational technology corporation. Through these measures, organizations can not only address current vulnerabilities but also adapt to emerging threats, ensuring the resilience of their digital assets in an ever-evolving threat landscape.

Integrated Posture Management and Workload Protection: Strategic Priority

Designing an integrated posture management and workload protection strategy is essential for organizations seeking comprehensive defense against evolving threats. This section explores the strategic implementation of such a system within a global financial institution, emphasizing the synergy between posture management and workload protection for robust security.

Business Scenario: Global Financial Institution

Our business scenario unfolds within a globally renowned financial institution managing a vast network of branches and digital services. The institution handles sensitive financial data, making security a top priority. With the increasing complexity of cyber threats and stringent regulatory requirements, the need for an integrated posture management and workload protection system becomes critical.

Challenges Faced:

- **Hybrid Infrastructure Complexity**

  The financial institution operates in a hybrid environment, utilizing both on-premises infrastructure and cloud services. Managing security configurations across this hybrid landscape poses a challenge due to the diversity of systems and environments.

- **Dynamic Nature of Cyber Threats**

  The institution faces a dynamic threat landscape with sophisticated cyber adversaries constantly evolving their tactics. Traditional security measures may not be sufficient to thwart advanced attacks, necessitating a proactive and adaptive security strategy.

- **Regulatory Compliance Requirements**

  As a financial entity, the institution is subject to stringent regulatory compliance mandates. Ensuring adherence to data protection laws and financial regulations is crucial to maintaining trust among customers and regulatory bodies.

Comprehensive Posture Management: Integrated Protection

The first step in the design process involves implementing a comprehensive posture management system. This system assesses the security configurations of the institution's entire infrastructure, including on-premises servers, cloud resources, and endpoints.

- **Automated Configuration Assessment**

  Deploy automated tools capable of continuously assessing the security posture across all assets. These tools should evaluate adherence to security best practices, regulatory requirements, and industry standards.

- **Centralized Posture Dashboard**

  Create a centralized dashboard that provides real-time insights into the security posture of the institution. This dashboard should offer a holistic view, enabling security teams to identify and address vulnerabilities promptly.

- **Dynamic Workload Protection**

  Concurrently, the institution implements a dynamic workload protection strategy, recognizing that traditional security measures may not suffice in the face of advanced threats.

- **Behavioral Analysis**

  Utilize advanced behavioral analysis tools to monitor the behavior of workloads and detect anomalous activities. This proactive approach helps identify potential threats, even if they exhibit novel patterns.

- **Zero Trust Architecture**

  Embrace a zero-trust architecture, where every workload, regardless of its location, is treated as potentially compromised. This involves continuous authentication, strict access controls, and micro-segmentation to limit lateral movement in case of a breach.

- **Integration for Synergy**

  The key to an effective strategy lies in the seamless integration of posture management and workload protection.

- **Automated Remediation**

  Connect the posture management system with workload protection measures to enable automated remediation. When vulnerabilities are identified in the posture assessment, the system should trigger actions to mitigate risks and strengthen defenses.

- **Threat Intelligence Integration**

  Integrate threat intelligence feeds into both posture management and workload protection systems. This ensures that security measures are updated in real-time based on the latest information about emerging threats.

- **Unified Security Operations Center (SOC)**

  Establish a unified SOC that brings together the monitoring and response functions for posture management and workload protection. This integration facilitates a coordinated response to security incidents and streamlines communication between teams.

Continuous Monitoring and Adaptation

Recognizing the dynamic nature of cybersecurity, the institution institutes continuous monitoring mechanisms.

- **Regular Security Audits**

  Conduct regular security audits to validate the effectiveness of the integrated strategy. These audits should include simulated attacks and real-time testing of response mechanisms.

- **Adaptive Security Policies**

  Implement adaptive security policies that can evolve based on the changing threat landscape. Machine learning and artificial intelligence can be employed to enhance the system's ability to adapt to new and emerging threats.

Benefits and Outcomes

In the realm of designing integrated posture management and workload protection, the benefits and outcomes are far-reaching. This approach fosters holistic security resilience, assuring regulatory compliance and reducing incident response time. Consequently, organizations gain not only enhanced cybersecurity but also bolstered customer trust through a fortified defense against emerging threats.

- **Holistic Security Resilience**

  The integrated posture management and workload protection strategy creates a holistic security resilience, addressing vulnerabilities at the configuration level and proactively protecting workloads against advanced threats.

- **Regulatory Compliance Assurance**

  The institution achieves and maintains regulatory compliance by continuously monitoring and adapting security measures to align with evolving data protection and financial regulations.

- **Reduced Incident Response Time**

  Automation and integration significantly reduce incident response time. The interconnected systems enable swift remediation, minimizing the impact of security incidents.

- **Enhanced Customer Trust**

  By demonstrating a commitment to robust security practices, the financial institution enhances customer trust. Clients feel assured that their financial data is secure and protected from unauthorized access.

Designing an integrated posture management and workload protection strategy is a strategic imperative for organizations, especially those dealing with sensitive data. The synergy between assessing and fortifying the security posture and proactively protecting dynamic workloads creates a formidable defense against evolving cyber threats. The case of our global financial institution serves as a testament to the effectiveness of such an integrated approach in navigating the complex landscape of cybersecurity with resilience and agility.

Securing Cloud Applications: A Real-time Scenario

Organizations increasingly rely on cloud applications to streamline operations, enhance collaboration, and deliver innovative services. However, the adoption of cloud applications also brings forth security challenges that require careful consideration and robust measures. In this narrative, we explore the imperative of securing cloud applications through a real-time scenario within a dynamic technology company.

Business Scenario: Dynamic Technology Company

Imagine a dynamic technology company at the forefront of developing cutting-edge applications for a global user base. The company utilizes a range of cloud applications, including customer relationship management (CRM), collaboration tools, and software development platforms, to drive innovation and meet the demands of a rapidly evolving market.

Challenges Faced:

- **Data Sensitivity and Compliance**

  The technology company handles sensitive customer data and intellectual property. Adhering to data protection regulations and industry compliance standards is paramount to maintain trust and avoid legal ramifications.

- **Dynamic Workforce Collaboration**

  With a geographically dispersed workforce, the company relies on cloud-based collaboration tools for seamless communication and project coordination. Ensuring secure collaboration becomes crucial to prevent data leaks and unauthorized access.

- **Application Development and Deployment**

  As a technology innovator, the company frequently develops and deploys applications in the cloud. Protecting the entire application lifecycle, from development to deployment, is essential to safeguard against vulnerabilities and cyber threats.

Securing Cloud Applications: Real-time Measures Implemented

- **Identity and Access Management (IAM)**

  The company implements robust IAM protocols to control and monitor access to cloud applications. Multi-factor authentication (MFA) is enforced, ensuring that only authorized individuals can access sensitive data and applications.

  - **Real-time Scenario**

    An engineer attempts to access the cloud development environment from a new location. The IAM system prompts for additional authentication, preventing unauthorized access even with compromised credentials.

- **Data Encryption and Privacy Controls**

  To protect sensitive data during transit and at rest, the company enforces encryption measures. Additionally, privacy controls are implemented to ensure compliance with data protection regulations.

  - **Real-time Scenario**

    A customer service representative accesses customer data through the CRM application. The data is encrypted during transmission, and access controls prevent unauthorized personnel from viewing sensitive customer information.

- **Continuous Monitoring and Threat Detection**

  Real-time monitoring tools are deployed to detect unusual activities or security threats within the cloud environment. Anomaly detection and threat intelligence feeds enhance the company's ability to identify and respond to potential security incidents promptly.

- **Real-time Scenario**

  The monitoring system detects an unusual surge in data access from a specific user account. Automated alerts are triggered, and the security team promptly investigates the incident, preventing a potential data breach.

- **Secure Application Development Practices**

  The company adopts secure coding practices and conducts regular security reviews throughout the application development lifecycle. This proactive approach helps identify and mitigate vulnerabilities before applications are deployed.

  - **Real-time Scenario**

    During a code review, a potential security vulnerability is identified in a new feature. The development team promptly addresses the issue before the application is released, preventing a potential avenue for exploitation.

- **Incident Response and Recovery Planning**

  The technology company establishes an incident response plan outlining the steps to be taken in the event of a security incident. Regular drills and simulations ensure that the response team is well-prepared to address any emerging threats.

  - **Real-time Scenario**

    A cloud application experiences a service disruption due to a distributed denial of service (DDoS) attack. The incident response team follows the established playbook, quickly mitigating the attack and restoring normal service.

- **Employee Training and Awareness**

  Recognizing that human error can contribute to security vulnerabilities, the company invests in ongoing training programs to educate employees about security best practices and the potential risks associated with cloud applications.

  - **Real-time Scenario**

    An employee receives a phishing email attempting to trick them into revealing login credentials. Due to security awareness training, the employee recognizes the phishing attempt, reports it to the IT security team, and avoids a potential security breach.

Benefits and Outcomes

Securing cloud applications in a real-time scenario introduces complex challenges, including the delicate balance of data sensitivity and compliance. Dynamic workforce collaboration further complicates matters, demanding robust security measures. Additionally, navigating the intricacies of application development and deployment in the cloud poses unique hurdles that organizations must address for a comprehensive and effective security strategy.

- **Enhanced Data Security**

  By implementing robust identity and access controls, encryption measures, and continuous monitoring, the technology company ensures the enhanced security of its sensitive data, mitigating the risk of unauthorized access and data breaches.

- **Regulatory Compliance**

  The company's commitment to data privacy controls and secure practices ensures compliance with data protection regulations and industry standards, preventing legal repercussions and fostering trust among customers and stakeholders.

- **Proactive Threat Mitigation**

  Continuous monitoring and threat detection mechanisms enable the company to proactively identify and mitigate security threats, preventing potential disruptions and safeguarding the integrity of its cloud applications.

- **Agile and Secure Development**

  Secure application development practices contribute to the creation of resilient and secure applications, reducing the risk of vulnerabilities and ensuring a smooth deployment process.

- **Responsive Incident Management**

  The established incident response plan and regular training drills empower the company to respond swiftly to security incidents, minimizing the impact and facilitating a quick recovery.

- **Cultivating a Security-aware Culture**

  Ongoing employee training and awareness efforts foster a security-aware culture within the organization, reducing the likelihood of human-related security incidents and creating a collective sense of responsibility for cybersecurity.

In the context of a dynamic technology company relying on cloud applications for innovation and collaboration, the strategic implementation of security measures is imperative. By addressing challenges related to data sensitivity, workforce collaboration, and application development, the company enhances its security posture and ensures the resilience of its cloud applications in the face of evolving cyber threats. This real-time scenario serves as a testament to the proactive measures and integrated strategies needed to secure cloud applications effectively.

Improving Your Security Posture: A Business Scenario

Businesses face constant threats that necessitate a proactive approach to security. Strengthening your security posture is crucial to mitigate risks, protect sensitive data, and ensure business continuity. This narrative explores the imperative of improving security posture through a real-world scenario within a multinational finance corporation.

Business Scenario: Multinational Finance Corporation

Imagine a multinational finance corporation with a global presence, managing a vast array of financial transactions and sensitive customer data. In the face of escalating cyber threats and increasing regulatory scrutiny, the corporation recognizes the urgency of improving its security posture to safeguard its reputation and maintain the trust of its clients.

Challenges Faced:

- **Global Operations and Compliance**

  Operating across various jurisdictions, the finance corporation must navigate complex regulatory landscapes. Compliance with diverse data protection and financial regulations poses a challenge, requiring a robust security posture to meet these varied requirements.

- **Digital Transformation and Cyber Threats**

  The corporation is undergoing a digital transformation to enhance operational efficiency and customer experience. However, the increased reliance on digital technologies exposes it to a broader range of cyber threats, necessitating an adaptive security posture.

- **Third-Party Risk**

  As part of its global operations, the corporation engages with numerous third-party vendors and partners. Managing the associated third-party risk is crucial to prevent potential vulnerabilities that could be exploited by cyber adversaries.

Improving Security Posture: Real-time Measures Implemented

In the pursuit of fortifying organizational resilience, real-time measures are paramount. Improving security posture demands swift and adaptive actions to counter emerging threats. Implementing proactive strategies and cutting-edge technologies ensures a dynamic defense mechanism, enabling organizations to respond effectively to evolving cyber challenges and safeguard their digital assets.

- **Comprehensive Security Assessment**

  The corporation initiates a comprehensive security assessment to evaluate its existing security controls and vulnerabilities. This assessment involves examining network configurations, access controls, and data protection measures.

  - **Real-time Scenario**

    The assessment reveals outdated software versions and misconfigurations in critical systems. The security team prioritizes remediation efforts based on the severity of these findings.

- **Adoption of Zero Trust Architecture**

  Recognizing the limitations of perimeter-based security, the corporation embraces a Zero Trust Architecture. This model assumes that threats can exist both inside and outside the network, requiring strict access controls and continuous authentication.

  - **Real-time Scenario**

    A user attempts to access sensitive financial data from a new device. The Zero Trust model prompts for additional authentication, preventing unauthorized access even with compromised credentials.

- **Continuous Monitoring and Threat Intelligence**

  The corporation implements continuous monitoring tools that provide real-time insights into network activities. Integration with threat intelligence feeds enhances the ability to detect and respond to emerging cyber threats promptly.

  - **Real-time Scenario**

    Anomalies in network traffic patterns are detected, indicating a potential malware infection. The automated system triggers alerts, enabling the security team to isolate the affected systems and initiate remediation.

- **Employee Training and Awareness**

  Recognizing that human error can be a significant security risk, the corporation invests in ongoing employee training programs. These programs educate staff about phishing threats, social engineering tactics, and the importance of adhering to security policies.

  - **Real-time Scenario**

    An employee receives a phishing email attempting to trick them into divulging login credentials. Due to security awareness training, the employee recognizes the phishing attempt, reports it to the IT security team, and avoids a potential security breach.

- **Incident Response Planning**

  The corporation develops and regularly updates an incident response plan outlining the steps to be taken in the event of a security incident. Simulated drills and exercises ensure that the response team is well-prepared to handle real-world scenarios.

  - **Real-time Scenario**

    A cyber attack results in a temporary disruption of services. The incident response team follows the established playbook, swiftly identifies the attack vector, contains the incident, and restores normal operations.

- **Vendor Security Assessment**

  Recognizing the importance of third-party risk management, the corporation conducts thorough security assessments of its vendors and partners. This involves evaluating their security controls, data protection practices, and incident response capabilities.

  - **Real-time Scenario**

    A vendor experiences a security breach that potentially exposes shared data. The corporation, having conducted a prior security assessment, swiftly collaborates with the vendor to contain the breach and reassesses its third-party risk management protocols.

Benefits and Outcomes:

- **Regulatory Compliance Assurance**

  The improved security posture ensures that the corporation adheres to diverse regulatory requirements, minimizing the risk of legal repercussions and maintaining trust with regulatory bodies.

- **Proactive Threat Mitigation**

  Continuous monitoring, threat intelligence integration, and a Zero Trust architecture enable the corporation to proactively identify and mitigate security threats, minimizing the impact and disruption caused by cyber attacks.

- **Human-Centric Security**

  Employee training and awareness programs create a human-centric security culture, reducing the likelihood of security incidents originating from human error and fostering a sense of collective responsibility for cybersecurity.

- **Vendor Risk Mitigation**

  Thorough security assessments of third-party vendors reduce the risk associated with external partnerships, ensuring that the corporation's extended ecosystem maintains robust security measures.

- **Efficient Incident Response**

  The incident response planning and regular drills contribute to an efficient and coordinated response to security incidents, minimizing downtime and restoring normal operations swiftly.

- **Enhanced Customer Trust**

  The proactive measures undertaken to improve security posture contribute to enhanced customer trust. Clients feel reassured that their financial data is protected against a wide spectrum of cyber threats, reinforcing the corporation's reputation.

In the face of evolving cyber threats and regulatory complexities, improving security posture is not merely a defensive measure; it's a strategic imperative for organizations, especially those operating in highly regulated industries like finance. The real-time scenario within the multinational finance corporation demonstrates that a holistic approach encompassing technology, people, and processes is essential to fortify the organization's defenses and navigate the dynamic cybersecurity landscape with resilience and agility.

Protecting Cloud Workloads: A Real-time Scenario

Organizations leverage the scalability and flexibility of cloud services to power their operations. However, the shift to the cloud also introduces new security challenges that demand robust measures to protect cloud workloads. This section explores the imperative of protecting cloud workloads through a real-time scenario within a forward-thinking technology company.

Business Scenario: Innovative Technology Company

Consider an innovative technology company that specializes in developing and delivering cloud-based applications. With a diverse portfolio catering to clients worldwide, the company relies heavily on cloud workloads to provide scalable and efficient services. In the face of growing cybersecurity threats, safeguarding these cloud workloads becomes paramount.

Challenges Faced:

- **Global Reach and Scalability:**

  The technology company's applications serve a global user base, requiring scalable and geographically distributed cloud workloads. Managing the security of these distributed workloads poses a challenge, especially with varying regulatory requirements across regions.

- **Cybersecurity Threat Landscape**

  As a technology innovator, the company is a prime target for cyber threats. The evolving nature of cyberattacks, including ransomware and advanced persistent threats (APTs), necessitates a proactive approach to protect cloud workloads from potential breaches.

- **Data Sensitivity and Compliance**

  Handling sensitive customer data demands compliance with data protection regulations. Ensuring that cloud workloads adhere to these regulations is essential for maintaining trust and avoiding legal repercussions.

Protecting Cloud Workloads: Real-time Measures Implemented

In safeguarding cloud workloads, real-time measures play a pivotal role in ensuring resilience against evolving threats. Implementing cutting-edge security protocols and continuous monitoring is imperative. This proactive approach not only fortifies the digital infrastructure but also bolsters the organization's ability to swiftly respond to emerging risks in the dynamic cloud environment.

- **Identity and Access Management (IAM)**

  The technology company implements robust IAM policies to control and monitor access to cloud workloads. Multi-factor authentication (MFA) is enforced to add an extra layer of security.

  - **Real-time Scenario**

    An employee attempts to access a critical cloud workload from an unrecognized device. IAM triggers MFA, verifying the user's identity and preventing unauthorized access.

- **Data Encryption and Tokenization**

  To protect data during transmission and storage, the company enforces encryption measures. Additionally, sensitive data within the cloud workloads is tokenized to add an extra layer of security.

  - **Real-time Scenario**: A database containing customer information is accessed for routine maintenance. Data within the database is tokenized, ensuring that even if accessed, the actual sensitive information remains secure.

- **Continuous Monitoring and Threat Detection**

  Real-time monitoring tools are deployed to detect abnormal activities or potential security threats within the cloud workloads. Threat detection algorithms and anomaly detection enhance the ability to identify and respond promptly.

  - **Real-time Scenario:** Unusual patterns of data access are detected, indicating a potential unauthorized intrusion. The monitoring system triggers alerts, enabling the security team to investigate and mitigate the threat.

- **Regular Security Audits and Penetration Testing**

  The company conducts regular security audits and penetration testing on its cloud workloads. This proactive approach helps identify vulnerabilities and weaknesses before they can be exploited.

  - **Real-time Scenario:** A scheduled penetration test identifies a misconfigured security group in the cloud workload settings. The configuration is promptly corrected, preventing potential external access.

- **Incident Response Planning**

  The technology company develops an incident response plan outlining the steps to be taken in case of a security incident. Regular simulations and drills ensure that the incident response team is well-prepared.

  - **Real-time Scenario:** An external threat actor launches a DDoS attack on one of the critical cloud workloads. The incident response team follows the established plan, deploying counter measures to mitigate the attack and minimize service disruption.

- **Automated Patch Management**

  Automated patch management systems are employed to ensure that all software and systems within the cloud workloads are up-to-date with the latest security patches.

  - **Real-time Scenario:** A vulnerability is identified in the operating system of a cloud server. The automated patch management system deploys the necessary updates, closing the security gap swiftly.

Benefits and Outcomes:

- **Enhanced Access Control**

  IAM policies and multi-factor authentication ensure that only authorized individuals can access and manage the cloud workloads, reducing the risk of unauthorized access.

- **Data Protection and Compliance**

  Encryption, tokenization, and adherence to regulatory standards safeguard sensitive data within the cloud workloads, ensuring compliance and fostering trust among customers and regulatory bodies.

- **Proactive Threat Mitigation**

  Continuous monitoring, threat detection, and regular security audits enable the company to proactively identify and mitigate potential security threats, minimizing the risk of data breaches.

- **Efficient Incident Response**

  The incident response planning and regular drills contribute to an efficient and coordinated response in case of a security incident, minimizing downtime and service disruption.

- **Vulnerability Management**

  Regular penetration testing and automated patch management contribute to effective vulnerability management, reducing the attack surface and minimizing the risk of exploitation.

- **Customer Trust and Reputation**

  The implemented security measures enhance customer trust by demonstrating a commitment to the security and privacy of their data, ultimately preserving the company's reputation as a reliable technology provider.

In the dynamic landscape of cloud computing, protecting cloud workloads is a foundational element of a comprehensive cybersecurity strategy. The real-time scenario within the innovative technology company illustrates the practical measures taken to safeguard cloud workloads, emphasizing the importance of continuous monitoring, proactive threat mitigation, and adherence to best practices. By implementing these measures, organizations can confidently leverage the benefits of cloud computing while fortifying their defenses against evolving cyber threats.

Defender for Cloud Planning and Operations: A Real-time Scenario

In the realm of cybersecurity, robust planning and seamless operations are crucial for safeguarding cloud environments against evolving threats. Microsoft Defender for Cloud, a comprehensive cloud security solution, plays a pivotal role in enhancing the security posture of organizations. Let us delve into a real-time scenario within a multinational corporation to understand how Defender for Cloud planning and operations contribute to a resilient cloud security strategy.

Business Scenario: Multinational Corporation in the Financial Sector

Imagine a multinational corporation operating in the financial sector, leveraging cloud services to drive innovation and streamline operations. With a vast digital infrastructure storing sensitive financial data, the corporation faces the challenge of securing its cloud environment against sophisticated cyber threats. The corporation adopts Microsoft Defender for Cloud to fortify its security posture in a dynamic threat landscape.

Challenges Faced:

- **Regulatory Compliance**

  The financial corporation operates in a highly regulated industry, subject to stringent data protection and financial regulations. Ensuring compliance with diverse regulatory frameworks is paramount to avoid legal consequences and maintain customer trust.

- **Hybrid Cloud Environment**

  The corporation maintains a hybrid cloud environment, combining on-premises infrastructure with cloud services. Managing security consistently across this hybrid landscape poses challenges, requiring a unified security solution.

- **Advanced Persistent Threats (APTs)**

  The corporation is a prime target for advanced persistent threats seeking to exploit vulnerabilities in the cloud infrastructure. Detecting and mitigating APTs in real-time is imperative to prevent data breaches and financial losses.

Defender for Cloud Planning and Operations: Real-time Measures Implemented

In the realm of cloud planning and operations, the implementation of Defender for Cloud introduces a paradigm shift by incorporating real-time measures. This cutting-edge approach ensures proactive and adaptive strategies, enhancing an organization's ability to respond dynamically to emerging threats and challenges within the cloud environment.

- **Unified Security Dashboard**

  The corporation begins by planning the deployment of Defender for Cloud, establishing a unified security dashboard. This centralized view provides real-time insights into security configurations, threat intelligence, and compliance status across the entire hybrid cloud environment.

  - **Real-time Scenario**

    An unauthorized attempt to access a critical financial database triggers an alert on the unified dashboard. The security team swiftly investigates and blocks the unauthorized access, preventing a potential data breach.

- **Compliance Management**

  Leveraging Defender for Cloud's compliance management features, the corporation conducts regular assessments to ensure adherence to industry-specific regulations. Automated compliance checks and reports simplify the process of maintaining compliance.

  - **Real-time Scenario**

    A regulatory audit requires evidence of data protection measures. Using Defender for Cloud, the corporation generates a comprehensive compliance report, showcasing adherence to regulatory requirements.

- **Threat Detection and Response**

  Defender for Cloud employs advanced threat detection capabilities, including behavioral analytics and machine learning, to identify potential security threats. Automated response mechanisms enable the security team to respond swiftly to emerging threats.

  - **Real-time Scenario**

    Unusual patterns of data exfiltration are detected, indicating a potential APT. Defender for Cloud automatically isolates the affected systems, limiting the impact of the threat while the security team investigates and mitigates.

- **Identity and Access Management (IAM)**

  The corporation enhances IAM through Defender for Cloud, implementing role-based access controls and continuous monitoring. Anomalies in user behavior trigger alerts, enabling proactive identification of compromised credentials.

  - **Real-time Scenario**

    Defender for Cloud alerts the security team to an employee's account displaying atypical access patterns. Investigation reveals a compromised credential, and immediate action is taken to secure the account and prevent further unauthorized access.

- **Secure Configuration Management**

  Continuous monitoring of cloud configurations is essential to prevent misconfigurations that could expose vulnerabilities. Defender for Cloud facilitates secure configuration management, providing recommendations and remediation guidance.

  - **Real-time Scenario**

    A misconfigured cloud storage bucket is identified through Defender for Cloud. The security team promptly adjusts the configuration to restrict public access, preventing potential data exposure.

- **Incident Response Planning**

  The corporation develops and regularly updates an incident response plan using insights from Defender for Cloud. Regular simulations ensure that the incident response team is well-prepared to handle security incidents effectively.

  - **Real-time Scenario**

    A security incident involving a phishing campaign is identified. The incident response team, guided by the established plan, swiftly isolates affected systems, conducts forensics, and implements measures to prevent similar incidents.

Benefits and Outcomes:

- **Efficient Compliance Management**

  Defender for Cloud streamlines compliance management, reducing the time and effort required for audits. The corporation maintains a continuous state of compliance, fostering trust with regulatory bodies.

- **Proactive Threat Mitigation**

  Advanced threat detection and automated response mechanisms enable the corporation to proactively identify and mitigate security threats, minimizing the impact of potential breaches.

- **IAM Strengthening**

  IAM enhancements through Defender for Cloud contribute to strengthened access controls. Anomalies in user behavior are promptly identified, reducing the risk of unauthorized access.

- **Secure Configuration Practices**

  Secure configuration management ensures that cloud resources are configured according to best practices, reducing the risk of misconfigurations and vulnerabilities.

- **Incident Response Readiness**

  Regular incident response planning and simulations, guided by insights from Defender for Cloud, enhance the corporation's readiness to respond effectively to security incidents, minimizing downtime and service disruptions.

- **Enhanced Security Posture**

  Overall, the implementation of Defender for Cloud planning and operations contributes to an enhanced security posture. The corporation can confidently navigate the complexities of the cybersecurity landscape, safeguarding sensitive financial data and maintaining the trust of clients and stakeholders.

In the face of complex regulatory requirements, hybrid cloud environments, and persistent cyber threats, the real-time scenario within the multinational finance corporation underscores the strategic importance of planning and operations with Microsoft Defender for Cloud. By leveraging its features for compliance management, threat detection, IAM, secure configuration, and incident response, organizations can fortify their cloud security posture and effectively protect valuable digital assets in a rapidly evolving threat landscape.

Evaluating Security Posture with Microsoft Defender for Cloud: A Real-time Case Study

Organizations face constant challenges in safeguarding their digital assets against evolving threats. The effective evaluation of security posture is paramount, and Microsoft Defender for Cloud emerges as a comprehensive solution to assess, monitor, and enhance security in cloud environments. Let us explore a real-time case study within a global e-commerce corporation to understand how the organization utilized Microsoft Defender for Cloud to evaluate and strengthen its security posture.

Business Scenario: Global E-commerce Corporation

Imagine a global e-commerce corporation with a vast online presence, processing a high volume of transactions and managing sensitive customer data. The corporation, facing an increasingly sophisticated threat landscape, recognizes the need for a robust cloud security solution to ensure the resilience of its digital infrastructure. In this scenario, the organization turns to Microsoft Defender for Cloud to evaluate and fortify its security posture.

Challenges Faced:

- **Diverse Cloud Environment**

  The e-commerce corporation operates in a multi-cloud environment, utilizing services from various cloud providers to meet its operational needs. Managing security across this diverse landscape introduces complexities, necessitating a unified solution.

- **Customer Data Protection**

  With a large customer base, the corporation handles vast amounts of sensitive data, including personal and financial information. Protecting this data against potential breaches is critical to maintain customer trust and compliance with data protection regulations.

- **Continuous Threat Landscape**

  The corporation faces a relentless threat landscape, including ransomware, phishing attacks, and attempts to exploit vulnerabilities in its cloud infrastructure. Real-time threat detection and response capabilities are essential to thwart emerging threats.

Microsoft Defender for Cloud Implementation: Real-time Measures Unified Security Dashboard

Microsoft Defender for Cloud is deployed to create a unified security dashboard, providing a centralized view of the organization's security posture across various cloud environments. The dashboard consolidates information on security configurations, threat intelligence, and compliance status.

Real-time Scenario

An alert on the dashboard highlights an unusual spike in data access from an employee account. The security team investigates promptly, discovering a compromised credential, and takes immediate action to prevent unauthorized access.

- **Threat Detection and Response**

  Leveraging Defender for Cloud's advanced threat detection capabilities, the organization implements real-time monitoring for suspicious activities. Automated response mechanisms enable swift action to mitigate potential threats.

  - **Real-time Scenario**

    An attempt to inject malicious code into a critical application is detected. Defender for Cloud automatically isolates the affected component, preventing the potential spread of malware and ensuring uninterrupted service.

- **Continuous Compliance Monitoring**

  The corporation utilizes Defender for Cloud to conduct continuous compliance monitoring. Automated checks and reports ensure that cloud configurations align with industry regulations and data protection standards.

  - **Real-time Scenario**

    A regulatory audit is scheduled, requiring evidence of adherence to data protection standards. Using Defender for Cloud, the organization generates a comprehensive compliance report, showcasing compliance with relevant regulations.

- **Identity and Access Management (IAM)**

  Defender for Cloud strengthens IAM by implementing continuous monitoring and access controls. Anomalies in user behavior trigger alerts, enabling proactive identification of compromised credentials or unauthorized access.

  - **Real-time Scenario**

    An employee's account displays unusual access patterns. Defender for Cloud alerts the security team, leading to the discovery of a phishing attempt. The compromised account is secured, preventing potential data exfiltration.

- **Secure Configuration Management**

  The organization employs Defender for Cloud to ensure secure configurations across its cloud resources. The solution provides recommendations and remediation guidance to address vulnerabilities and misconfigurations.

  - **Real-time Scenario**

    A misconfigured storage bucket exposing sensitive customer data is identified. Defender for Cloud guides the security team in adjusting the configuration promptly, preventing potential data exposure.

- **Incident Response Planning**

  Microsoft Defender for Cloud insights contribute to the development of an incident response plan. Regular simulations and drills using real-world scenarios ensure that the incident response team is well-prepared to handle security incidents.

  - **Real-time Scenario**

    A distributed denial of service (DDoS) attack is launched against the e-commerce platform. The incident response team, guided by the established plan and insights from Defender for Cloud, successfully mitigates the attack and maintains service availability.

Benefits and Outcomes:

- **Unified Visibility and Control**

  Microsoft Defender for Cloud provides the e-commerce corporation with unified visibility into its security posture, facilitating centralized control and management of security configurations across diverse cloud environments.

- **Proactive Threat Mitigation**

  Advanced threat detection and automated response mechanisms enable the organization to proactively identify and mitigate security threats, reducing the potential impact of breaches and ensuring uninterrupted operations.

- **Continuous Compliance Assurance**

  Automated compliance monitoring ensures that the organization continuously adheres to data protection regulations and industry standards, reducing the risk of legal consequences and fostering customer trust.

- **IAM Strengthening**

  IAM enhancements through Defender for Cloud contribute to strengthened access controls, enabling the proactive identification and remediation of compromised credentials or unauthorized access.

- **Secure Configuration Practices**

  Secure configuration management ensures that cloud resources are configured securely, reducing the risk of vulnerabilities and misconfigurations that could be exploited by malicious actors.

- **Efficient Incident Response**

  The incident response planning and simulations, guided by insights from Defender for Cloud, enhance the organization's readiness to respond effectively to security incidents, minimizing downtime and service disruptions.

- **Enhanced Customer Trust**

  The proactive security measures implemented with Microsoft Defender for Cloud contribute to enhanced customer trust. Clients feel reassured that their data is protected against a wide array of cyber threats.

The real-time case study within the global e-commerce corporation underscores the strategic importance of Microsoft Defender for Cloud in evaluating and fortifying security posture in a cloud-centric environment. By leveraging the solution's capabilities for threat detection, compliance monitoring, IAM, secure configuration management, and incident response planning, organizations can navigate the complexities of the cybersecurity landscape with resilience and confidence.

In the ever-evolving landscape of cybersecurity, understanding the potential pathways that adversaries might exploit to compromise an organization's assets is paramount. Attack Path Analysis (APA) emerges as a proactive approach to identify and mitigate potential security risks. Let us explore a real-time scenario within a financial institution to comprehend how Attack Path Analysis plays a pivotal role in unraveling cyber threats.

Business Scenario

Financial Institution Security Posture: Imagine a large financial institution managing vast amounts of customer data, financial transactions, and sensitive information. The institution, aware of the evolving nature of cyber threats, recognizes the need for a comprehensive security strategy. In this scenario, Attack Path Analysis becomes a crucial component to evaluate and fortify the organization's security posture.

Challenges Faced:

- **Complex Network Architecture**

  The financial institution operates within a complex network architecture, involving interconnected systems, databases, and communication channels. Managing the security implications of this intricate structure poses a significant challenge.

- **Regulatory Compliance**

  The financial sector is subject to stringent regulatory requirements. Ensuring compliance with data protection laws and industry standards is imperative to avoid legal consequences and maintain trust with clients.

- **Sophisticated Cyber Threats**

  Adversaries targeting financial institutions employ sophisticated tactics, such as advanced malware, social engineering, and targeted attacks. The organization needs to stay ahead of these threats to safeguard its assets and maintain operational resilience.

Attack Path Analysis Implementation: Real-time Measures

Implementing real-time measures for Attack Path Analysis enhances proactive threat mitigation. Let us explore this in detail:

- **Network Mapping and Asset Identification**

  The financial institution begins by mapping its network and identifying critical assets. Attack Path Analysis tools are employed to visualize the interconnected elements of the network, including servers, databases, and communication nodes.

  - **Real-time Scenario**

    An Attack Path Analysis reveals that a server hosting a customer database is indirectly connected to an external vendor's system. This information prompts a closer inspection of the vendor's security measures and access permissions.

- **Vulnerability Assessment**

  Automated vulnerability assessments are conducted to identify potential weaknesses in the network and systems. This involves scanning for outdated software, misconfigurations, and known vulnerabilities that could be exploited by attackers.

  - **Real-time Scenario**

    A vulnerability assessment detects an unpatched software component in a critical server. The IT team promptly schedules a patch update to address the vulnerability and mitigate potential risks.

- **User Permissions and Access Controls**

  Attack Path Analysis focuses on evaluating user permissions and access controls within the organization. This includes assessing who has access to critical systems, data, and the potential pathways a user might take to escalate privileges.

- **Real-time Scenario**

  A routine audit reveals that an employee's access permissions are misconfigured, providing unintended access to sensitive financial reports. The permissions are immediately adjusted to align with the principle of least privilege.

- **Social Engineering and Phishing Analysis**

  Understanding the human factor in security, the institution incorporates social engineering and phishing analysis into the Attack Path Analysis. This involves assessing the susceptibility of employees to phishing attempts and other social engineering tactics.

  - **Real-time Scenario:**

    A simulated phishing campaign reveals that a significant number of employees click on malicious links. This prompts the organization to enhance its cybersecurity awareness training and implement additional email filtering measures.

- **Incident Response Planning**

  Attack Path Analysis informs the development and refinement of the institution's incident response plan. Scenarios identified through APA are incorporated into tabletop exercises, ensuring that the incident response team is well-prepared for potential security incidents.

  - **Real-time Scenario**: A simulated ransomware attack, identified through Attack Path Analysis, allows the incident response team to isolate affected systems, communicate with stakeholders, and initiate the recovery process.

- **Continuous Monitoring and Threat Intelligence**

  Real-time monitoring tools and threat intelligence feeds are integrated into the Attack Path Analysis process. This ensures that the organization stays abreast of emerging threats and can adjust security measures accordingly.

  - **Real-time Scenario**

    Threat intelligence indicates an uptick in attacks targeting financial institutions. The security team, informed by this intelligence, proactively enhances network monitoring and adjusts security policies to counter potential threats.

Benefits and Outcomes:

Embarking on continuous monitoring and threat intelligence initiatives delivers a myriad of benefits and outcomes crucial for maintaining robust cybersecurity. This proactive approach not only bolsters the organization's defenses but also ensures real-time insights into potential threats. The continuous monitoring and incorporation of threat intelligence result in heightened situational awareness, rapid threat detection, and strategic decision-making capabilities.

- **Identification of Critical Pathways**

  Attack Path Analysis identifies critical pathways that adversaries might exploit to reach high-value assets. This allows the financial institution to prioritize security measures and focus resources on mitigating specific risks.

- **Proactive Vulnerability Management**

  The institution adopts a proactive stance toward vulnerability management by regularly assessing and addressing potential weaknesses. This reduces the attack surface and minimizes the risk of exploitation through known vulnerabilities.

- **User-centric Security Measures**

  Understanding the importance of user behavior, Attack Path Analysis facilitates the implementation of user-centric security measures. This includes refining access controls, conducting awareness training, and addressing social engineering risks.

- **Effective Incident Response**

  Incident response planning informed by Attack Path Analysis ensures that the organization is well-prepared to handle security incidents. The institution can respond swiftly and effectively, minimizing the impact of potential breaches.

- **Continuous Adaptation to Threats**

  Integration with threat intelligence enables the financial institution to adapt continuously to emerging threats. This proactive approach ensures that security measures evolve alongside the dynamic nature of cybersecurity threats.

- **Regulatory Compliance Assurance**

  Attack Path Analysis contributes to continuous compliance by identifying potential areas of non-compliance and allowing the institution to address them promptly. This ensures that the organization aligns with data protection laws and industry standards.

The real-time case study within a financial institution illustrates how the proactive identification and mitigation of security risks through Attack Path Analysis contribute to a resilient security posture. By understanding potential attack pathways, organizations can stay ahead of adversaries, fortify their defenses, and ensure the integrity of their critical assets in the face of evolving cyber threat

Posture Evaluation with Microsoft Defender for Cloud Secure Score: A Business Scenario

Microsoft Defender for Cloud Secure Score emerges as a valuable solution, providing a quantitative measure of an organization's security hygiene in cloud environments. Let us explore a business scenario within a global technology enterprise to understand how Secure Score is utilized for posture evaluation and improvement.

Business Scenario: Global Technology Enterprise

Imagine a global technology enterprise that leverages cloud services to drive innovation and deliver cutting-edge solutions to clients worldwide. With a vast digital infrastructure, the organization recognizes the critical importance of securing its cloud environment against a myriad of cyber threats. In this scenario, Microsoft Defender for Cloud Secure Score becomes a central element in the organization's efforts to evaluate and enhance its security posture.

Challenges Faced:

Embarking on the journey of posture evaluation with Microsoft Defender for Cloud Secure Score introduces a set of distinctive challenges. This business scenario entails complexities associated with leveraging this tool effectively, understanding its nuanced recommendations, and aligning them with organizational objectives. Navigating these challenges becomes pivotal for optimizing security measures.

- **Diverse Cloud Environment**

  The technology enterprise operates in a multi-cloud environment, utilizing services from various providers to meet its diverse operational needs. Managing security consistently across this intricate landscape poses challenges, demanding a unified approach.

- **Regulatory Compliance**

  As a global entity, the organization is subject to diverse data protection regulations and industry standards. Ensuring compliance across different regions while maintaining operational efficiency is a complex yet essential task.

- **Emerging Cyber Threats**

  The technology sector is a prime target for cyber adversaries aiming to exploit vulnerabilities in cloud infrastructure. Staying ahead of evolving threats and ensuring the resilience of digital assets is imperative for the organization's reputation and client trust.

Posture Evaluation with Microsoft Defender for Cloud Secure Score: Real-time Measures

Posture Evaluation with Microsoft Defender for Cloud Secure Score provides an invaluable real-time measure of an organization's security resilience. Leveraging this tool, businesses can continuously assess and enhance their security posture, allowing for proactive identification and remediation of vulnerabilities, thereby bolstering their overall cybersecurity defenses.

- **Secure Score Assessment**

  The technology enterprise begins by leveraging Microsoft Defender for Cloud Secure Score to conduct a comprehensive assessment of its security posture. The Secure Score dashboard provides a numerical representation of the organization's current security state based on implemented security controls and best practices.

- **Real-time Scenario:** The initial Secure Score reveals that the organization has implemented only a subset of the recommended security controls. Areas such as identity and access management and data protection are identified for improvement.

- **Identity and Access Management (IAM) Enhancement**

  Recognizing the critical role of IAM in securing cloud environments, the organization focuses on improving its Secure Score in this area. Steps include enforcing multi-factor authentication (MFA), reviewing user permissions, and enhancing access controls.

  - **Real-time Scenario:** The implementation of MFA across critical systems and the adjustment of user permissions result in a notable increase in the Secure Score. The organization is now better protected against unauthorized access attempts.

- **Data Encryption and Protection Measures**

  To bolster its Secure Score, the enterprise prioritizes data protection measures. This includes the implementation of encryption for data in transit and at rest, as well as the classification of sensitive information to control access effectively.

  - **Real-time Scenario:** Encryption protocols are implemented for communication channels, and sensitive data is classified according to its level of confidentiality. These measures contribute to an improved Secure Score in the data protection category.

- **Continuous Monitoring and Threat Detection**

  The organization integrates continuous monitoring tools and advanced threat detection features to enhance its ability to respond to emerging cyber threats. This proactive approach aligns with the organization's goal of improving its Secure Score by promptly addressing potential security incidents.

  - **Real-time Scenario:** An automated threat detection system identifies suspicious activity indicative of a potential malware infection. The incident response team, alerted by the monitoring tools, swiftly mitigates the threat, preventing further compromise and boosting the Secure Score.

- **Regular Security Audits and Policy Reviews**

  Microsoft Defender for Cloud Secure Score encourages the enterprise to conduct regular security audits and reviews of its security policies. This ensures that security measures remain aligned with evolving threats and industry best practices.

  - **Real-time Scenario:** A scheduled security audit reveals a misconfiguration in a cloud service. The configuration is promptly corrected, and the security policies are updated, contributing to an increased Secure Score.

- **Incident Response Simulation**

  In an effort to enhance its incident response capabilities, the organization incorporates simulated drills based on real-world scenarios into its security strategy. The insights gained from these simulations contribute to refining the incident response plan.

  - **Real-time Scenario:** A simulated ransomware attack allows the incident response team to practice containment, eradication, and recovery processes. The lessons learned from the simulation lead to adjustments in the incident response plan and further improvements in the Secure Score.

Benefits and Outcomes:

- **Quantifiable Security Measurement**

  Microsoft Defender for Cloud Secure Score provides the organization with a quantifiable measurement of its security posture. This numeric representation facilitates clear communication about the state of security to stakeholders, including executives and regulatory bodies.

- **Prioritization of Security Controls**

  Secure Score assists the enterprise in identifying and prioritizing security controls that require attention. This enables a strategic allocation of resources to areas that have the most significant impact on overall security posture.

- **Continuous Improvement**

  The iterative nature of Secure Score allows the organization to continuously improve its security posture. Regular assessments, adjustments, and enhancements contribute to an ongoing cycle of security maturity.

- **Alignment with Best Practices**

  The organization aligns its security measures with industry best practices, leveraging the recommendations provided by Microsoft Defender for Cloud. This alignment not only improves the Secure Score but also ensures adherence to recognized standards.

- **Operational Efficiency and Compliance**

  Enhancements in IAM, data protection, and incident response contribute to operational efficiency. Simultaneously, the organization ensures compliance with diverse regulatory requirements, reducing the risk of legal consequences.

- **Proactive Threat Mitigation**

  The integration of continuous monitoring and threat detection measures enables the enterprise to proactively identify and mitigate potential threats. This proactive stance minimizes the impact of security incidents and contributes to an elevated security posture, bolstering overall resilience against evolving cyber threats.

- **Secure Score**

  In the dynamic landscape of cloud security, Microsoft Defender for Cloud Secure Score serves as a valuable tool for organizations seeking to evaluate and enhance their security posture. The real-time case study within the global technology enterprise demonstrates how Secure Score facilitates a systematic approach to security improvement, providing a numeric representation of security maturity and guiding organizations toward a resilient and proactive cybersecurity stance. Through continuous assessment, adjustment, and alignment with best practices, organizations can leverage Secure Score to navigate the complexities of cloud security and stay ahead of evolving cyber threats.

Designing Cloud Workload Protection with Microsoft Defender for Cloud: A Business Scenario

Microsoft Defender for Cloud emerges as a comprehensive solution for designing robust cloud workload protection strategies. Let us delve into a business scenario within a forward-thinking healthcare organization to understand how the design of cloud workload protection using Microsoft Defender for Cloud is crucial in safeguarding critical data and ensuring compliance.

Business Scenario: Innovative Healthcare Organization

Imagine an innovative healthcare organization leveraging cloud services to streamline patient care, manage electronic health records (EHRs), and facilitate collaborative research. The organization recognizes the immense value of cloud computing in enhancing operational efficiency but is equally mindful of the unique security challenges in the healthcare sector. In this scenario, Microsoft Defender for Cloud plays a pivotal role in designing a robust cloud workload protection strategy.

Challenges Faced:

- **Health Data Sensitivity**

  The healthcare organization deals with highly sensitive patient data, including medical records and personally identifiable information (PII). Protecting this data is paramount to maintain patient trust and comply with healthcare data protection regulations.

- **Multi-Cloud Complexity**

  The organization operates in a multi-cloud environment to ensure flexibility and scalability. Managing security consistently across different cloud providers introduces complexities, requiring a unified approach to cloud workload protection.

- **Continuous Threat Landscape**

  Healthcare entities are prime targets for cyber threats due to the value of health data. The organization faces a continuous threat landscape, including ransomware attacks, data breaches, and the potential for unauthorized access to critical systems.

Designing Cloud Workload Protection with Microsoft Defender for Cloud: Real-time Measures

Designing Cloud Workload Protection with Microsoft Defender for Cloud involves strategic planning for robust real-time security measures. The integration of a Unified Security Dashboard serves as a pivotal component, offering comprehensive visibility and control. This proactive approach ensures a dynamic defense system against emerging threats, enhancing overall cloud workload protection.

- **Unified Security Dashboard**

  The healthcare organization starts by designing a unified security dashboard using Microsoft Defender for Cloud. This centralized view provides real-time insights into the security posture of cloud workloads, including virtual machines, databases, and storage.

  - **Real-time Scenario:**

    An alert on the dashboard indicates suspicious activity in the EHR database. Microsoft Defender for Cloud identifies the potential threat, allowing the security team to investigate and mitigate the risk promptly.

- **Identity and Access Management (IAM)**

  Recognizing the critical role of IAM in securing cloud workloads, the organization designs policies to enforce the principle of least privilege. Multi-factor authentication (MFA) is implemented to enhance user authentication.

  - **Real-time Scenario**

    An attempt to access patient records with compromised credentials triggers MFA, preventing unauthorized access. The organization strengthens IAM controls based on insights from Microsoft Defender for Cloud.

- **Data Encryption and Tokenization**

  To protect sensitive health data, the organization designs encryption measures for data in transit and at rest. Additionally, Microsoft Defender for Cloud aids in the implementation of tokenization to enhance data protection within cloud workloads.

  - **Real-time Scenario**

    A potential data breach is thwarted as encrypted patient data remains secure during a network intrusion. Tokenization ensures that even if accessed, the actual patient information remains protected.

- **Continuous Monitoring and Threat Detection**

  Real-time monitoring and threat detection mechanisms are integrated into the cloud workload protection strategy. Microsoft Defender for Cloud employs machine learning algorithms to identify abnormal activities and potential security threats.

  - **Real-time Scenario**

    Unusual patterns of access are detected in a research project's cloud workload. Microsoft Defender for Cloud triggers alerts, enabling the security team to investigate and prevent a possible data exfiltration attempt.

- **Secure Configuration Management**

  The organization designs secure configuration management practices using Microsoft Defender for Cloud recommendations. Regular assessments ensure that cloud workloads adhere to security best practices and are resilient to misconfigurations.

  - **Real-time Scenario**

    A misconfigured storage bucket is identified through Defender for Cloud. The security team promptly adjusts the configuration to restrict public access, preventing potential exposure of sensitive research data.

- **Incident Response Planning**

  A robust incident response plan is designed based on insights from Microsoft Defender for Cloud. Simulations and tabletop exercises ensure that the organization is well-prepared to respond effectively to security incidents.

  - **Real-time Scenario:** A ransomware attack is simulated, allowing the incident response team to practice isolating affected systems and initiating the recovery process. The lessons learned contribute to refining the incident response plan.

Benefits and Outcomes:

- **Holistic Cloud Workload Protection**

  Microsoft Defender for Cloud facilitates a holistic approach to cloud workload protection. The organization can design comprehensive security measures that encompass identity management, data protection, configuration management, and threat detection.

- **Real-time Threat Mitigation**

  The integration of continuous monitoring and threat detection enables real-time identification and mitigation of potential security threats. This proactive approach minimizes the impact of incidents and ensures the integrity of health data.

- **Improved Identity Security**

  IAM enhancements, including MFA implementation, contribute to improved identity security. Unauthorized access attempts are thwarted, and the organization maintains granular control over user permissions within cloud workloads.

- **Data Protection and Compliance**

  Encryption measures and tokenization contribute to robust data protection practices. The organization can demonstrate compliance with healthcare data protection regulations, fostering trust among patients and regulatory bodies.

- **Efficient Incident Response**

  The incident response plan, informed by Microsoft Defender for Cloud insights, ensures efficient and coordinated responses to security incidents. Simulations allow the organization to practice and refine its incident response procedures.

- **Secure Configuration Practices**

  Secure configuration management practices reduce the risk of misconfigurations within cloud workloads. The organization aligns with security best practices, minimizing vulnerabilities that could be exploited by malicious actors.

- **Continuous Security Improvement**

  Microsoft Defender for Cloud provides a continuous feedback loop for security improvement. The organization can regularly assess its cloud workload protection measures, adjust security controls, and adapt to emerging threats.

In the context of an innovative healthcare organization, designing cloud workload protection with Microsoft Defender for Cloud proves instrumental in addressing the unique challenges posed by sensitive health data and a multi-cloud environment. The real-time scenario illustrates the practical measures taken to safeguard cloud workloads, emphasizing the importance of a comprehensive and proactive approach to security. By leveraging the capabilities of Microsoft Defender for Cloud, organizations in various sectors can confidently embrace the benefits of cloud computing while fortifying their defenses against evolving cyber threats.

Database Workload Protections: Safeguarding Critical Data in Real-Time Scenarios

Database workload protections are essential to fortify against evolving threats and ensure the integrity and confidentiality of stored data. Let us explore a real-time scenario within a financial institution to understand the significance of robust database workload protections.

Business Scenario: Financial Institution Database Security

Imagine a large financial institution managing vast amounts of customer information, transaction records, and sensitive financial data. The institution's databases are a treasure trove for cybercriminals seeking to exploit vulnerabilities. In this scenario, implementing database workload protections becomes critical to maintaining trust, ensuring regulatory compliance, and safeguarding the institution's reputation.

Challenges Faced:

- **Regulatory Compliance**

  The financial institution operates in a highly regulated environment, subject to stringent data protection laws and financial industry regulations. Compliance with these standards is not just a requirement but a fundamental aspect of maintaining the institution's credibility.

- **Persistent Cyber Threats**

  Financial institutions are prime targets for cyber threats, including ransomware attacks, data breaches, and attempts to compromise financial transactions. The institution faces a constant barrage of sophisticated attacks seeking to exploit vulnerabilities in its databases.

- **Operational Resilience**

  The databases are the backbone of the institution's operations. Any compromise could lead to service disruptions, financial losses, and damage to the institution's reputation. Ensuring the operational resilience of the databases is a top priority.

Database Workload Protections: Real-Time Measures

- **Advanced Threat Detection**

  Implementing advanced threat detection mechanisms within the database infrastructure is crucial. Real-time monitoring tools, such as intrusion detection systems and behavior analytics, are employed to identify unusual patterns indicative of potential threats.

  - **Real-Time Scenario:** An anomaly in database access patterns is detected, suggesting a potential unauthorized attempt to exfiltrate sensitive financial data. The advanced threat detection system triggers an alert for immediate investigation.

- **Encryption and Tokenization**

  To protect data at rest and in transit, the financial institution employs encryption and tokenization techniques. Encryption ensures that even if unauthorized access occurs, the data remains unreadable. Tokenization replaces sensitive data with non-sensitive equivalents.

- **Real-Time Scenario:** A security audit reveals an attempt to access encrypted financial records. The encryption measures successfully thwart the attempt, maintaining the confidentiality of the data and preventing a potential data breach.

- **Access Controls and Least Privilege Principle**

  Implementing strict access controls based on the principle of least privilege is vital for database security. Regularly reviewing and adjusting user permissions ensures that only authorized individuals have access to specific data and functionalities.

  - **Real-Time Scenario:** An employee's access privileges are inadvertently escalated, providing unintended access to critical financial reports. The institution, alerted by the access control system, promptly adjusts permissions to align with the least privilege principle.

- **Continuous Monitoring of Configuration Settings**

  Regularly monitoring and auditing database configuration settings is essential to identify and rectify any misconfigurations that could expose vulnerabilities. Automated tools provide insights into the adherence of configurations to security best practices.

  - **Real-Time Scenario:** An analysis of database configurations reveals a misconfigured setting that could potentially expose transaction logs. The security team promptly adjusts the configuration to mitigate the risk and enhance database workload protections.

- **Database Activity Auditing**

  Enabling database activity auditing allows the institution to track and review activities within the database environment. This includes monitoring changes to data, access attempts, and other critical events, providing an audit trail for forensic analysis.

  - **Real-Time Scenario:** Unusual activity in a database triggers an audit alert. Upon investigation, it is revealed that an insider was attempting to manipulate financial records. The institution takes immediate action to prevent fraudulent activities.

- **Incident Response Planning**

  A well-defined incident response plan specific to database security incidents is essential. Regularly conducting simulated drills based on real-world scenarios ensures that the response team is well-prepared to mitigate and contain security incidents promptly.

  - **Real-Time Scenario:** A simulated ransomware attack on the database is conducted. The incident response team, guided by the established plan, effectively isolates the affected systems, analyzes the extent of the attack, and initiates recovery procedures.

Benefits and Outcomes:

- **Proactive Threat Mitigation**

  Advanced threat detection mechanisms enable the financial institution to proactively identify and mitigate potential threats in real-time. This proactive stance minimizes the impact of security incidents and safeguards sensitive financial data.

- **Data Confidentiality Assurance**

  Encryption and tokenization measures ensure the confidentiality of financial data. Even in the event of unauthorized access, the data remains protected, mitigating the risk of data breaches and ensuring compliance with data protection regulations.

- **Effective Access Controls**

  Strict access controls based on the least privilege principle enhance the security posture of the institution. Unauthorized access attempts are swiftly identified and addressed, reducing the risk of data misuse or manipulation.

- **Configuration Management**

  Continuous monitoring of configuration settings and prompt adjustments to misconfigurations contribute to a secure database environment. This proactive approach minimizes the attack surface and strengthens database workload protections.

- **Forensic Analysis and Accountability**

  Database activity auditing provides an audit trail for forensic analysis. In the event of a security incident, the institution can conduct a thorough investigation, identify the root cause, and hold individuals accountable for malicious activities.

- **Operational Resilience**

  The implementation of database workload protections ensures the operational resilience of the institution. In the face of cyber threats, the databases remain secure, minimizing the risk of service disruptions and financial losses.

- **Regulatory Compliance Adherence**

  By incorporating robust security measures, the financial institution demonstrates adherence to regulatory requirements. This not only ensures legal compliance but also fosters trust with regulatory bodies and stakeholders.

In the dynamic landscape of cybersecurity, database workload protections are indispensable for organizations, especially those dealing with sensitive information such as financial data. The real-time scenario within a financial institution underscores the importance of proactive measures, advanced threat detection, encryption, access controls, and incident response planning in securing databases. By incorporating these strategies, organizations can fortify their database environments, mitigate potential risks, and ensure the confidentiality and integrity of critical data in the face of persistent cyber threats.

Integrating Hybrid and Multicloud Environments with Azure Arc: A Business Scenario

Microsoft Azure Arc emerges as a transformative solution, allowing businesses to seamlessly extend Azure services and management across hybrid and multicloud environments. Let us explore a business scenario within a global manufacturing enterprise to understand how Azure Arc facilitates the integration of diverse environments for enhanced operational efficiency and agility.

Business Scenario: Global Manufacturing Enterprise

Imagine a global manufacturing enterprise with a diverse set of requirements, ranging from managing on-premises data centers for critical production systems to utilizing multiple cloud providers for various applications. The organization faces challenges related to consistency in operations, compliance, and efficient resource management across this hybrid and multicloud landscape. In this scenario, Azure Arc becomes instrumental in unifying and simplifying the management of resources across these diverse environments.

Challenges Faced:

- **Diverse Infrastructure**

  The manufacturing enterprise operates a mix of on-premises servers, cloud resources from Azure, AWS, and Google Cloud, and edge devices at production facilities. Managing this diverse infrastructure introduces complexities in terms of consistency and centralized control.

- **Operational Consistency**

  Ensuring operational consistency across environments is crucial for maintaining production efficiency. The organization needs a solution that provides a unified approach to manage and govern resources, irrespective of their location or cloud provider.

- **Compliance and Governance**

  Compliance with industry regulations and internal governance policies is a top priority. The organization must consistently apply policies, monitor configurations, and ensure security controls across its entire infrastructure, including edge locations.

Integrating with Azure Arc: Real-Time Measures

- **Unified Management Dashboard**

Azure Arc is deployed to create a unified management dashboard, providing a single pane of glass for overseeing resources across on-premises data centers, Azure, and other cloud providers. This centralized view allows IT administrators to gain insights into the state of all connected resources.

  - **Real-Time Scenario:** An alert on the dashboard highlights a potential security vulnerability in an on-premises server. Azure Arc provides visibility, and the security team can remediate the issue centrally, ensuring a consistent security posture.

- **Policy Enforcement and Compliance**

  Azure Policy is utilized to enforce consistent policies across the hybrid and multicloud environment. Policies related to security, compliance, and resource configurations are defined centrally and applied uniformly, ensuring adherence to regulatory requirements.

  - **Real-Time Scenario:** An audit reveals a non-compliant configuration in an AWS instance. Azure Arc, with its policy enforcement capabilities, triggers corrective actions to bring the AWS resource in line with the organization's compliance standards.

- **Application Management and Deployment**

  Azure Arc enables the organization to extend Azure services to on-premises and multicloud environments. This includes deploying and managing applications consistently across the entire landscape, leveraging Azure Kubernetes Service (AKS) for containerized workloads.

  - **Real-Time Scenario:** A new version of a critical production application needs to be deployed both on Azure and an on-premises server. Azure Arc facilitates a seamless deployment process, ensuring the application behaves consistently in both environments.

- **Infrastructure as Code (IaC)**

  Infrastructure as Code principles are embraced, using Azure Resource Manager (ARM) templates. This allows the organization to define and deploy infrastructure resources across hybrid and multicloud environments in a declarative manner.

  - **Real-Time Scenario:** The manufacturing enterprise needs to scale up its compute resources during a peak production period. With Azure Arc and IaC, the IT team deploys additional virtual machines on-premises and in the cloud using a standardized template.

- **Edge Computing Integration**

  Azure Arc extends its capabilities to edge locations, allowing the organization to manage and deploy applications on edge devices seamlessly. This is particularly crucial for scenarios where real-time processing is required at production facilities.

  - **Real-Time Scenario:** Edge devices at manufacturing plants generate large volumes of sensor data. Azure Arc enables the deployment of edge applications for real-time analytics, improving operational efficiency and reducing latency.

- **Hybrid Networking and Connectivity**

  Azure Arc provides tools for configuring hybrid networking, ensuring secure and seamless connectivity between on-premises, cloud, and edge environments. This includes the ability to define network policies and manage virtual networks consistently.

  - **Real-Time Scenario:** A new production facility is established in a remote location. Azure Arc facilitates the extension of the organization's virtual network to the new site, enabling secure communication and resource access.

Benefits and Outcomes:

- **Operational Efficiency**

  Azure Arc enables the global manufacturing enterprise to achieve operational consistency by providing a unified platform for managing resources across diverse environments. This consistency translates to streamlined operations, reduced complexity, and improved efficiency.

- **Compliance Assurance**

  Centralized policy enforcement through Azure Arc ensures that the organization adheres to regulatory requirements and internal governance policies consistently. This reduces the risk of compliance violations and potential legal consequences.

- **Application Agility**

  With Azure Arc, the organization gains the agility to deploy and manage applications seamlessly across on-premises, Azure, and other cloud providers. This flexibility allows for rapid application development and deployment cycles

- **Infrastructure Flexibility**

  Leveraging Infrastructure as Code (IaC) principles, the manufacturing enterprise can adapt its infrastructure to changing needs. Azure Arc's support for IaC enables the organization to scale resources, deploy new services, and maintain infrastructure consistency.

- **Edge Computing Advancements**

  Azure Arc extends the organization's capabilities to the edge, facilitating the deployment of applications for real-time processing at manufacturing plants. This empowers the enterprise to harness the benefits of edge computing for improved operational insights.

- **Unified Networking and Connectivity**

  The organization benefits from Azure Arc's capabilities for configuring hybrid networking. This ensures secure and consistent connectivity, allowing seamless communication between on-premises data centers, cloud resources, and edge locations.

- **Cost Optimization**

  By unifying management and leveraging Azure Arc's capabilities, the enterprise can optimize costs through efficient resource utilization, streamlined operations, and the ability to scale resources based on demand.

In the complex and dynamic landscape of hybrid and multicloud environments, Azure Arc serves as a powerful enabler for organizations seeking to achieve operational consistency, compliance, and agility. The real-time scenario within a global manufacturing enterprise highlights how Azure Arc seamlessly integrates diverse infrastructure, providing a unified platform for management and deployment.

Designing a Solution for External Attack Surface Management: Safeguarding Business Assets in Real-Time

Designing a robust solution for external attack surface management is imperative in identifying and securing potential points of vulnerability. Let us explore a real-time business scenario within a global financial institution to understand the significance of such a solution and how it can be effectively implemented.

Business Scenario: Global Financial Institution

Imagine a large global financial institution with a vast digital infrastructure that includes online banking services, customer portals, and interconnected systems for financial transactions. The institution is acutely aware of the escalating threats in the digital realm, ranging from sophisticated cyber attacks to potential exploits of external-facing assets. In this scenario, designing a solution for external attack surface management becomes paramount to safeguarding customer data, maintaining trust, and upholding the integrity of financial operations.

Challenges Faced:

- **Dynamic External Landscape**

  The financial institution operates in a dynamic digital environment where external assets, such as web applications, APIs, and public-facing services, are constantly evolving. Managing this dynamic landscape poses challenges in identifying and securing potential attack vectors.

- **Regulatory Compliance**

  As a financial entity, the organization is subject to stringent regulatory requirements regarding the security and privacy of customer information. Compliance mandates necessitate a comprehensive solution that not only identifies vulnerabilities but also ensures adherence to industry regulations.

- **Sophisticated Cyber Threats**

  The financial sector is a prime target for sophisticated cyber threats, including phishing attacks, web application exploits, and distributed denial of service (DDoS) attacks. The institution faces the constant challenge of staying ahead of evolving threat vectors.

Designing the Solution for External Attack Surface Management: Real-Time Measures

- **Continuous Discovery and Asset Inventory**

  Implementing a solution that provides continuous discovery of external-facing assets is crucial. Automated tools are employed to maintain an up-to-date asset inventory, including domains, subdomains, and publicly accessible services.

- **Real-Time Scenario:** A new subdomain is discovered through continuous monitoring. The solution updates the asset inventory, ensuring that security measures are extended to cover the newly identified external surface.

- **Vulnerability Assessment and Prioritization**

  Conducting regular vulnerability assessments on external assets helps identify potential weaknesses. The solution incorporates prioritization mechanisms based on the criticality of assets and the severity of vulnerabilities, allowing the organization to address high-risk areas promptly.

  - **Real-Time Scenario:** A vulnerability scan reveals a critical flaw in the online banking portal. The solution flags this as a high-priority issue, prompting immediate remediation efforts to secure the sensitive financial platform.

- **Threat Intelligence Integration**

  Integrating threat intelligence feeds enhances the solution's capability to identify emerging threats and potential attack patterns. This real-time intelligence allows the organization to proactively adjust security measures based on the latest threat landscape.

  - **Real-Time Scenario:** Threat intelligence indicates an increase in DDoS attacks targeting financial institutions. The solution dynamically adjusts firewall configurations to strengthen defenses against potential volumetric attacks.

- **Web Application Firewall (WAF) Implementation**

  Deploying a WAF is essential to protect web applications from common exploits and vulnerabilities. The solution includes the configuration of a WAF with rule sets tailored to the financial institution's applications, providing an additional layer of defense.

  - **Real-Time Scenario**: A WAF alert triggers as it detects a SQL injection attempt on the customer portal. The solution automatically blocks the malicious traffic, preventing a potential compromise of customer data.

- **Incident Response Planning**

  A well-defined incident response plan specific to external attack surface incidents is essential. Simulated exercises and tabletop drills are conducted regularly to ensure that the incident response team is prepared to address security incidents promptly.

  - **Real-Time Scenario:** A simulated phishing campaign results in an influx of suspicious emails. The incident response team, guided by the established plan, swiftly identifies and isolates the threat, preventing a potential compromise of employee credentials.

- **Compliance Monitoring and Reporting**

  The solution includes robust mechanisms for monitoring and reporting compliance with industry regulations. Regular audits are conducted to ensure that security measures align with regulatory requirements, and reports are generated for stakeholders and regulatory bodies.

  - **Real-Time Scenario:** An audit reveals a configuration deviation that could lead to non-compliance. The solution generates a report, and corrective actions are taken immediately to address the deviation and maintain regulatory adherence.

- **User Awareness and Training**

  Recognizing the human factor in security, the solution incorporates user awareness and training programs. Employees are educated on recognizing phishing attempts, secure browsing practices, and the importance of reporting suspicious activities.

  - **Real-Time Scenario:** An employee reports a suspicious email that appears to be a phishing attempt. The solution acknowledges the report, and the security team investigates, preventing a potential breach through user vigilance.

Benefits and Outcomes:

- **Proactive Vulnerability Management**

  Continuous discovery and vulnerability assessments enable proactive identification and management of potential weaknesses. The organization can prioritize and remediate vulnerabilities promptly, reducing the attack surface.

- **Dynamic Adaptation to Threats**

  Integration with threat intelligence feeds allows the organization to dynamically adapt to emerging threats. The solution adjusts security measures in real-time, ensuring a proactive defense against evolving attack vectors.

- **Incident Response Readiness**

  Regular incident response drills and planning ensure that the organization is well-prepared to address security incidents. This readiness minimizes response times and reduces the impact of potential external attacks.

- **Compliance Assurance**

  Compliance monitoring and reporting mechanisms provide assurance that security measures align with industry regulations. The organization can demonstrate a commitment to compliance, fostering trust with regulatory bodies and stakeholders.

- **User-Centric Security Culture**

  User awareness and training programs contribute to a security-conscious culture within the organization. Employees become a frontline defense against phishing and social engineering attempts, enhancing overall security posture.

- **Reduced Risk of Data Breaches**

  By implementing a comprehensive solution for external attack surface management, the financial institution significantly reduces the risk of data breaches and unauthorized access to sensitive financial information.

The real-time scenario within a global financial institution emphasizes the importance of proactive measures, continuous monitoring, and dynamic adaptation to emerging threats. By implementing a robust solution, organizations can fortify their external attack surface, mitigate risks effectively, and maintain the trust and confidence of customers and stakeholders in an ever-changing cybersecurity landscape.

Conclusion

A robust hybrid and multi-cloud security framework is imperative in today's dynamic digital landscape. By combining the strengths of various cloud environments, organizations can enhance their security posture, ensuring data integrity, confidentiality, and availability. Implementing comprehensive measures is essential to mitigate evolving cyber threats and safeguard sensitive information. In the next chapter, we will discuss secure endpoint solution design.

Multiple Choice Questions

1. What is a primary benefit of implementing a hybrid and multi-cloud security framework?

   a. Increased network latency.

   b. Enhanced scalability and flexibility.

   c. Limited data accessibility.

   d. Reduced security protocols.

2. In a hybrid and multi-cloud environment, what does the term "hybrid" refer to?

   a. Exclusively on-premises infrastructure.

   b. A combination of on-premises and cloud resources.

   c. Sole reliance on public cloud services.
   d. Strictly private cloud architecture.
3. How does a multi-cloud security framework contribute to resilience?
   a. By concentrating all resources in a single cloud provider.
   b. By reducing the complexity of security protocols.
   c. By distributing workloads across multiple cloud providers.
   d. By eliminating the need for encryption.
4. What is a key consideration in securing data in a hybrid and multi-cloud environment?
   a. Ignoring encryption practices.
   b. Centralizing all data storage.
   c. Implementing robust encryption and access controls.
   d. Allowing unrestricted data access.
5. Why is visibility crucial in managing security in a hybrid and multi-cloud framework?
   a. To obscure potential security threats.
   b. To streamline security protocols.
   c. To monitor and analyze activities across diverse cloud environments.
   d. To limit user access to cloud resources.

Answers

1. b
2. b
3. c
4. c
5. c

Chapter 14
Secure Endpoint Solution Design

Introduction

Crafting a secure endpoint solution is imperative to safeguarding organizational assets. This chapter delves into the intricate process of designing robust endpoint security measures, ensuring protection against diverse cyber threats. From endpoint detection and response (EDR) to antivirus software integration, this exploration navigates the strategies and technologies essential for fortifying endpoints and mitigating the risks posed by malicious actors in the ever-evolving cybersecurity landscape.

Structure

In this chapter, we will cover the following topics:

- Introduction to Endpoint Security
- Strengthening Cybersecurity Defenses: Leveraging Endpoint Detection and Response (EDR) for Business Resilience
- Safeguarding Business Assets: The Imperative of Deploying Modern Anti-Malware Software
- Cybersecurity Vigilance: The Crucial Role of Regular Anti-Malware Updates in Business Defense
- Fortifying the Digital Fortress: Specifying Server Security Requirements in a Real-World Context
- Navigating Cyber Waters: Strengthening Network Security in a Real-World Setting
- Orchestrating Cyber Vigilance: The Crucial Role of Logging and Monitoring in a Corporate Landscape
- Gatekeepers of Security: Navigating Identity and Access Control in a Real-World Context

- Safeguarding Confidentiality: A Dive into Data Protection in a Real-World Scenario
- Strengthening Cyber Resilience: Navigating Vulnerability Management in a Real-World Setting
- Orchestrating Security Harmony: Inventory and Asset Management in a Real-World Scenario
- Fortifying Digital Defenses: Secure Configuration in a Real-World Scenario
- Sentinel Protectors: Malware Defense Strategies in a Real-World Scenario
- Harmonizing Security: Strategic Specification of Requirements for Mobile Devices and Clients in a Global Corporation
- Seamless Integration: Leveraging Existing and New Devices in a Business Environment
- Safeguarding Sensitive Data: A Case Study on Least-Privileged Access in a Financial Institution

Introduction to Endpoint Security

Endpoint security is a critical component of comprehensive cybersecurity strategies, focusing on protecting individual devices, or endpoints, within a network. These endpoints include laptops, desktops, smartphones, and other devices connected to the network. The primary goal of endpoint security is to safeguard these entry points from cyber threats and unauthorized access.

In an era of increasing cyber threats, endpoint security is crucial as endpoints serve as potential gateways for malicious activities. Traditional antivirus solutions were once the primary defense, but modern endpoint security extends beyond mere virus detection. It encompasses a range of technologies such as firewalls, intrusion prevention systems, and behavioral analysis tools.

Endpoint security not only guards against external threats but also addresses internal risks, such as unauthorized access or data leakage. With the proliferation of remote work and mobile devices, securing endpoints becomes even more challenging and critical. Endpoint security solutions often incorporate advanced features like real-time monitoring, threat intelligence, and automated response mechanisms to proactively detect and thwart potential attacks.

As businesses evolve, understanding the significance of endpoint security is paramount to building a resilient defense against cyber threats, ensuring the protection of sensitive data, and maintaining the integrity of the overall network infrastructure.

Security Control: Endpoint security

Endpoint security is a pivotal security control within the broader landscape of cybersecurity, focusing on fortifying individual devices that serve as entry points to a network. These devices, which include computers, smartphones, and tablets, represent potential vulnerabilities that malicious actors may exploit. The objective of endpoint security is to create a robust defense mechanism that safeguards these endpoints from a variety of cyber threats.

One key aspect of endpoint security is antivirus protection, which aims to detect and eliminate malicious software like viruses, worms, and trojans. However, contemporary endpoint security extends beyond traditional antivirus solutions. It involves a multifaceted approach, integrating technologies like firewalls, intrusion detection, and prevention systems, and advanced behavioral analytics.

Firewalls play a crucial role in endpoint security by monitoring and controlling incoming and outgoing network traffic. They establish a barrier between a secure internal and external networks, potentially untrusted networks, preventing unauthorized access and protecting sensitive data.

Intrusion Detection and Prevention Systems (IDPS) are designed to identify and respond to potential security threats. These systems analyze network and/or system activities for patterns indicative of malicious intent or unauthorized access. By promptly detecting and mitigating threats, IDPS contributes significantly to endpoint security.

Behavioral analytics is another integral component, focusing on monitoring and analyzing user behavior. By establishing a baseline of normal activities, any deviations that may signal a security threat can be quickly identified. This proactive approach enhances the overall effectiveness of endpoint security by enabling rapid response to potential breaches.

Endpoint security is particularly vital in the current landscape where remote work and the use of personal devices are prevalent. It ensures that each device connected to the network adheres to security policies, reducing the risk of data breaches and unauthorized access.

Endpoint security serves as a critical security control by fortifying individual devices against a myriad of cyber threats. Its multifaceted approach, encompassing antivirus protection, firewalls, intrusion detection, and behavioral analytics, creates a resilient defense mechanism crucial for safeguarding sensitive data and maintaining the integrity of the overall network infrastructure.

Strengthening Cybersecurity Defenses: Leveraging Endpoint Detection and Response (EDR) for Business Resilience

Businesses encounter an expanding array of cyber threats, heightening the importance of robust cybersecurity measures. One increasingly prominent approach is the adoption of Endpoint Detection and Response (EDR) solutions, offering proactive and adaptive defense mechanisms against sophisticated cyber threats.

Consider a hypothetical multinational corporation entrusted with sensitive client data and proprietary information critical to its operations. As the organization expands its digital presence and embraces remote work, its endpoints become potential targets for cyber adversaries. In this dynamic environment, implementing EDR becomes essential to bolster the business's defenses against evolving threats.

EDR functions as a comprehensive cybersecurity solution, continuously monitoring and analyzing endpoint activities for any signs of unusual patterns or suspicious behavior. In our scenario, the EDR system is configured to establish a baseline of normal activities across the organization's diverse endpoints, including employee laptops, servers, and mobile devices.

Moreover, EDR solutions not only detect threats but also facilitate incident response through capabilities such as threat hunting, containment, and remediation. By providing these incident response capabilities, EDR strengthens the organization's ability to swiftly address and mitigate cyber threats, thereby enhancing overall cybersecurity posture.

One day, the EDR system detects anomalous behavior on an employee's laptop, indicating a potential security breach. The system immediately triggers an alert, enabling the organization's cybersecurity team to swiftly investigate the incident. With real-time visibility into the endpoint's activities, the EDR solution aids in identifying and containing the threat before it escalates.

Moreover, EDR does not merely stop at detection. It responds to incidents with automated actions, isolating compromised endpoints and neutralizing threats promptly. This capability is especially critical in our scenario, where quick response time can mitigate the impact of a security incident on the organization's sensitive data and maintain business continuity.

As the business landscape continues to evolve, adopting EDR is not just a cybersecurity necessity but a strategic imperative. It enhances resilience, reduces response times, and empowers organizations to stay one step ahead of cyber threats. In conclusion, the incorporation of Endpoint Detection and Response in our business scenario showcases its pivotal role in fortifying cybersecurity defenses and ensuring the continued trust and security of sensitive information in an increasingly interconnected world.

Safeguarding Business Assets: The Imperative of Deploying Modern Anti-Malware Software

Businesses engage in an ongoing battle against malicious software aiming to exploit vulnerabilities and compromise sensitive information. Employing modern anti-malware software emerges as a pivotal strategy, offering robust defense against a wide array of cyber threats. Let us delve deeper into the importance of adopting this technology through a hypothetical business scenario.

Imagine a financial institution tasked with managing extensive client data and financial transactions. In this scenario, the potential consequences of a malware attack are significant, ranging from financial loss to reputational harm. To bolster its defenses, the institution opts to integrate state-of-the-art anti-malware software across its network infrastructure.

Modern anti-malware solutions extend beyond traditional virus detection methods, incorporating advanced techniques like heuristic analysis, behavior monitoring, and machine learning algorithms. These sophisticated capabilities empower the software to detect and combat even the most elusive malware strains that might evade detection by conventional antivirus programs. In our scenario, the financial institution harnesses these cutting-edge features to establish a proactive defense against emerging threats.

Continuous updates and real-time threat intelligence play pivotal roles in modern anti-malware solutions. The software receives regular updates to identify new threats, ensuring the organization remains resilient against the latest malware variants. With these capabilities, our financial institution stays ahead of the evolving threat landscape, safeguarding its assets and the sensitive information entrusted by clients.

In the event of a malware outbreak, the software's swift response mechanisms come into play. The anti-malware solution promptly isolates infected devices, containing the threat and preventing its spread throughout the network. This agility is critical in minimizing potential damage and downtime.

While the adoption of modern anti-malware software is essential for businesses, it is worth delving into the technical intricacies of these advanced techniques. Heuristic analysis involves identifying malware based on behavioral patterns rather than specific signatures, while behavior monitoring tracks and analyzes suspicious activities in real-time. Machine learning algorithms enhance detection accuracy by learning from vast datasets. By understanding these techniques and their specific benefits in detecting and combating malware, businesses can further strengthen their technical grasp and cybersecurity defenses. Ultimately, embracing advanced anti-malware solutions not only mitigates risks but also fosters trust, positioning businesses to navigate the digital landscape securely.

Cybersecurity Vigilance: The Crucial Role of Regular Anti-Malware Updates in Business Defense

A fundamental strategy in this defense is ensuring that anti-malware software and signatures are consistently updated. In our hypothetical business scenario, a tech-driven company at the forefront of innovation recognizes the critical importance of staying ahead in the cyber arms race.

Imagine a scenario where this tech company is entrusted with developing cutting-edge software solutions for various clients. The value of their intellectual property and the sensitive data they handle necessitate a robust cybersecurity posture. In response to the dynamic nature of cyber threats, the company places a high priority on regular updates for its anti-malware software.

The anti-malware solution adopted by the company not only provides real-time protection but also receives regular updates containing the latest malware signatures. These updates are imperative as they empower the software to recognize and neutralize newly emerged threats promptly. In our scenario, the company's commitment to ensuring these updates is akin to fortifying their digital walls against constantly evolving cyber adversaries.

Failure to keep anti-malware software and signatures current can leave a business vulnerable to zero-day attacks and sophisticated malware that exploits undiscovered vulnerabilities. Recognizing this risk, our tech company diligently schedules and deploys updates across its entire network infrastructure. This proactive approach not only shields against known threats but also enhances the organization's resilience to emerging and novel cyber risks.

In the event of a cyber incident, having up-to-date anti-malware signatures proves pivotal. It enables swift detection and response, limiting the potential impact on the company's operations and preserving the integrity of their software development processes.

The scenario of our tech-driven company underscores the critical importance of ensuring regular updates for anti-malware software and signatures. By staying vigilant and proactive in this aspect of cybersecurity, businesses can establish a resilient defense, mitigate risks, and ensure the sustained security of their digital assets in an ever-evolving threat landscape.

Fortifying the Digital Fortress: Specifying Server Security Requirements in a Real-World Context

Ensuring the security of servers is a foundational aspect of safeguarding critical data and maintaining business operations. This section explores the significance of specifying server security requirements within the context of a modern business facing the complexities of a digital landscape.

Consider a multinational e-commerce enterprise handling vast amounts of customer data, financial transactions, and proprietary business information. This scenario places the company's servers at the epicenter of potential cyber threats, making the establishment of stringent security requirements imperative.

Server security requirements encompass a comprehensive set of measures, including access controls, encryption protocols, regular audits, and intrusion detection systems. In our real-world scenario, the e-commerce company identifies the need to not only meet industry standards but also to surpass them to mitigate evolving cyber threats.

Access controls become a paramount concern as the company specifies that only authorized personnel with defined roles should have access to sensitive servers. Multi-factor authentication is implemented, adding an extra layer of defense against unauthorized access attempts. This proactive measure minimizes the risk of internal and external threats compromising server integrity.

Encryption protocols are also a crucial element of the server security requirements. The e-commerce enterprise mandates the use of robust encryption algorithms for data in transit and at rest, ensuring that even if a breach were to occur, the stolen data remains indecipherable to unauthorized entities.

Regular audits and vulnerability assessments become routine practices to identify and rectify potential weaknesses in the server infrastructure. This ongoing diligence not only aligns with industry compliance standards but also bolsters the company's resilience against emerging cyber threats.

Intrusion detection systems are implemented to actively monitor server activities, promptly identifying and responding to anomalous behavior. This real-time monitoring capability proves invaluable in our scenario, as it allows the company to thwart potential threats before they can compromise the integrity of customer data or disrupt operations.

The real-world scenario of our multinational e-commerce enterprise underscores the critical nature of specifying robust server security requirements. By implementing comprehensive measures, businesses can fortify their digital fortress, ensuring the confidentiality, integrity, and availability of critical data in the face of ever-evolving cybersecurity challenges.

Navigating Cyber Waters: Strengthening Network Security in a Real-World Setting

Network security stands as the linchpin in safeguarding digital assets against a myriad of cyber threats. In a dynamic network, servers host critical data while mobile devices and laptops offer remote access to cloud-based servers and applications. Smart systems and IoT devices enhance efficiency by collecting and analyzing data, while POS devices facilitate transactions. Printers provide physical documentation, and wearables offer personalized insights. Network devices ensure seamless connectivity, while desktops remain foundational workstations. Cloud-based apps enable collaboration and productivity. This interconnected ecosystem requires robust security and management to ensure reliability and data integrity, underscoring the complexity and importance of modern network infrastructure.

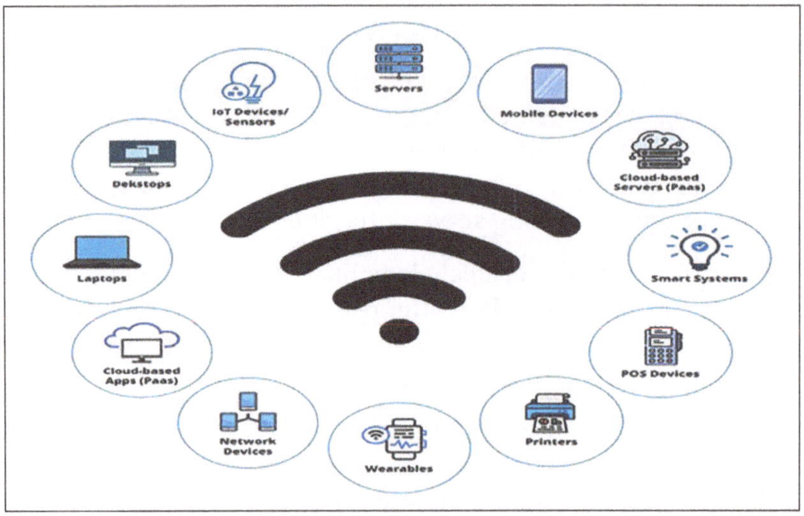

Figure 14.1: *Real-World setting of Network*

Let us delve into a real-world scenario of a multinational financial institution, where the implementation of robust network security measures is paramount.

Our financial institution handles vast amounts of sensitive customer information, financial transactions, and proprietary data. Recognizing the potential risks associated with cyber threats, the institution undertakes a comprehensive approach to network security to ensure the confidentiality, integrity, and availability of its critical assets.

The first layer of defense involves robust perimeter security measures. Firewalls and intrusion detection systems are strategically placed at the network boundaries to monitor and control incoming and outgoing traffic. In our scenario, these defenses act as sentinels, scrutinizing data packets for malicious activity and thwarting potential threats before they can breach the network.

Secure access controls play a pivotal role, with the financial institution adopting stringent measures to authenticate and authorize individuals accessing the network. Multi-factor authentication and role-based access restrictions ensure that only authorized personnel can navigate through different segments of the network, minimizing the risk of unauthorized access.

Continuous monitoring is a key component of the network security strategy. Security Information and Event Management (SIEM) systems are implemented to provide real-time analysis of security alerts generated throughout the institution's network. This proactive approach allows the cybersecurity team to promptly identify and respond to potential security incidents, maintaining the integrity of the network.

Regularly updating and patching network devices and software is imperative. In our scenario, the financial institution establishes a systematic process for applying patches promptly, mitigating vulnerabilities that could be exploited by cyber adversaries seeking to infiltrate the network.

Employee awareness and training also contribute significantly to network security. The financial institution conducts regular cybersecurity training sessions to educate staff on the latest threats, social engineering tactics, and best practices for maintaining a secure network environment.

The real-world scenario of our multinational financial institution highlights the critical role of network security in protecting against cyber threats. By implementing a multi-faceted approach encompassing perimeter defenses, access controls, continuous monitoring, regular updates, and employee training, businesses can navigate the cyber waters with resilience, ensuring the security of their digital assets and maintaining the trust of their customers.

Orchestrating Cyber Vigilance: The Crucial Role of Logging and Monitoring in a Corporate Landscape

Let's explore a real-world scenario involving a multinational financial institution, where robust network security measures are of paramount importance.

Our financial institution manages vast amounts of sensitive customer information, financial transactions, and proprietary data. Understanding the potential risks associated with cyber threats, the institution adopts a comprehensive approach to network security, ensuring the confidentiality, integrity, and availability of its critical assets.

The initial layer of defense involves implementing robust perimeter security measures. Firewalls and intrusion detection systems are strategically positioned at network boundaries to monitor and regulate incoming and outgoing traffic. In this scenario, these defenses serve as vigilant guardians, scrutinizing data packets for any signs of malicious activity and preventing potential threats from breaching the network.

Secure access controls play a crucial role, with the financial institution enforcing stringent measures to authenticate and authorize individuals accessing the network. Multi-factor authentication and role-based access restrictions are employed to ensure that only authorized personnel can traverse different segments of the network, minimizing the risk of unauthorized access.

Continuous monitoring forms a cornerstone of the network security strategy. Security Information and Event Management (SIEM) systems are deployed to conduct real-time analysis of security alerts generated across the institution's network. This proactive approach enables the cybersecurity team to swiftly identify and respond to potential security incidents, thereby preserving the integrity of the network.

Regularly updating and patching network devices and software is imperative. In this scenario, the financial institution implements a systematic process for promptly applying patches, mitigating vulnerabilities that could be exploited by cyber adversaries seeking to infiltrate the network.

Employee awareness and training also play a significant role in enhancing network security. The financial institution conducts regular cybersecurity training sessions to educate staff on the latest threats, social engineering tactics, and best practices for maintaining a secure network environment.

The real-world scenario of our multinational financial institution underscores the critical importance of network security in safeguarding against cyber threats. By adopting a multi-faceted approach encompassing perimeter defenses, access controls, continuous monitoring, regular updates, and employee training, businesses can navigate the cyber landscape with resilience, ensuring the security of their digital assets and upholding the trust of their customers.

Gatekeepers of Security: Navigating Identity and Access Control in a Real-World Context

Let us explore a real-world scenario within a multinational corporation to understand the critical role IAC plays in safeguarding sensitive data, intellectual property, and business continuity.

Imagine a global financial institution managing vast amounts of customer information, financial transactions, and proprietary systems. In this scenario, the institution recognizes the paramount importance of implementing stringent IAC measures to prevent unauthorized access and protect against potential cyber threats.

Central to the IAC strategy is the adoption of robust authentication mechanisms. Multi-factor authentication (MFA) is implemented across all access points, requiring employees to verify their identity using multiple factors such as passwords, biometrics, and one-time passcodes. This proactive approach significantly enhances the security posture, reducing the risk of unauthorized access even in the event of compromised credentials.

Role-based access control (RBAC) becomes a cornerstone of the institution's security framework. Different employees have varying roles and responsibilities, each demanding distinct levels of access to sensitive information. By aligning access privileges with job functions, the institution ensures that employees only have the permissions necessary for their roles, minimizing the attack surface and mitigating the risk of insider threats.

Continuous monitoring of user activities further fortifies the IAC strategy. The financial institution deploys real-time monitoring tools that track user behavior, identifying anomalies or suspicious patterns indicative of potential security incidents. This vigilance allows for prompt detection and response, preventing unauthorized access before it escalates into a more significant breach.

Regular reviews and audits of user access permissions are integral to the institution's IAC strategy. By periodically reassessing and updating access privileges based on changes in job roles or responsibilities, the financial institution mitigates the risk of lingering, unnecessary access that could be exploited by malicious actors.

The real-world scenario of our multinational financial institution underscores the pivotal role of Identity and Access Control in the cybersecurity landscape. By implementing robust authentication measures, adopting role-based access controls, continuously monitoring user activities, and conducting regular reviews, businesses can establish a comprehensive IAC framework. This framework not only safeguards sensitive information but also ensures the seamless functioning of operations in an environment where security is paramount.

Safeguarding Confidentiality: A Dive into Data Protection in a Real-World Scenario

Information is a valuable asset for any organization, data protection emerges as a critical aspect of cybersecurity strategies. Let us explore a real-world scenario within a healthcare organization to understand how robust data protection measures are essential in preserving the confidentiality and integrity of sensitive patient information.

Imagine a large hospital system handling electronic health records (EHRs) for thousands of patients. In this scenario, the hospital recognizes the significance of safeguarding patient data against potential breaches, unauthorized access, and ensuring compliance with privacy regulations like the Health Insurance Portability and Accountability Act (HIPAA).

Encryption becomes a cornerstone of the data protection strategy. The hospital employs robust encryption algorithms to secure patient data both in transit and at rest. This cryptographic layer acts as a shield, rendering sensitive information indecipherable to unauthorized entities, even if intercepted during transmission or in the event of a security breach.

Access controls are meticulously implemented to regulate who can access patient records and under what circumstances. Role-based access controls (RBAC) ensure that only authorized healthcare professionals with a legitimate need can view specific patient information. This granular approach minimizes the risk of unauthorized access, mitigating the potential impact of insider threats or external cyber attacks.

Regular data backups are a fundamental component of the hospital's data protection strategy. In the event of data loss due to accidental deletion, hardware failures, or cyber incidents, the institution can swiftly restore critical patient information from secure backups, ensuring continuity of care and minimizing disruptions.

Auditing and monitoring tools are deployed to keep a vigilant eye on data access and usage. The hospital utilizes real-time alerts to notify administrators of any unusual activities or potential security incidents. This proactive approach allows for prompt detection and response, enhancing the overall security posture of the organization.

Continuous staff training on data protection practices is prioritized. Employees, from healthcare professionals to administrative staff, are educated on the importance of maintaining patient confidentiality, recognizing phishing attempts, and adhering to established security protocols. This human-centric approach reinforces the organization's commitment to a culture of data protection.

The real-world scenario of our healthcare organization underscores the critical nature of data protection in preserving the confidentiality and integrity of sensitive information. By implementing robust encryption, access controls, regular backups, monitoring tools, and fostering a culture of awareness among staff, businesses can navigate the complex landscape of data protection, ensuring compliance with regulations and maintaining the trust of stakeholders.

Strengthening Cyber Resilience: Navigating Vulnerability Management in a Real-World Setting

Vulnerability management stands as a critical practice to identify, assess, and mitigate potential weaknesses in an organization's digital infrastructure. Let us explore a real-world scenario within a financial institution to understand the pivotal role of vulnerability management in safeguarding against cyber threats.

Imagine a large bank managing an extensive network of financial transactions, customer data, and sensitive information. In this scenario, the bank recognizes the imperative of a robust vulnerability management program to fortify its cyber defenses and maintain the trust of its clients.

Regular vulnerability assessments become a cornerstone of the bank's strategy. Automated scanning tools are employed to systematically identify weaknesses in software, network configurations, and system architectures. By conducting these assessments on a recurring basis, the bank can proactively address vulnerabilities before they can be exploited by malicious actors.

Prioritization of vulnerabilities is a key aspect of the scenario. The bank employs risk-based methodologies to assess the potential impact and exploitability of identified vulnerabilities. This approach ensures that the cybersecurity team focuses its resources on addressing the most critical and high-risk vulnerabilities promptly, minimizing the overall risk exposure.

Patch management is tightly integrated into the vulnerability management framework. Once vulnerabilities are identified, the bank swiftly deploys patches and updates to remediate the weaknesses. This agile response minimizes the window of opportunity for attackers to exploit vulnerabilities, enhancing the overall security posture of the institution.

A robust incident response plan complements vulnerability management efforts. In the event of a security incident related to a known vulnerability, the bank's cybersecurity team is well-prepared to swiftly detect, contain, and eradicate the threat. This holistic approach not only emphasizes prevention but also positions the organization to effectively respond to emerging cyber threats.

Continuous improvement is embedded in the bank's vulnerability management strategy. Periodic reviews and assessments of the program's effectiveness, coupled with ongoing staff training, ensure that the institution remains adaptive to evolving cyber risks and industry best practices.

The real-world scenario of our financial institution exemplifies the critical importance of vulnerability management in navigating the complexities of modern cybersecurity. By implementing regular assessments, prioritizing vulnerabilities, integrating effective patch management, and fostering a proactive incident response culture, businesses can fortify their cyber resilience and sustain a secure digital environment for critical financial operations and customer trust.

Orchestrating Security Harmony: Inventory and Asset Management in a Real-World Scenario

Effective inventory and asset management play a pivotal role in maintaining an organization's resilience against potential threats. Let us delve into a real-world scenario within a multinational technology company to understand how meticulous management of digital assets fosters a proactive and secure operational environment.

Imagine a technology giant managing a vast array of digital devices, servers, and software applications critical to its global operations. In this scenario, the company recognizes that a comprehensive inventory and asset management system is crucial for both operational efficiency and cybersecurity.

The first step in the company's strategy involves creating a detailed inventory of all digital assets. Automated asset discovery tools scan the network to identify and catalog every device connected to the corporate infrastructure. This includes servers, workstations, routers, IoT devices, and software applications. The resulting inventory provides a holistic view of the digital landscape, forming the foundation for effective asset management.

Asset categorization and classification become integral to the scenario. Each identified asset is categorized based on its criticality to business operations, sensitivity of the data it handles, and its role within the organization. This classification allows the company to prioritize security measures, focusing more robust protections on mission-critical assets and sensitive information.

Lifecycle management is a key aspect of the company's strategy. From procurement to decommissioning, each asset undergoes a systematic lifecycle process. This includes regular updates, patching, and ensuring compliance with security policies. For example, if a server or application reaches the end of its lifecycle, it is retired securely to prevent potential security risks associated with outdated technology.

Regular audits and continuous monitoring complement the inventory and asset management framework. The company employs automated tools to monitor changes in the digital landscape, ensuring that any new asset additions or unexpected modifications trigger alerts for further investigation. This proactive approach helps identify unauthorized or potentially malicious changes promptly.

Security measures are tailored to the specifics of each asset category. Mission-critical assets may have heightened security protocols, while less critical assets may have standard protections. This targeted approach ensures a balanced allocation of resources, optimizing security efforts without compromising operational efficiency.

The real-world scenario of our multinational technology company exemplifies the critical role of inventory and asset management in cybersecurity. By creating a comprehensive inventory, categorizing assets, implementing lifecycle management, conducting regular audits, and tailoring security measures to asset specifics, organizations can navigate the complexities of the digital landscape with efficiency and resilience.

Fortifying Digital Defenses: Secure Configuration in a Real-World Scenario

Let us explore a real-world scenario within a global financial institution to understand the critical role secure configuration plays in maintaining a robust and resilient security posture.

Our scenario unfolds in a large bank managing extensive financial transactions, customer data, and critical infrastructure. Recognizing the imperative of secure configuration, the bank implements a comprehensive strategy to ensure that all its systems and devices are configured securely, minimizing vulnerabilities and reducing the risk of exploitation.

Central to the bank's approach is the deployment of configuration management tools. Automated solutions are implemented to systematically apply and enforce secure configurations across servers, network devices, databases, and endpoints. This ensures a standardized, secure baseline for all digital assets, reducing the attack surface and enhancing the overall security posture of the institution.

The bank employs industry best practices for secure configurations, adhering to guidelines from authoritative sources like the Center for Internet Security (CIS) or the National Institute of Standards and Technology (NIST). Configuration baselines are established for different types of assets, specifying secure settings for operating systems, applications, and network devices. Regular updates to these baselines are integrated into the bank's security processes, reflecting evolving security standards and emerging threats.

Continuous monitoring plays a pivotal role in the scenario. The bank implements real-time monitoring tools to detect and alert on any deviations from secure configurations. This proactive approach allows the cybersecurity team to swiftly identify potential security incidents or unauthorized changes, enabling prompt remediation before they can escalate.

Regular vulnerability assessments are tightly integrated into the secure configuration strategy. Automated scans are conducted to identify misconfigurations that could expose vulnerabilities. The findings from these assessments inform the bank's continuous improvement cycle, allowing them to refine and enhance their secure configuration practices in response to emerging threats.

Employee awareness and training are integral components of the bank's secure configuration strategy. Staff members, from IT administrators to end-users, are educated on the importance of adhering to secure configuration standards, recognizing the impact of misconfigurations, and reporting any suspicious activities promptly.

The real-world scenario of our global financial institution underscores the critical role of secure configuration in cybersecurity. By deploying automated configuration management tools, adhering to industry best practices, implementing continuous monitoring, conducting regular vulnerability assessments, and fostering a culture of awareness among staff, businesses can fortify their digital defenses and navigate the complex landscape of cybersecurity with resilience and confidence.

Sentinel Protectors: Malware Defense Strategies in a Real-World Scenario

Let us explore a real-world scenario within a multinational corporation to understand the pivotal role of malware defense in maintaining a secure nd resilient cybersecurity posture.

Our scenario unfolds in a technology conglomerate managing intellectual property, client data, and mission-critical systems. Recognizing the potential risks associated with malware attacks, the company implements a multifaceted approach to defend against various types of malicious software.

The company's strategy commences with endpoint protection solutions. Advanced antivirus software is deployed across all devices within the corporate network, employing heuristic analysis and real-time scanning to detect and neutralize known and emerging malware threats. Regular updates to virus definitions ensure that the antivirus software remains equipped to combat the latest variants of malicious code.

Email security plays a crucial role in the scenario. The company employs robust email filtering and threat detection mechanisms to identify and quarantine phishing attempts, malicious attachments, and links leading to malware-infected websites. Employee training programs complement these technical measures, educating staff on recognizing and avoiding social engineering tactics employed by malware distributors.

Network-based defenses are tightly integrated into the company's malware defense strategy. Firewalls and intrusion detection systems monitor and control network traffic, identifying and blocking communication with known malicious servers. Web filtering tools prevent access to malicious websites, further reducing the risk of malware infections originating from the internet.

Behavioral analytics enhances the company's ability to detect zero-day threats. The incorporation of machine learning and anomaly detection algorithms allows the cybersecurity team to identify deviations from normal user behavior, signaling potential malware infections or insider threats.

Regular vulnerability assessments and patch management are critical components of the scenario. The company ensures that operating systems and applications are promptly updated with the latest security patches, mitigating vulnerabilities that could be exploited by malware seeking to infiltrate the network.

Incident response and recovery planning are integrated into the malware defense strategy. In the event of a successful malware attack, the company is well-prepared to contain and eradicate the threat swiftly, minimizing the impact on operations and data integrity.

The real-world scenario of our multinational technology conglomerate highlights the multifaceted nature of effective malware defense. By combining endpoint protection, email security, network defenses, behavioral analytics, regular patching, and incident response planning, businesses can fortify their digital defenses against the diverse and evolving landscape of malware threats.

Harmonizing Security: Strategic Specification of Requirements for Mobile Devices and Clients in a Global Corporation

This narrative delves into a real-world scenario within a multinational corporation to elucidate the strategic importance of specifying requirements for mobile devices and clients in fortifying cybersecurity.

Scenario Overview

Imagine a technology conglomerate operating on a global scale, with a workforce dispersed across continents. The corporation is acutely aware of the pivotal role mobile devices play in day-to-day operations, making it imperative to establish stringent security standards. To address this, the company devises a comprehensive strategy, blending policy development, advanced technology deployment, and employee awareness initiatives.

- **Policy Development:**

  The cornerstone of the corporation's approach is the formulation of a meticulous Mobile Device Management (MDM) policy. This policy delineates clear and enforceable requirements for mobile devices and clients accessing the corporate network. Device configurations, encryption standards, and secure authentication mechanisms are specified to create a standardized, secure baseline across the organization. This policy serves as the foundational framework for ensuring the security of mobile devices and mitigating potential vulnerabilities.

- **Endpoint Security Solutions**

  Recognizing the evolving threat landscape, the corporation deploys advanced endpoint security solutions across all mobile devices and clients. These solutions are equipped to detect, mitigate, and prevent various forms of malware, ransomware, and cyber threats. Regular updates and real-time threat intelligence integration ensure the efficacy of the endpoint security strategy, providing a proactive defense against emerging risks. The deployment of such solutions is particularly crucial in the face of sophisticated cyber threats that could compromise the confidentiality and integrity of corporate data.

- **Authentication Standards**

  A stringent approach to authentication is a key focus area. Multi-factor authentication (MFA) is mandated for all access points, requiring employees to undergo additional identity verification steps when accessing corporate resources from mobile devices. This not only enhances the overall security posture but also addresses the potential risks associated with mobile devices being lost or stolen.

- **Regular Audits and Monitoring**

  To maintain continuous compliance and security, the corporation employs automated tools for regular audits and monitoring of mobile devices. These tools assess adherence to security policies, detect anomalies in usage patterns, and promptly alert administrators to any suspicious activities. Real-time monitoring is essential for swift responses to potential security incidents, reducing the dwell time of threats and minimizing the impact of data breaches.

- **Employee Training and Awareness**

  Recognizing the human element in cybersecurity, the corporation invests in comprehensive training and awareness programs for its employees. Staff members are educated on best practices for securing their mobile devices, recognizing and reporting phishing attempts, and understanding the importance of adhering to security policies. This proactive approach fosters a culture of cybersecurity consciousness throughout the organization, making employees active contributors to the overall security posture.

The real-world scenario of our multinational technology conglomerate exemplifies how specifying requirements for mobile devices and clients is not just a technical imperative but a strategic necessity. By combining policy development, advanced security solutions, stringent authentication standards, regular audits, and employee awareness initiatives, businesses can create a harmonized and resilient cybersecurity framework that mitigates risks and ensures the secure integration of mobile devices in the corporate environment.

Seamless Integration: Leveraging Existing and New Devices in a Business Environment

Let us explore a real-world scenario within a multinational technology corporation to understand how strategic device integration can enhance productivity, foster innovatifon, and ensure a seamless transition.

Scenario:

Imagine a technology giant at the forefront of innovation, constantly pushing the boundaries of what is possible in the digital realm. As the company expands its operations, there arises a need to harmonize the use of existing devices with the integration of new cutting-edge technologies. This scenario emphasizes the importance of optimizing the synergy between legacy devices and the latest technological advancements to drive business success.

- **Utilizing Existing Devices:**

  The technology corporation acknowledges the value embedded in its existing devices, ranging from servers and workstations to legacy infrastructure components. The first step is to conduct a thorough assessment of the capabilities of these devices, identifying areas where they still excel and aligning them with specific business functions. Legacy systems with proven reliability continue to play a crucial role in day-to-day operations, serving as the backbone of critical processes.

- **Strategic Integration of New Devices:**

  Recognizing the need for innovation and staying ahead in the competitive landscape, the technology corporation strategically introduces new devices into its ecosystem. These may include state-of-the-art servers, cutting-edge workstations, or the latest IoT devices tailored to enhance efficiency and support emerging business needs. The integration is meticulous, ensuring compatibility with existing infrastructure and seamless interoperability.

- **Unified Network Architecture:**

  To facilitate the harmonious coexistence of existing and new devices, the corporation invests in a unified network architecture. This ensures that all devices, regardless of their vintage or capabilities, can communicate seamlessly.

The adoption of standardized communication protocols and comprehensive network security measures guarantees a secure and interconnected environment where data flows efficiently and securely between devices.

- **Adaptive Software Solutions:**

  To maximize the potential of both existing and new devices, the technology corporation invests in adaptive software solutions. These applications are designed to be platform-agnostic, accommodating diverse operating systems and hardware specifications. This approach allows employees to work seamlessly across devices, promoting collaboration and productivity.

- **Employee Training and Change Management:**

  Understanding that device integration is not solely a technological shift but also a cultural one, the corporation prioritizes employee training and change management. Training programs are implemented to familiarize employees with the features of new devices and promote a smooth transition. Clear communication channels are established to address any concerns and ensure that the workforce feels confident in adopting the integrated device environment.

- **Continuous Monitoring and Optimization:**

  The technology corporation recognizes that device integration is an ongoing process. Continuous monitoring of device performance, regular software updates, and periodic assessments of the overall device ecosystem are conducted. This iterative approach ensures that the integrated environment remains dynamic, responsive, and aligned with the evolving needs of the business.

The real-world scenario of our multinational technology corporation showcases the strategic integration of existing and new devices to create a harmonious and productive business environment. By leveraging the strengths of legacy systems, introducing cutting-edge technologies, adopting a unified network architecture, investing in adaptive software solutions, prioritizing employee training, and embracing continuous optimization, businesses can achieve a synergistic balance that propels them towards sustained success in a rapidly evolving digital landscape.

Safeguarding Sensitive Data: A Case Study on Least-Privileged Access in a Financial Institution

The principle of least-privileged access stands as a fundamental strategy to minimize risks and protect sensitive data. This case study explores the implementation of least-privileged access within a prominent financial institution, SecureBank, showcasing its strategic significance in fortifying digital defenses.

Case Study:

SecureBank, a leading financial institution operating globally, recognizes the critical importance of safeguarding customer data, financial transactions, and sensitive information against cyber threats. In pursuit of a robust security posture, SecureBank adopts the principle of least-privileged access across its digital infrastructure.

- **User Role Segmentation:**

SecureBank initiates the implementation of least-privileged access by meticulously segmenting user roles based on job responsibilities. A thorough analysis is conducted to determine the necessary level of access for each employee, from front-end customer service representatives to backend database administrators. This segmentation forms the foundation for least-privileged access control.

- **Role-Based Access Control (RBAC):**

To operationalize least-privileged access, SecureBank adopts Role-Based Access Control (RBAC). Employee roles are defined with granular permissions, ensuring that individuals only have access to the specific resources and data necessary for their designated tasks. RBAC enhances precision in access control, reducing the risk of unauthorized activities.

- **Regular Access Reviews:**

Recognizing that organizational structures and job responsibilities evolve, SecureBank institutes a routine access review process. Periodic assessments are conducted to validate that employees retain access only to the resources essential for their roles. Any discrepancies or deviations trigger immediate corrective actions, ensuring alignment with the least-privileged access principle.

- **Multi-Factor Authentication (MFA):**

To augment access controls, SecureBank enforces multi-factor authentication (MFA) as an additional layer of security. Beyond the principle of least-privileged access, MFA adds an extra barrier, requiring users to provide multiple forms of verification. This multifaceted approach significantly mitigates the risk of unauthorized access attempts.

- **Dynamic Privilege Elevation:**

In scenarios where temporary access escalation is necessary, SecureBank employs dynamic privilege elevation mechanisms. This allows employees to obtain elevated permissions for specific tasks, reducing the likelihood of prolonged access to sensitive resources and maintaining the core tenets of least-privileged access.

- **Employee Training and Awareness:**

SecureBank recognizes that a successful implementation of least-privileged access requires the collaboration of its workforce. Comprehensive training programs and awareness campaigns are conducted to educate employees about the importance of adhering to the principle. Staff members gain a clear understanding of their roles, responsibilities, and the role they play in maintaining a secure digital environment.

- **Incident Response Integration:**

In the event of a security incident, SecureBank integrates least-privileged access into its incident response protocols. Rapid containment strategies involve reverting access permissions to the bare minimum required for critical operations. This ensures that even in the face of a security breach, the potential impact is limited by the principles of least-privileged access.

SecureBank's case study exemplifies the strategic implementation of least-privileged access in a financial institution. By adopting user role segmentation, RBAC, regular access reviews, MFA, dynamic privilege elevation, employee training, and incident response integration, SecureBank fortifies its digital infrastructure against unauthorized access attempts. This comprehensive approach not only protects sensitive financial data but also serves as a model for applying the least-privileged access principle in critical sectors where data security is paramount.

Conclusion

The design of a secure endpoint solution is paramount in safeguarding organizations against evolving cyber threats. By implementing robust endpoint security measures, including advanced threat detection, encryption, and continuous monitoring, businesses can establish a resilient defense against potential breaches. The protection of sensitive data, intellectual property, and user privacy hinges on a proactive and comprehensive approach to endpoint security. As technology advances, organizations must remain vigilant in adapting their security strategies to ensure the integrity of their endpoints. A well-designed secure endpoint solution not only mitigates risks but also fosters a secure and productive digital environment. In the next chapter, we will discuss network security design issues.

Multiple Choice Questions

1. What is the primary goal of secure endpoint solution design?

    a. Enhancing network speed.

    b. Safeguarding against cyber threats.

   c. Maximizing software compatibility.
   d. Minimizing endpoint user experience.
2. Which of the following is a key component of secure endpoint solutions?
   a. Ignoring software updates.
   b. Weak password policies.
   c. Advanced threat detection.
   d. Limited user education.
3. How does encryption contribute to secure endpoint solutions?
   a. Slows down system performance.
   b. Secures data from unauthorized access.
   c. Increases vulnerability to malware.
   d. Impacts internet connectivity.
4. Why is continuous monitoring essential in endpoint security?
   a. It consumes excessive system resources.
   b. It helps with occasional check-ups.
   c. It identifies and addresses security issues in real-time.
   d. It only works during office hours.
5. What is the significance of user education in secure endpoint solution design?
   a. It increases the risk of security breaches.
   b. It minimizes system compatibility.
   c. It enhances user awareness and reduces security threats.
   d. It slows down endpoint performance.

Answers

1. b
2. c
3. b
4. c
5. c

CHAPTER 15
Secure Network Design

Introduction

Secure network design is paramount in safeguarding digital assets and ensuring resilient cyber defenses. It involves structuring networks with layered security protocols, firewalls, and intrusion detection systems. A well-designed network minimizes attack surfaces, employs strong access controls, and encrypts sensitive data in transit. By incorporating principles like the least privilege and segmentation, secure network design mitigates the risk of unauthorized access and lateral movement. Regular audits and updates further bolster its effectiveness, creating a robust foundation that withstands evolving cyber threats, ensuring data confidentiality, integrity, and availability in today's dynamic and interconnected digital landscape.

Structure

In this chapter, we will cover the following topics:

- Safeguarding Digital Frontiers: Secure Network Design Imperative
- Secure Digital Highways: Network Security Group Traffic Filtering
- Safeguarding Enterprise Integrity: Network Posture Management

Safeguarding Digital Frontiers: Secure Network Design Imperative

As businesses rely more on interconnected systems, networks become vulnerable to malicious activities. A secure network design is not just a technological necessity but a strategic imperative, aiming to safeguard sensitive information, ensure operational continuity, and maintain user trust. This involves implementing robust firewall configurations, encryption protocols, intrusion detection systems, and comprehensive access controls. This chapter explores the critical elements, strategies, and best practices of secure network design, emphasizing its pivotal role in contemporary cybersecurity. Our goal is to provide insights into secure network design and empower organizations to navigate cybersecurity complexities, ensuring the resilience and integrity of their digital infrastructures.

Strategic Network Segmentation: Cybersecurity Enhancement

Businesses are increasingly dependent on robust network infrastructures to streamline operations and facilitate communication. However, the escalating threat landscape demands a proactive approach to cybersecurity. Network segmentation emerges as a crucial design solution to fortify an organization's defenses against cyber threats. This strategy involves dividing a network into distinct segments, each with its own security protocols, creating hurdles for potential attackers and minimizing the impact of security breaches.

Consider a hypothetical scenario where a multinational corporation, TechGuard Solutions, operates in various geographical locations with diverse business units. To safeguard sensitive data, intellectual property, and customer information, TechGuard Solutions recognizes the need for a comprehensive network segmentation strategy.

Scenario Overview

TechGuard Solutions has experienced a surge in cyber threats, ranging from ransomware attacks to data breaches. The existing flat network structure proves vulnerable to lateral movements by malicious actors. To address these challenges, the company decides to implement a robust network segmentation plan.

Design Solutions for Network Segmentation:

Designing solutions for network segmentation involves creating isolated zones within a network to enhance security. By implementing this strategy, organizations can restrict lateral movement, minimize attack surfaces, and safeguard critical assets. Network segmentation bolsters resilience against cyber threats, ensuring a more robust defense and mitigating potential breaches.

- **Identification of Critical Assets**

  TechGuard Solutions conducts a thorough inventory of its assets, identifying critical servers, databases, and systems that require enhanced protection.

  Segmentation focuses on isolating these assets into separate network zones, limiting unauthorized access.

- **Role-Based Access Control (RBAC):**

  RBAC is implemented to ensure that employees have access only to the resources necessary for their roles.

  Granular access control policies are defined, preventing lateral movement within the network and reducing the attack surface.

- **Implementation of VLANs:**

  Virtual Local Area Networks (VLANs) are deployed to create isolated segments within the overall network.

  This ensures that even if one segment is compromised, the damage is contained, and lateral movement becomes challenging for attackers.

- **Network Monitoring and Intrusion Detection:**

  Continuous monitoring tools and intrusion detection systems are employed to identify anomalous activities across network segments.

  Real-time alerts and automated responses enhance the organization's ability to swiftly counteract potential threats.

- **Regular Audits and Updates:**

  Scheduled audits are conducted to assess the effectiveness of the segmentation strategy and identify areas for improvement.

  Security protocols and segmentation policies are regularly updated to align with evolving cyber threats.

The implementation of a robust network segmentation strategy, tailored to the specific needs of TechGuard Solutions, becomes imperative in the face of escalating cyber threats. This proactive approach not only fortifies the organization's cybersecurity posture but also ensures the continuity of operations and the safeguarding of sensitive information in an interconnected digital landscape.

Secure Digital Highways: Network Security Group Traffic Filtering

In the contemporary business landscape, where data flows are the lifeblood of organizations, ensuring the secure passage of information becomes paramount. With the rise in cyber threats, businesses need robust solutions to filter and control network traffic effectively. Network Security Groups (NSGs) emerge as a vital component in this endeavor, providing a strategic approach to managing traffic and fortifying digital assets. Let us explore a business scenario where a dynamic enterprise, CyberShield Innovations, leverages NSGs to enhance its network security.

Scenario Overview

CyberShield Innovations, a technology firm specializing in cybersecurity solutions, operates in a cloud-centric environment, utilizing various applications and services. The company has recently experienced an uptick in cyber-attacks, with sophisticated threat actors attempting to exploit vulnerabilities in their network infrastructure. In response, CyberShield Innovations recognizes the need to implement robust traffic filtering solutions using Network Security Groups.

Design Solutions for Traffic Filtering with Network Security Groups

Designing solutions for traffic filtering with Network Security Groups (NSGs) is pivotal in fortifying network defenses. NSGs enable granular control over inbound and outbound traffic, allowing organizations to define rules, restrict access, and safeguard critical assets.

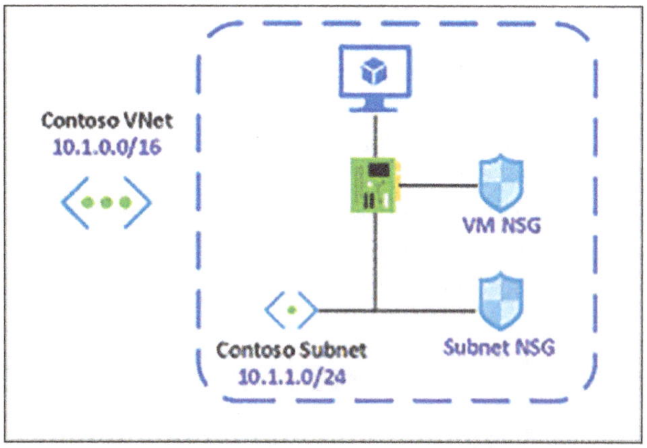

Figure 15.1: *Network Security Group (Source* : Network Security Groups with Azure Site Recovery - Azure Site Recovery | Microsoft Learn)

This strategic approach enhances cybersecurity, ensuring a robust defense against unauthorized access and potential threats.

- **Granular Rule Definition:**

  CyberShield Innovations meticulously defines NSG rules based on the principle of least privilege. Each rule outlines specific protocols, source and destination IP addresses, and port ranges, enabling granular control over traffic flow.

- **Application of Zero Trust Principles:**

  Zero Trust is embraced as a guiding principle, requiring explicit verification for every access attempt. NSGs are configured to deny all traffic by default, allowing only explicitly permitted communications, reducing the attack surface.

- **Segmentation of Resources:**

  CyberShield Innovations divides its network into segments, each associated with a distinct NSG. This ensures that even if one segment is compromised, the impact is contained, preventing lateral movements by attackers.

- **Integration with Azure Services:**

  Leveraging the capabilities of Azure, CyberShield Innovations integrates NSGs seamlessly with other Azure services, such as Azure Firewall and Azure Virtual Network, creating a cohesive security infrastructure.

- **Regular Audits and Adjustments:**

  Continuous monitoring and periodic audits of NSG configurations are conducted to adapt to evolving threats and business requirements.

  Adjustments to NSG rules are made promptly based on threat intelligence and network performance metrics.

In the face of escalating cyber threats, CyberShield Innovations proactively strengthens its network security posture through the strategic implementation of Network Security Groups. By adopting a meticulous approach to traffic filtering, CyberShield Innovations not only safeguards its digital assets but also ensures the integrity and confidentiality of critical information. This design solution allows the organization to navigate the digital highways securely, fostering innovation and growth while mitigating the risks associated with an interconnected business landscape.

Safeguarding Enterprise Integrity: Network Posture Management

The advent of diverse devices, remote work scenarios, and intricate network architectures necessitates a proactive approach. Network Posture Management (NPM) emerges as a crucial component in securing organizational networks by ensuring that all devices adhere to predefined security standards. This section explores the design solutions for network posture management within a hypothetical business scenario.

Scenario Overview

Consider a global financial institution, SecureBank Corp, which manages vast amounts of sensitive financial data. With an increasing number of remote employees accessing the network from various locations and devices, SecureBank Corp recognizes the critical importance of implementing robust network posture management.

Strengthening Financial Fortresses: A Guide to Network Posture Management at SecureBank Corp

"Strengthening Financial Fortresses: A Guide to Network Posture Management at SecureBank Corp" illuminates the strategic approach to fortifying digital defenses in the financial sector. This comprehensive guide explores robust network design, encryption, and access controls, offering a blueprint for SecureBank Corp to ensure the resilience of its digital infrastructure in the face of evolving cyber threats.

Design Solutions for Network Posture Management:

- **Device Profiling and Classification:**

  SecureBank Corp initiates a comprehensive device profiling process, classifying devices based on their type, operating system, and security features.

  This allows the organization to create distinct network policies tailored to different device categories.

- **Endpoint Security Policies:**

  Well-defined endpoint security policies are established, specifying the required security configurations for devices to connect to the network.

  These policies encompass antivirus software, operating system patches, and other essential security measures.

- **Continuous Monitoring and Assessment:**

  SecureBank Corp employs continuous monitoring tools to assess the security posture of devices in real-time.

  Any deviations from the established security standards trigger automated responses, such as quarantining the device or alerting the IT security team.

- **Integration with Identity and Access Management (IAM):**

  Network posture management is seamlessly integrated with IAM systems to ensure that only authenticated and authorized users with compliant devices gain access to sensitive resources.

  This enhances overall access control and reduces the risk of unauthorized access.

- **Automated Remediation:**

  Automated remediation processes are implemented to bring non-compliant devices back into adherence with security standards.

  This minimizes manual intervention and accelerates the response time to security posture deviations.

- **User Education and Awareness:**

  SecureBank Corp conducts regular awareness programs to educate users about the importance of adhering to security standards.

  Employees are encouraged to keep their devices updated and report any security concerns promptly.

SecureBank Corp navigates the intricacies of a dynamic and interconnected financial landscape, the implementation of network posture management stands as a linchpin in fortifying its cybersecurity defenses. By adopting a proactive stance and integrating sophisticated solutions, the organization ensures that its network remains resilient against evolving cyber threats, thereby safeguarding its reputation, client trust, and the integrity of financial data.

Network Monitoring: Business Resilience Vigilance

Proactive monitoring is the key to identifying potential issues, ensuring optimal performance, and safeguarding against cyber threats. This section explores the design solutions for network monitoring within the context of a hypothetical business scenario.

Scenario Overview

Imagine a thriving e-commerce enterprise, SwiftCart, which relies heavily on its online platform for customer transactions. SwiftCart experiences occasional disruptions in its services, impacting user experience and revenue. To address these challenges, SwiftCart recognizes the critical need for an advanced network monitoring system.

SwiftGuard: Elevating E-Commerce Stability with Advanced Network Monitoring

SwiftGuard revolutionizes e-commerce stability through advanced network monitoring. By vigilant surveillance of network activities, it ensures seamless operations, timely issue detection, and enhanced user experiences. SwiftGuard's proactive approach elevates the reliability of e-commerce platforms, safeguarding against disruptions and bolstering the overall performance and resilience of digital storefronts.

Design Solutions for Network Monitoring:

- **Comprehensive Traffic Analysis**

SwiftCart implements advanced traffic analysis tools to monitor the flow of data across its network.

By understanding patterns and identifying anomalies, the organization gains insights into potential bottlenecks, performance issues, or malicious activities.

- **Real-time Performance Monitoring**

  SwiftCart adopts real-time performance monitoring tools to track the health and performance of its network infrastructure.

  Key metrics, such as bandwidth utilization, latency, and packet loss, are continuously monitored to ensure optimal service delivery.

- **Incident Detection and Response**

  SwiftCart integrates intelligent incident detection mechanisms to identify security breaches or abnormal activities promptly.

  Automated response protocols are established to mitigate threats and minimize the impact of potential security incidents.

- **End-to-End Visibility**

  The network monitoring solution provides end-to-end visibility, covering not only the data center but also remote offices, cloud environments, and external connections.

  This holistic approach ensures that SwiftCart can identify and address issues across its entire digital ecosystem.

- **Scalability and Flexibility**

  Recognizing the dynamic nature of its business, SwiftCart's network monitoring solution is designed to scale seamlessly with the company's growth.

  The system can adapt to changes in network architecture, accommodating new technologies and expanding infrastructure.

- **Predictive Analytics**

  SwiftCart leverages predictive analytics to forecast potential issues based on historical data.

  By proactively addressing impending challenges, the organization minimizes downtime and enhances overall network reliability.

- **User Experience Monitoring**

  SwiftCart prioritizes user experience by implementing monitoring tools that assess website and application performance from the end-user perspective.

  This ensures a seamless customer experience and helps identify and resolve issues before they impact users.

SwiftCart navigates the competitive landscape of e-commerce, the implementation of advanced network monitoring solutions becomes a linchpin for sustained success. By adopting a proactive and comprehensive approach to network monitoring, SwiftCart not only ensures the stability and reliability of its digital infrastructure but also fortifies its defenses against potential disruptions and cyber threats. SwiftGuard stands as a testament to the company's commitment to delivering a secure, seamless, and optimal online shopping experience for its customers.

Conclusion

The intricate tapestry of secure network design is woven with threads of resilience, foresight, and strategic vigilance. As organizations traverse the dynamic landscape of digital connectivity, the imperative to fortify against cyber threats becomes indisputable. A well-crafted secure network design is not a mere technological scaffold but a shield that safeguards sensitive data, preserves operational continuity, and instills confidence in users. By embracing robust encryption, access controls, and vigilant monitoring, organizations can forge a cyber-resilient environment. As we conclude this exploration, the call to prioritize secure network design echoes as a fundamental commitment to the integrity, reliability, and sustained success of modern enterprises.

Multiple Choice Questions

1. What is a primary objective of secure network design?
    a. Maximizing network speed.
    b. Minimizing encryption.
    c. Safeguarding against cyber threats.
    d. Ignoring access controls.
2. Which technology is commonly used for securing data in transit in a secure network design?
    a. Telnet
    b. HTTP
    c. SSL/TLS
    d. FTP
3. What is the purpose of access controls in secure network design?
    a. Slowing down network performance.
    b. Restricting unauthorized access.

   c. Encouraging open network policies.
   d. Minimizing encryption standards.
4. Which component plays a crucial role in detecting and preventing unauthorized access in a secure network design?
   a. Firewalls
   b. Open Wi-Fi networks
   c. Unrestricted user permissions
   d. Inactive intrusion detection systems
5. How does secure network design contribute to user trust?
   a. By ignoring encryption protocols.
   b. By minimizing access controls.
   c. By preserving data integrity and confidentiality.
   d. By encouraging open network policies.

Answers

1. c
2. c
3. b
4. a
5. c

Index

A

Anti-Malware 284, 285
Application Development
  about 156
  aspects,
    implementing 157, 158
  benefits 158
  business, scenario 156
  case study 158
  future, outcome 160
  methodology,
    evaluating 160
  posture, evaluating 159
  security, enhancing 157
Application Programming
    Interfaces (APIs)
  about 174
  business, scenario 174
  future, considering 175
  key, considering 174
Attack Chain Modeling 53, 54
Attack Chain Modeling,
    aspects
  Denial-of-service 55
  malware, distributing 55
  MitM, attack 54
  phishing, attack 54
  ransomware,
    attack 54
  social engineering,
    attack 55
  SQL, injection 54
  zero-day, exploits 55
Azure Arc
  about 270
  benefits 272, 273
  challenges 270
  concepts 270
  real-time, measuring 271, 272
Azure Automation
  about 63
  challenges 64
  concepts 64
  enterprises, collaborating 65
  objectives 65
  results 66
Azure Landing Zones
  about 28
  benefits 29
  core components 28
  purpose 28
Azure Landing Zones, role
  application,
    modernization 30
  governance,
    provisioning 30
  network, connectivity 30
  operations,
    optimizing 30
  security, compliance 30
  strategy, planning 30
  zones, landing 30
Azure Storage
  about 192
  benefits 192
  capabilities 193
  fundamental, aspects 192

Azure Storage, concepts
authentication 193
encrypting 193
firewalls, virtual network 194
Geo-redundancy 194
network, security 193
private, link 193
regulatory, compliance 194
security center, monitoring 194
Shared Access Signatures (SAS) 194
threat, detecting 194

B

Best Practices 4
Best Practices, characteristics
competitive, advantage 5
continuous, improving 5
continuous, learning 5
effectiveness, efficiency 5
expert consensus 5
industry, compliance 5
risk mitigation 5
standardization 5
Business Resilience
about 56, 57
challenges 57
concepts 57
objectives 57
Business Resilience, strategy
awareness, improving 59
continuous, monitoring 58
customer trust, enhancing 59
cybersecurity, assessment 58
cybersecurity, collaborating 58
employee, awareness 58
framework, implementing 58
incident, implementing 58
incident response, planning 58
industry, recognizing 59
supply chain, security 58

C

CAF (Cloud Adoption Framework)
about 20
aspects 23, 24
business scenario 25
components 20-22
objectives 22, 23
security, enhancing 24, 25
CAF, role
adoption 26
benefits 26
governance 25
operations 26
organization, managing 26
planning 25
security, compliance 26
strategy 25
well-architecture, framework 26
CAF, secure methodology
data, protecting 27
disaster, recovery 28
IAM, managing 27
legal, compliance 27
network, security 27
security, governance 27
security, operations 28
threat, protecting 27
Cloud Adoption Framework (CAF) 8
Cloud Applications
about 237
benefits 240
concepts 237
real-time, measuring 238, 239
Cloud Applications, challenges
app, deploying 238
data sensitivity, compliance 237
workforce, collaborating 238

Cloud Infrastructure Entitlement Management (CIEM)
about 110
challenges 111
cloud security, collaborating 112
concepts 111
objectives 112
results 112
Cloud Workloads
about 244
benefits 247
business, scenario 262
challenges 245
concepts 245
real-time, measuring 245-247
security, integrating 263-265
Container Orchestration
about 213
access control, utilizing 213
applications, optimizing 217, 218
audits, compliance 222, 223
business, scenario 213
isolating 220, 221
log, auditing 217
network, security 216
secrets, managing 221
security, runtime 215
Cybersecurity Architect 2
Cybersecurity Architect, best practices
access, controlling 6
alerts, monitoring 7
documentation, compliance 7
encrypting 6
incident response, planning 6
patch, managing 6
regular audit, testing 7
response, exercise 7
risk assessment 6
security, awareness 6
security framework 6
vendor risk, managing 6
Cybersecurity Architect, roles
adaptation, improving 4
architecture, designing 3
budgeting 4
collaborating 4
compliance, managing 3
documenting 4
incident response, planning 3
risk assessment, analyzing 3
security awareness, training 4
security strategy, developing 3
surveillance, monitoring 4
technology, evaluation 3
Cyber Waters
about 286
key, components 287
risks, associating 286
role, optimizing 287
security, measuring 286

D

Database Workload Protections
about 266
benefits 269, 270
business, scenario 266
challenges 267
real-time, measuring 267, 268
Data Maps
about 185
benefits 186
business, scenario 187-189
data, protecting 186, 187
real-time, scenario 185, 186
Data Protection Solution, case studies 190
Data Security
about 180
benefits 184, 185
business, scenario 183, 184
crucial, element 181
data governance, designing 183
data, protecting 181
fundamental, principles 181
mechanisms, authenticating 182, 183

Designing Solutions
anomaly, detecting 128
continuous, improving 129
endpoint, protecting 128
incident response, planning 129
real time, monitoring 128
response, automating 129
scenario 128
threat intelligence, integrating 129
DevOps Era
case, studies 154
challenges 154
concepts 154
Dynamic Business Environment
about 76
challenges 76
objectives 76, 77
results 77, 78
strategies 77

E

EASM
about 273
benefits 276
challenges 274
concepts 274
real-time, measuring 274, 275
Endpoint Detection and Response (EDR)
about 282
assets, managing 292, 293
confidentiality, safeguarding 289, 290
cyber, vigilance 287, 288
data, safeguarding 298-300
Gatekeepers, security 288, 289
harmonizing, security 295, 296
seamless, integrating 297, 298
sentinel, protecting 294, 295
vulnerability, navigating 290, 291
Endpoint Security
about 280
behavior, analyzing 281
key aspects 281
role, optimizing 281
security control, utilizing 281
Enterprise Access Model 104
Enterprise Access Model, components
MDM 105
network segmentation 105
PAM 105
RBAC 104
SSO 105

F

FortifyBank 97, 99

G

Global E-commerce
about 88, 89
challenges 89
concepts 89
identity, managing 90
results 90, 91

H

healthcare organization 263
healthcare organization, challenges
health data, sensitivity 263
multi-cloud, complexity 263
threat landscape, implementing 263
Hybrid Cloud Environment
about 86
access, policies 87
benefits, results 88
challenges 86
cloud, expansions 87
concepts 86
federation, identity 87
Microsoft Entra ID, integrating 86

Hybrid Cloud Management
about 225
challenges, considering 226, 227
concepts 225, 226
Hybrid Cloud Management, benefits
agility, flexibilities 226
cost, efficiency 226
data security, compliance 226
scalability 226

I

IaaS, challenges
access management, identifying 205
cloud service, collaborating 206
compliance, managing 206
data, encrypting 205
network, security 205
response, communicating 206
security, governance 205
IaaS (Infrastructure as a Service) 203
Identity Governance Solutions
about 106
concepts 106
governance, collaborating 107
objectives 106, 107
results 107

K

Key Management Service (KMS) 97

M

MCCP (Microsoft Cloud Compliance Program)
about 78
infrastructure, securing 80
microsoft priva, analyzing 79, 80
MCRA, business scenario 40, 41
MCRA, capabilities
data, protecting 43
IAM 44
network, security 44
regulations, compliance 44
remediation, automating 44
risk, identifying 43
threat, detecting 44
MCRA, controls
access, managing 44
automation, recommending 45
community, involving 45
compliance, checking 45
data, encrypting 44
DLP 44
guidance, best practices 45
monitoring 45
network, security 45
security, score 44
threat, detecting 45
MCRA, features
access, managing 45
compliance, checking 46
data, encrypting 45
data loss, preventing 46
guidance, best practices 46
network, security 46
secure, score 45
threat, detecting 46

MCRA, key components
access management, identifying 36
data, protecting 37
network, security 36
threat, detecting 37
MCRA (Microsoft Cybersecurity Reference Architecture) 36
MCSB, business scenario 42, 43
MCSB, capabilities
compliance, auditing 48
data, protecting 48
IAM, implementing 48
incident response, planning 48
network, security 48
patch, managing 48
threat, detecting 48
MCSB, key components
assessment, scoring 39
automating 40
best practices 39
community, involving 40
continuous, improving 40
documenting 40
regulations, compliance 40
security, controlling 39
tools, integrating 40
MCSB, key features
continuous, monitoring 38
DevSecOps, automating 39
regulation, compliance 38
security, configuring 38
MCSB (Microsoft Cloud Security Benchmark) 37
Microsoft 365 141
Microsoft 365, services
Microsoft Team 142
OneDrivc, business 142
online, exchanging 142
online, sharepoint 142
Microsoft Cloud Benchmark
about 229
aspects 231
benefits 230, 231
business, scenarios 229, 230
challenges 231
concepts 229
results 233
vulnerabilities, implementing 232
Microsoft Cloud Security Benchmark (MCSB) 8
Microsoft Cybersecurity Reference Architecture (MCRA) 7
Microsoft Defender
about 252
attack path, analyzing 256, 257
benefits 254, 255
business, scenario 255, 256
cloud secure, scoring 260, 261
posture, evaluating 259
real-time, scenario 253, 254
Microsoft Entra ID 85
MITRE ATT&CK 55, 56
Modern Authentication
about 91
dynamic security 93
identity, managing 93
problem statement, analyzing 91
RBAC, authorization 92
strategies, implementing 92
Multi-Cloud, business case
cloud-native, tools 119, 120
continuous, monitoring 119
cross-platforms, responsing 120
governance, compliance 120
orchestration, automating 120
threat intelligence, integrating 120

Multicloud Management
about 227
challenges 228
concepts 227
strategic, implementing 229
Multicloud Management, benefits
cost, optimizing 228
flexibility, choice 228
performance, optimizing 228
risk, mitigating 228

O

Office 365 Security
about 143
ATP, utilizing 144
capabilities 144
cloud app, security 144
EOP, analyzing 144
key features 143
key , terminology 149, 150
threat, intelligence 144
Office 365 Security, case studies
awareness, training 146
compliance, auditing 146
defender, analyzing 146
OneDrive, sharepoint 145
online, exchanging 145
Office 365 Security, scenario
centralized security, managing 147
cloud, protecting 148
cloud, security 147
email, security 147
endpoint, comprehensing 147
microsoft defender, implementing 148
response, automating 147, 148
security center, managing 148
threat intelligence, integrating 147, 148

P

PaaS, challenges
API, security 204
container, secuirity 205
secure, developing 204
PaaS (Platform as a Service)
about 202
principles 202
security, measuring 203
PAM, principles
audit, monitoring 103
least, privilege 103
password, managing 104
provision, deprovision 104
secure, authenticating 103
session, managing 104
PAM (Privileged Access Management) 103
posture management system 235, 236
posture management system, benefits
compliance, assurance 236
holistic security, resillience 236
response time, reducing 237
trust, enhancing 237
Privileged Access 103

R

ransomware attack
about 59
aspects 61
challenges 61
concepts 60
cybersecurity, enhancing 62
data security, enhancing 61, 62
objective 61
operations, optimizing 60
result 63

Regulatory Compliance
- about 70
- challenges 70
- concepts 70
- objectives 70, 71
- results 71, 72
- roles, utilizing 75, 76
- strategies 71

S

SaaS, challenges
- access controls, authenticating 204
- audits, monitoring 204
- data, encrypting 204

SaaS, objectives
- compliance, ensuring 202
- customizing 202
- data, managing 202
- support, training 202
- user, configuring 202

SaaS, responsibilities
- disaster, recovery 202
- infrastructure, managing 201
- performance, optimizing 202
- security, measuring 202
- updating 202

SaaS (Software as a Service) 201

Safeguarding Cyber Frontiers
- about 133
- continuous, monitoring 133
- education, awareness 134
- forensic analysis, reporting 134, 135
- patch, managing 134
- procedures, responsing 134
- scenario 133
- threat intelligence, integrating 133

Safeguarding Cyber Frontiers, benefits
- employee awareness, enhancing 135
- incident, responsing 135
- proactive threat, detecting 135
- vulnerability, reducing 135

Secure Network
- cybersecurity, enhancing 303, 304
- imperative, safeguarding 302
- posture, managing 306-308
- resilience, vigilance 308, 309
- traffic, filtering 304-306

secure tenant administration
- about 108
- challenges 108
- collaborate, strategic 109
- concepts 108
- objectives 109
- results 109, 110

Securing Compliance
- about 72
- challenge 73
- concepts 73
- objectives 73
- results 74
- robust cyber, defense 74

Security Operations (SecOps)
- about 117
- concepts 118, 119
- data, collecting 117, 118
- data, normalizing 118
- data, persistence 118
- data, visualizing 118

Security Posture
- about 241
- benefits 243, 244
- business, scenario 241
- case studies 251, 252
- real-time, measuring 242, 243

Security Posture, challenges
cyber threats, transforming 241
global operation, compliance 241
third party, risk 241
SIEM Solutions
about 125
correlation, analysis 126
data collection, aggregating 125
forensic analysis, reporting 127
incident response, automating 126
normalization, parsing 126
real-time, monitoring 126
SIEM Solutions, benefits
operational, efficiency 127
scalability, integrating 127
streamline, compliance 127
threat detection, enhancing 127
SOAR Solution
about 130
access, managing 131
business scenario 130
incident orchestration 131
report, analyzing 132
security tools, integrating 130
threat intelligence, integrating 131
threat, response 131
SOAR Solution, benefits
adaptability, changing 132
incident, responsing 132
threat detection, enhancing 132
workload, reducing 132
SQL
about 195
benefits 198
business, scenario 195
concepts 195
SQL, challenges
complex, infrastructure 196
data, sensitivity 196
threats, cybersecurity 196

T

TechSecure
business, scenario 169
case study, results 155, 156
code, securing 155
continuous security, recognizing 155
cost-efficient, measuring 169, 171
DevOps security, integrating 155
future, considering 171
lifecycle, strategies 170
mechanisms, authenticating 155
Threat Detection Coverage
about 136
behavior, analyzing 137
Email security, phishing 137
endpoint, security 136
intelligence, integrating 138
network traffic, analyzing 137
response, planning 138
risk assessment, inventory 136
scenario 136
Threat Detection Coverage, benefits
cyber impact, minimizing 138
response time, reducing 138
threats, adaptability 139
threat visibility, enhancing 138
Threat Modeling
about 161
application, evaluating 166
case study 161
future, considering 163
real-time, scenario 164, 165
secureFin, embarking 162
TechMart, implementing 167, 168
tools, analyzing 163

Threat Modeling, key features
mitigation, strategies 164
risk, assessment 164
STRIDE, framework 164
system diagrams 164
threat, identifying 164
Threat Modeling, significance
lifecycle, integrating 162
proactive risk, managing 162
resources, optimizing 162
vulnerability, identifying 161

U

Unified Operations
continuous, improving 122
cross function, collaborating 122
data, centralizing 122
employee, empowerment 123
integration, processing 121
manufacture, setting up 121
real-time, visibility 122
streamline workflow 122
technological integrating 122
Unified Operations, threats
audit trall, creating 124
business scenario 123
compliance, reporting 124
flexibility, scalability 125
incident response, forensics 125
log, centralizing 123
real time, monitoring 124
SIEM 124

W

Web Workloads
about 206
business, scenario 207
key, security 207
response, communicating 211-213
threats, monitoring 209
vulncrability, managing 208
Well-Architected Framework 31, 32

X

XYZ Corporation 104

Z

Zero Trust
about 93, 94
access policies 95, 96
business, scenario 95
Zero Trust Deployment, application
BYOD 11
cloud, security 11
E-commerce, data protecting 12
financial services, banking 12
healthcare data, security 12
infrastructure, protecting 11
IoT Device, security 11
supply chain, security 11
Zero Trust Deployment, frameworks
azure security, benchmark 10
CIS 10
DSS PCI 10
ISO 27001 10
NIST 10
Zero Trust Deployment, key objectives
attack surface, minimizing 9
continuous, monitoring 9
data, protecting 9
just-in-time-access 9
secure remote, accessing 9
trust, verifying 9
Zero Trust RaMP 7
Zero Trust RaMP, resources
CAF 8
MCSB 8
MCRA 7
WAF 8
Zero Trust Security
about 12
data, securing 15
endpoint, securing 15
infrastructure, securing 14
model, optimizing 13
network, securing 13